Stanley Gibbo

CHANNEL ISLANDS
POSTAL HISTORY
Catalogue

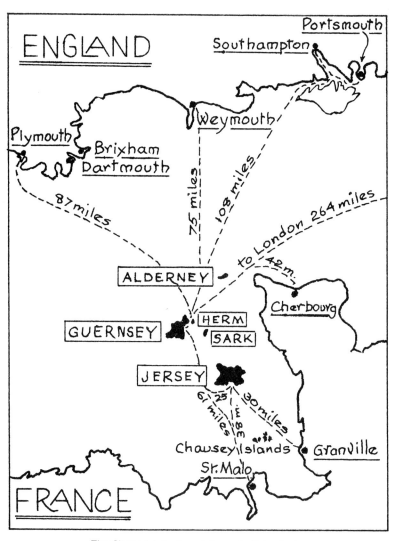

The Channel Islands and the main Entry Ports

Stanley Gibbons
CHANNEL ISLANDS
POSTAL HISTORY
Catalogue

FIRST EDITION

Stanley Gibbons Publications Ltd
London and Ringwood

**By Appointment to Her Majesty the Queen
Stanley Gibbons Ltd., London
Philatelists**

1st edition—December 1991

The material contained in this catalogue was previously published as part of the *Stanley Gibbons Specialised Catalogue of Stamps and Postal History*, which first appeared in April 1979.

Item No. 2826(91)

Printed in Great Britain by
BPCC Wheatons Ltd., Exeter, Devon.

Contents

Preface

Those discussing the greater involvement of this country in European affairs tend, perhaps through politeness to our French partners, to forget the previous historical context when the writ of English kings ran in large areas of western France in addition to their lands across the Channel. Since William the Conqueror's troops streamed ashore at Pevensey in 1066 two groups of islands, tucked away to the west of the Cotentin Peninsula, have maintained their allegiance to the Kings and Queens of England as the successors to the Dukes of Normandy.

The Channel Islands have always been involved with Europe, Jersey is after all only 15 miles from the French coast, and both Bailiwicks were occupied by Germany between 1940 and 1945. One result of such links is that their postal history forms a unique study.

The *Stanley Gibbons Channel Islands Specialised Catalogue*, published in 1979 and 1983, was partly devoted to postal history. During the past eight years there have been many new discoveries and research has thrown further light on a number of aspects. To record these it has been decided to publish the postal history chapters as a catalogue in their own right. Postage stamp issues of both Guernsey and Jersey are covered by the annual Stanley Gibbons checklist, *Collect Channel Islands and Isle of Man Stamps*.

In the preparation of this catalogue we have been fortunate, once again, to have the assistance of the Channel Islands Specialists' Society. Corrections and additions have been made throughout, but major revisions have been undertaken to Chapters 10 (Postage Due and Instructional Marks), 14 (Sub-offices of Jersey and Guernsey), 18 (The German Occupation) and 19 (Red Cross Message Service). In response to a number of requests listings of slogan postmarks and special handstamps have been restored to Chapter 15. The text has been completely reset and there are many new illustrations. Prices have been carefully revised to reflect the buoyant state of the present market in this material.

The postal history of the Channel Islands is a fascinating study and it is hoped that this new edition will encourage more collectors to participate in it.

David J. Aggersberg

Acknowledgements

We are most grateful for the participation of the Channel Islands Specialists' Society in the preparation of this catalogue. John Simpson has, once again, acted as co-ordinator and major contributions have been made by Ian Griggs (German Occupation), David Gurney (Sub-offices and Red Cross Message Service), Gerald Marriner (Postage Due markings) and T. Peters (Jersey packet stamps). The postal authorities of both Guernsey and Jersey have also assisted by providing details of slogan postmarks and special handstamps which have been in use on the islands. Tom Green's advice as to current market values has been invaluable in the preparation of this book.

William Heinemann Ltd., the London publishers, have permitted very generous use of the text and illustrations in *Stamps and Postal History of the Channel Islands*, the standard handbook by William Newport published by that company. We are indebted to John St. John for this valuable co-operation.

For Section 19 on the Red Cross Message Service, Picton Publishing of Chippenham, Wiltshire, have provided illustrations, permitting their reproduction from *The Red Cross Mail Service for Channel Island Civilians 1940–45*. For this courtesy we thank the author, Donald McKenzie, and the publisher, David Picton-Phillips.

Illustrations of Types **G11***a*, **G51**, **G53***a*, **G83**, **G85/6**, **G104**, **G153**, **G192**, **G200**, **G206**, **P9**, and Guernsey C, F and G from Section 15 are reproduced from *615 Postmarks of the Guernsey Head Post Office* by permission of the author, Leopold Mayr.

The illustration for Type **J14** was provided by *Philatelic Magazine* and for Type **J56** by Robson Lowe Ltd. We express our thanks to both.

STANLEY GIBBONS PUBLICATIONS LTD.

Stanley Gibbons Addresses

HEAD OFFICE, 399 STRAND, LONDON WC2R 0LX

Auction Room and Specialist Stamp Departments. Open Monday–Friday 9.30 a.m. to 5 p.m.

Shop. Open Monday 9.30 a.m. to 5.30 p.m., Tuesday–Friday 8.30 a.m. to 5.30 p.m. and Saturday 10.00 a.m. to 4.00 p.m.
Telephone 071-836 8444 for all departments.

RINGWOOD OFFICE

Stanley Gibbons Publications and Promotions, 5, Parkside, Christchurch Road, Ringwood, Hants BH24 3SH. Telephone 0425 472363.

OVERSEAS BRANCHES

Stanley Gibbons (Australia) Pty. Ltd., P.O. Box 863J, Melbourne 3001, Australia. Telephone (01 0613) 670 3332 and Telex AA 37223.

Stanley Gibbons (Singapore) Pte. Ltd., Raffles City, P.O. Box 1689, Singapore 9117, Republic of Singapore. Telephone (010 65) 336 1998.

Stanley Gibbons Publications Ltd. has overseas agents and distributors for Australia, Austria, Belgium, Canada, Denmark, France, Germany, Hong Kong, Israel, Japan, Luxembourg, Netherlands, New Zealand, Scandinavia, South Africa, Switzerland, United States and West Indies. Please contact the Ringwood address for details.

Introductory Notes

Prices

Prices in this catalogue are expressed in pounds and pence sterling. One pound comprises 100 pence (£1 = 100p).

In the Catalogue lists our method of indicating prices is:

Numerals for pence, e.g. 20 denotes 20p (20 pence).

Numerals for pounds and pence, e.g. 4·50 denotes £4·50 (4 pounds and 50 pence).

For £100 and above, prices are in whole pounds.

References can be found in the text to the previous British currency (to February 1971):

£1 = 20s. One pound = twenty shillings *and*

1s. = 12d. One shilling = twelve pence.

Just as with adhesives, the condition of a cover or entire affects the value. Damage, tears or soiling will reduce the market value. The visual aspect is likewise important, covers of attractive general appearance command higher prices than duller counterparts. In more detail, categories covered by this Catalogue are as follows:

Agents' Letters. We have listed all the known agents and we price letters bearing their names and endorsements. Not all agents endorsed the letters handled by them with their names and charges and in many cases collectors have to be content with letters simply addressed in the care of a particular agent. Prices are for complete letters or outer wrappers.

Pre-adhesive Markings. Prices for postal markings prior to 1840 are for clear and complete marks on complete letters (entires) or outer wrappers. Poor strikes are worth considerably less and really superb marks on attractive entires are worth substantially more than the Catalogue price.

Mulreadys and Penny Blacks and Reds. Prices for Mulready envelopes and lettersheets and for Penny Blacks and Reds are for those with clear Maltese Cross cancellations and with the Jersey or Guernsey datestamp. Covers with stamps should have four-margined examples. Poor adhesives or indistinct cancellations are worth considerably less.

*Cancellations and Markings from 1844. Prices for these later cancellations are for clear marks on covers or postcards.

*Parcel Post strikes on piece. Parcel post strikes, particularly the large "label" types, are difficult to find whole. Prices are for good and complete examples. For the parcel post labels add to the price of the label itself the value of the markings and the used price of any high-denomination postage stamps.

*Special Handstamps and Slogan Postmarks. Prices are for clear examples on covers or postcards franked at normal postal rates.

*Cachets. Prices for cachets are for those clearly struck on covers or postcards that have passed through the post. Those on unused postcards, which were often applied before the cards were sold, are—unless exceptionally scarce—worth one-half of used examples.

*Mail with France. The prices in Section 17 refer to letters originating in the Channel Islands or sent to the Islands where the marking was also simultaneously in use on mail from or to the U.K. The P-F and P-D markings will need their value increasing according to other postal markings on the cover. Prices for the French lozenge obliterations are for those on the most commonly used 3d. and 4d. adhesives. Covers bearing other values are worth considerably more.

Red Cross Messages. In Section 19 prices are for forms showing the most common types of cachet. Those with scarce cachets should add the figure from the separate price-list of cachets also given.

Internee Mail. In Section 20 postcards in pristine condition and lettersheets in fine condition are worth 20% more than Catalogue. Covers are priced as bearing the cheapest variety of censor mark, where applicable. Covers with additional or more expensive marks are priced at the value of the dearest mark.

Stamps on piece and Loose stamps. We do not normally price stamps on piece or loose stamps with particular cancellations. The exceptions (they are stated in the listings) are for extremely rare marks or for items like parcel post cancellations where "on piece" would be the usual mode of collecting.

   *For the era of adhesives, account must be taken not only of the marking, but also of the postage stamps on the cover. The price-lists show the value of the marking. For categories asterisked above, however, find the prices for postage stamps in used condition from the Stanley Gibbons Catalogue. If the figure exceeds the price of the marking it should be *added* to obtain the total valuation. If it is less, the cover (including its stamps) is valued as shown in our price-lists for the marking.
   It often happens that common markings are found used in conjunction with rarer ones. In valuing such covers take the highest priced mark and add half the value of all the others listed at £10 or over.

Correspondence.
   Letters should be addressed to the Catalogue Editor, Stanley Gibbons Publications Ltd., 5 Parkside, Christchurch Road, Ringwood, Hants. BH24 3SH, and return postage is appreciated when a reply is sought. New information and unlisted items for consideration are welcomed.

Postage Stamps.
   A full listing of the wartime stamps for the Channel Islands, the Great Britain regionals and the independent postal administration issues for Guernsey and Jersey is provided by the annual Stanley Gibbons checklist *Collect Channel Islands and Isle of Man Stamps.*

Abbreviations and Symbols

c.d.s. circular datestamp
d.c.   double circle
f.d.c. first day cover
mm   millimetres
No.   number
s.c.   single circle
†   Not known to exist
–   (in price column) Exists, but no market price is known
In columns of type numbers, a blank implies that the number quoted immediately above is repeated.

Bibliography

Periodical Publications
Channel Islands Specialists' Society. *Bulletin*, 1950–
Channel Islands Specialists' Society. *Les Isles Normandes*, 1975–
Club of Channel Islands Collectors (New York). *The Channel Islands Reporter*
States of Guernsey Post Office Board. *Guernsey Philatelic News*, 1970–
Jersey Postal Administration. *Jersey Stamp Bulletin*, 1970–

General Works
R. C. ALCOCK AND F. C. HOLLAND. *The Postmarks of Great Britain and Ireland* (Cheltenham, 1940) and Supplements.
R. C. ALCOCK AND F. C. HOLLAND. *The Maltese Cross Postmarks* (Cheltenham, 1959). Revised edition as *Maltese Cross Cancellations of the United Kingdom* (1971).
O. G. BOWLBY. "Maritime Postal Markings". *The Philatelist*, November 1949.
FRANCIS J. FIELD. *Airmails of the British Isles* (Sutton Coldfield, 1946).
C. GRASEMANN AND G. W. P. McLACHLAN. *English Channel Packet Boats* (London, 1939).
JOHN G. HENDY. *The History of the Early Postmarks of the British Isles* (London, 1905).
JOHN G. HENDY. *The History of the Postmarks of the British Isles from 1840 to 1876* (London, 1909).
ROBSON LOWE. *The Encyclopaedia of British Empire Postage Stamps*, Vol. 1, Great Britain and the Empire in Europe, 2nd edition (London, 1952). Reprinted, inclusive of Supplements, as Vols. 34 and 35 of *Billig's Philatelic Handbook* (North Miami, Florida, 1973).
CYRIL R. H. PARSONS, COLIN G. PEACHEY AND GEORGE R. PEARSON. *Slogan Postmarks of the United Kingdom* (Aylesbury, Bucks, 1974–80). Three volumes.
GEORGE R. PEARSON. *Special Event Postmarks of the United Kingdom*, 3rd edition (Hemel Hempstead, 1984).
P. L. PEMBERTON. "British Stamps with French Postmarks". *Philatelic Journal of Great Britain*, July 1936, September 1936, December 1936, July 1937, July 1938, April 1939, June 1939.
ALAN W. ROBERTSON. *Maritime Postal History of the British Isles* (Pinner, Middlesex, 1955–64). Reprinted by Harry Hayes (Batley, Yorkshire, 1974).
RAYMOND SALLES. *La Poste Maritime Française*, Tome 1, Les Entrees Maritime et Les Bateaux à Vapeur (Paris, 1961).
ARNOLD M. STRANGE. *A List of Books on the Postal History, Postmarks and Adhesive Postage and Revenue Stamps of Great Britain*, 2nd edition (London, 1971).
DR. J. T. WHITNEY. *Collect British Postmarks*, 5th edition (Benfleet, 1990).
R. M. WILLCOCKS. *The Postal History of Great Britain and Ireland; a Summarized Catalogue to 1840* (London, 1972).
R. M. WILLCOCKS. *England's Postal History to 1840* (London, 1975).

Channel Islands
CHARLES CRUICKSHANK. *The German Occupation of The Channel Islands* (London, 1975). Official history, non-philatelic.
YVES MAXIME DANAN. *Emissions Locales et Affranchissements de Guerre des Iles de la Manche* (Paris, 1969).
YVES MAXIME DANAN. *Histoire Postale des Iles de la Manche*. Tome 1 and Tome 2 (Paris, 1976 and 1978).
DAVID GURNEY. *The Channel Islands Sub-Post Offices and their Postmarks* (Ilford, 1983 and later supplements).
R. E. HARRIS. *Islanders Deported*, Parts 1 and 2 (Ilford, 1980, 1983).
R. A. HAYES. *Modern Channel Islands Flight Covers (from 1969)* (Jersey, 1974).
RICHARD MAYNE. *Mailships of the Channel Islands 1771–1971* (Chippenham, 1971).
LEOPOLD MAYR. *615 Postmarks of the Guernsey Head Post Office* (Vienna, 1990).
DONALD McKENZIE. *The Red Cross Mail Service for Channel Islands Civilians 1940–45* (Chippenham, 1975).
WILLIAM NEWPORT. *Stamps and Postal History of the Channel Islands* (London, 1972).
J. M. Y. TROTTER. "Early Guernsey Postal History and Private Agents for Guernsey Letters". *Transactions of the Société Guernesiaise*, 1950. *Postal History Society Bulletin*, 1950.
M. WIENEKE. *The German Field Post Office in the Channel Islands* (Jersey, 1981).

CHANNEL ISLANDS SPECIALISTS' SOCIETY

The Channel Islands Specialists' Society exists to help all who are interested in any aspects of Channel Islands philately. Its members have conducted a considerable amount of research and, as a result of this, the Society has published a number of books, which are available to members at a special price. It has nearly 400 members in all parts of the world.

For details of membership apply to:

**Brian Cropp
17, Westlands Avenue,
Huntercombe, SLOUGH,
Berks., SL1 6AG**

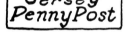

1. Letter Forwarding Agents

Before the establishment of Post Offices in Jersey and Guernsey and the provision of a regular packet service to the islands in 1794, letters for those places were sent to an agent, usually at Southampton, but occasionally at Portsmouth or another South Coast port. The agent paid the inland postage and then handed the letters to the captain of a ship sailing for the Channel Islands. On arrival at Jersey or Guernsey the captain handed over the letters to another agent, from whom they were collected by the addressee upon payment of the British inland postage plus a fee of 3d.—1d. for the ship's master and 1d. for each agent. Letters from the Channel Islands to England were handed over to the Post Office at Southampton by the ship's captain and therefore cost only 2d. on top of the postage.

The majority of the agents were merchants, but some were also ship owners and one or two shopkeepers or bankers. Many of the London coffee houses also acted as agents and bags for particular ship's captains were often to be found in them.

There were also agents in Bristol, Falmouth, Gosport, Plymouth, Poole and Weymouth, but most of these started up after the packet service was established and ran in competition with it.

The Southampton agent doing the largest business in the latter half of the eighteenth century was William Seward who, alone, or with a partner, was an agent

Letter for Guernsey with agent's endorsement on flap

from 1756 to 1793. He charged the usual 1d. except in cases where he had paid more than a shilling postage, when the charge was generally 2d.

Brixham was used as a port for Guernsey mails when the wind was south-westerly, which was directly adverse from the Needles. James Ahier was at work in Weymouth from 1798, and was joined by Nicholas Robilliard in 1802. In the following year Robilliard took over altogether and carried on until 1810. A considerable quantity of mail from Britain and overseas went through his hands and it is suspected that he paid members of the packet crews to smuggle letters into the Channel Islands for him.

In the early 1790s letters from Guernsey to London often went via Dartmouth, although no agents are at present known in this town.

Most of the agents endorsed their letters "Forwarded by your humble servant (signature)" and one such is illustrated. A number of them also added their charge in manuscript, after deleting the inland postage charge and substituting a higher one; then the Guernsey or Jersey agent would cross out that figure and add his own and the captain's penny, writing the final sum to be collected from the addressee. Letters addressed to local firms were often charged on account rather than individually. One or two of the early Southampton agents worked at such cheap rates as $\frac{1}{4}$d. and $\frac{1}{2}$d., so that one finds letters charged at such curious sums as $3\frac{1}{4}$d. An oval rubber stamp struck in blue by N. M. Priaulx, of Southampton, in 1840 is recorded.

There were also agents in France and many other European countries and their endorsements can be found on letters. The following is a list of agents whose endorsements are known.

LETTER FORWARDING AGENTS

Agent	Dates	Price for entire
Southampton		
Caesar Knapton	1673	£180
Grevichy	1689	£250
Aaron Deveule	1703	£150
Richard Taunton	1711–33	£100
John Grove	1713–41	90·00
Bandinell & Co.	1718	£120
Bandinell & Hilgrove	1718–19	£100
Thomas Bandinell	1719–29	£100
T. Le Cocq	1726	£180
Peter Cailleteau	1735–58	95·00
Esther Cailleteau & Co.	1758	£100
Bonner	1737–45	95·00
Seward & Marett	1756–58	95·00
William Seward	1758–86	85·00
Seward & Priaulx	1784	80·00
Seward & Le Feuvre	1785–88	80·00
Seward & Co.	1785–95	80·00
Seward & Pipon	1791–93	80·00
Clement Hilgrove	1771–79	80·00
Hilgrove & Durell	1779–85	70·00
Thomas Durell	1786–93	65·00
P. Le Feuvre	1791–1817	55·00
P. Le Feuvre & Son	1818	80·00
W. I. Le Feuvre	1820–35	80·00
Nicholas Priaulx	1793	£120
Priaulx & Bienvenu	1796–1829	80·00
Priaulx & Sons	1829	80·00
N. M. Priaulx (oval rubber stamp)	1830–40	£100
Helleur	1839	£140

Agent	Dates	Price for entire
Brixham		
John N. Tozer	1738	£250
Samuel Tozer	1790–94	£250
Thomas Parkinson	1781–83	£250
Weymouth		
James Ahier	1798–1804	£100
Ahier & Robilliard	1802	£120
Nicholas Robilliard	1803–10	90·00
Thomas Martin	1803–05	£120
John Sandford Jnr.	1813	£140
Falmouth		
Thos. Dunstan	1790	£250
George C. Fox & Son	1805	£180
Jos. Banfield	1806–10	£180
Bristol		
Edward Gwatkin	1759	£250
Ball, Davis, Vaughan & Co.	1804	£250
Portsmouth		
James Wilkinson	1741–46	£250
John Carey	1812	£250
Gosport		
William Carver	1798	£250
Lyme		
Henry Chard	1793	£250
Poole		
Thomas Nicholson	1723	£250
Plymouth		
Francis De la Combe	1758	£250
Noel	1794	£250
St. Austell		
Henry Lambes	1783	£225
London		
M. Perchard	1757	£120
Cazelet & Sons	1783	£100
Peyerimhoff, De Mierro & Crispen	1784	£130
P. Perchard	1791	£100
Perchard & Brock	1792-95	£100
Le Mesurier & Secretin	1793	£100
Battier Zornlen	1793–95	95·00
Perchard, Brock & Le Mesurier	1795–98	95·00
Brock & Le Mesurier	1798–1810	95·00
Paul, Havilland & Le Mesurier	1799–1802	£100
Wombell, Gautier & Co.	1806	£100
E. Boehm & J. Tayler	1807	£100
Ed. Rodd	1807	£100
Boyd, Miller & Co.	1808	£100
Geo. H. Aylwyn	1810	£110
Fred De Lisle	1811–12	£110

Agent	Dates	Price for entire
Andrews & Tariner	1812	£120
Sandeman, Gooden & Foster	1814–20	£110
J. Levy Jnr.	1815	£110
Jno. McNeill & Co.	1817–18	90·00
Bell & Grant	1833–34	90·00
Samuel Dobrée & Sons	1834–51	80·00

Jersey

Philip Hamon, appointed Postmaster to States	1787	£200
Pierre Mallet	1792	£250
Madame Anne Ashley	1793	£250
Josué Priaulx	1798	£250
Hemery Bros. & Co.	1810	£200
Winter, Nicholle & Co.	1814	£200
J. Le Bailley	1822	£200
William Fruing	1825–49	£200
Amiraux Le Breton & Co.	1826	£225
P. & I. Janvrin	1830	£200
Ph. & Fr. Junovin & Fils	1830	£200
T. & P. Duhamel	1833–35	£200
Godefroy Sons & Co.	1842	£200

Guernsey

Maugher	1718	£200
Mrs. Ann Watson (Govt. Postmistress	1780–94	£150
	1794–1814)	
John le Page	1806	£150
Harry Dobrée	1810–18	£150
William Lihou	1812	£150
E. Shale	1812	£180
Isaac de Lisle	1812	£225
James & John Cochran	1820	£225
Sinclair	1823	£225
George S. Syvret & Matthieu Barbet (Foreign P.O.)	1823–41	£180
(also for some years before and after these dates)		
John Le Marchant	1826	£150
Aaron Symes	1828–39	£100
Harris	1828	£100
Francis de Putron	1830–37	£140
Edward Le Pelley	1837	£140
Priaulx Lauga & Co.	1840	£120

St. Malo

Mace Cohue	1676	£150
J. Monie	1678	£150
Jean Hardy	1682–85	£150
Sebire, Laisne & Cie.	1763–83	£120
Beaugard & De Segray	1772–73	£120
Jacques La Dure	1777–90	£120
Barbier, Robbereckts & Cie.	1802	£150
Monsieur Blaize	1790–93	£100
Louis Blaize & Cie.	1802–27	90·00
Louis Blaize	1802–32	90·00
Dupuy, Fromy Frs.	1815–16	£120
J. B. Gaultier	1826–27	£100

Agent	Dates	Price for entire
Fontan Frs.	1825–30	£100
Mme Veuve Fontan Jun.	1827	£100
Mauger Frères	1827–29	90·00
Matthieu Barbet	1829–32	£100
Calais		
A. Mancel	1815	£200
C. Sturmer	1823	£225
Morlaix		
P. Aurrere & Fils.	1815	£200
H. Dobrée Jnr.	1816	£200
Le Havre		
Charles Sturmer	1814–15	£200
Cherbourg		
Captain Poullain	1820–23	£130
J. Boulabert	1823	£160
De Bonfils	1827	£160
Paris		
Thomas De Lisle & Co.	1842	£100
Bayonne		
Francis Giffard & Son	1815	£200
Alicante		
John Carey	1812	£200
Cadiz		
R. W. Meade	1812	£200
Gortdon, Shaw & Co.	1812	£200
Lisbon		
Sealys & Goodall	1813	£180
Naples		
Bardon, Maingy & Price	1817–18	£180
Rome		
Pierre Meraj	1802	£180
Trieste		
J. Janvrin	1822	£110
Gibraltar		
Robinson & Lihou	1809	£180
Matthew G. Price	1810	£180
Dobrée, Price & Co.	1811–12	£180
Robert Anderson & Co.	1832	£180
Malta		
E. C. Puslow	1815	£200
Bolzano (Botzen)		
G. Giacomo Graff	1803	£200

Agent	Dates	Price for entire
Altona		
John Hutchinson	1804	£200
Hamburg		
J. B. Paschen & Co.	1793	£160
H. D. Schaffler	1803	£160
J. A. Schroders	1836	£130
Elsinore		
Balfour & Rainols	1807	£160
St. Thomas		
Bergeert & Ulhorn	1813	£160

2. Establishment of the Postal Service

Between 1779 and 1783 there was an attempt to carry mails, mainly of a military nature, to the Channel Islands as a war measure and the cutter *Express*, of 40 tons, sailed from Portsmouth or Southampton "as often as practicable". In 1783 she returned to Dover to continue in service on the Dover-Calais run. Letters carried on this service *and so endorsed* are rare.

(Price from £200)

In 1791 the Postmaster of Southampton was ordered to make a census of all letters addressed to the Channel Islands over a period of four weeks, and from this it was deduced that the number of letters to be carried annually would be around 30,000. On this basis it was considered that a packet service would not be self-supporting, but that, in view of the importance of the islands during a war with France, such a service should be established as a matter of state.

On 3 February 1794 (and other dates during the month) a notice regarding a packet service to the Channel Islands was published in the *London Gazette* and the first packet, the 80-ton cutter *Royal Charlotte*, sailed from Weymouth for Guernsey on 13 February. An Act of Parliament establishing the packet service was passed on 28 March 1794: 34 Geo. III, Cap. XVIII (1794). It also fixed rates of postage and authorised the Postmaster General to establish post offices and post roads in the islands. The Act was registered by the Royal Court of Guernsey on 6 October 1794, but was never registered by the Royal Court of Jersey and so was not law there.

A Post Office Surveyor, Christopher Saverland, went over on the first packet, and appointed Mrs. Ann Watson Postmistress of Guernsey and Charles William Le Geyt Postmaster of Jersey.

Postage Rates

The packet rates between Weymouth and the Channel Islands in 1794 were 2d. per single letter, 4d. per double letter, 6d. per treble letter and 8d. per ounce letter. In November 1805 they were raised to 3d. per single letter and pro rata. The inter-island rates were the same as those above.

The postage from London to Weymouth was 5d. which, with the packet charge, made 7d. for a single letter to the Channel Islands in 1794. It rose to 9d. on 5 January 1797, to 10d. on 5 April 1801, to 1s. on 12 November 1805 and to 1s. 1d. on 4 December 1812.

A private boat, organised by agents Ahren and Robilliard, plied mid-week between Weymouth and Guernsey for a few years from 1802. A cover is known from this service endorsed in manuscript "p bye-boat".

(Price from £325)

3. Pre-adhesive Markings

JERSEY

Jersey's first postal marking, which was introduced in 1794 and remained in use until October 1802, consisted simply of the word "JERSEY" arranged in a concave curve (Type **J1**). From 1797 a straight-line stamp was used concurrently with the previous mark for a while and continued in use until 1820. During this time two quite different types existed. Type **J2** measures 32 × 5mm, has a full loop to the "J" and wide letters. Type **J3** is 30 × 5mm; the loop to "J" gradually diminishes and it sometimes has a small dot over it.

The scroll type came into use in 1810 and, again, two distinct types exist. The first (Type **J4**) was used from 1810 to 1830 except for the years 1817–22. It can be distinguished by the lettering, which is large, the shape of the "J" of "JERSEY" and finally the full stop. The second type (Type **J5**), which came into use in 1817 and remained until 1830, has smaller lettering, shows a more distinctive "J" and the full stop after "JERSEY" is omitted.

With the setting up in Jersey of the Penny Post in the 1830s a new handstamp was introduced (Type **J6**). This mark was used until 1840, usually in conjunction with village number markings (Types **J7–10**). These latter handstamps, numbered 1 to 4, were used on their own after 1840. The parishes represented were St. Aubin, Gorey, St. Peter's and St. Clement's respectively and of these St. Aubin (No. 1) is the commonest. Numbers 5 and 6 were also allocated, it is believed to St. Saviour's and Trinity.

The year 1830 also saw the introduction of Jersey's first datestamp. This handstamp was applied to the backs of letters and remained in use until 1849. *See* Section 9.

(J1)   (J2)

JERSEY

(J3)

(J4)   (J5)

(J6)

(J7)

(J7a)

(J8)

(J9)

(J10)

Cat. No.	Type No.	Dates of use	Colour	Price on cover
JC1	**J1**	1794–1802	Black	£350
JC2	**J2**	1797–1806	Black	£300
JC3	**J3**	1807–20	Black	£300
JC4	**J4**	1810–17 and 1822–30	Black	£120
JC5	**J5**	1817–30	Black	£120
JC6	**J6**	1831–40		
		a. Used alone	Black	£250
		b. Used with Nos. JC7		
		or JC7a	Black	£350
		c. Used with Nos. JC8,		
		9 or 10	Black . . . . . *from*	£450
JC7	**J7**	1840–45 (with serifs)	Black	£200
JC7a	**J7a**	1851 (without serifs)	Black	£200
JC8	**J8**	1840–45	Black	£300
JC9	**J9**	1840–51	Black	£400
JC10	**J10**	1840	Black	£450

GUERNSEY

The first handstamp used in Guernsey after the establishment of the Post Office in 1794 was very similar to that of Jersey, taking the form of the word "GUERNSEY" set out as a concave curve (Type **G1**). Three distinct settings exist, the first, measuring 46mm wide being used from 1794 to 1801, the second, 49mm wide, from 1802 to 1808 and the third, the smallest, being only 37mm wide, from 1808 to 1810. This last type is considerably scarcer than either of the first two types and is always much fainter than the other two.

The next handstamp to be used was the scroll type. Two types of this strike exist. The first (Type **G2**), in use from 1810 to 1817 and in 1829–30, included a full stop after the word "GUERNSEY", though the easiest way of distinguishing it from the later type is by the positioning of the letter "G" which is very close to the left-hand edge of the frame. The second type (Type **G3**) was used from 1817 to 1830, and here the full stop is omitted and the letter "G" is much further away from the frame edge.

Though long out of use the Type **G2** scroll evidently survived, as it is known struck on Telegraph forms in 1870–72.

The Guernsey Penny Post was established between January and March 1836, but no handstamps have yet been found. Hendy records that it served La Valle and Torteval.

From 1830 a circular datestamp with serifed letters was used and this marking continued in use after the introduction of Uniform Penny Postage in 1840. *See* Section 9.

(G1)

(G2)   (G3)

Cat. No.	Type No.	Dates of use	Colour	Price on cover
GC1	**G1** (46mm wide)	1794–1801	Black	£350
GC2	**G1** (49mm wide)	1802–08	Black	£350
GC3	**G1** (37mm wide)	1808–10	Black	£550
GC4	**G2**	1810–17, 1829–30	Black	£130
		a. Used on telegram forms (1870–2)	Black	£200
GC5	**G3**	1817–30	Black	£130

4. Ship Letters

JERSEY

The establishment of the Post Office in Jersey in 1794 brought with it the same procedures which were uniform throughout the United Kingdom. In the case of letters which were carried by private ships it meant that these letters would be subject to the standard ship letter charges.

From 1793 British ports were issued with concave "SHIP-LRE" handstamps, but no example from Jersey has so far been recorded.

As a result of the organization of the London Ship Letter Office in 1799 a new type of handstamp was introduced and around 1802 Jersey received its copy (Type **J11**). It consisted of a double oval and crown bearing the words "SHIP-LETTER/JERSEY". This strike is extremely rare and so far only one example has been recorded (it is in the British Museum). This was because there was considerable opposition to the charges imposed upon letters carried by private ships whose owners in the main were themselves islanders. The letters forwarded from overseas were for the most part addressed to islanders and they objected to this "outrageous procedure". Most of the mail was therefore not handed over to the Post Office, but was delivered by other means, accounting for the lack of usage of this handstamp.

In 1834 a new handstamp (Type **J12**) was introduced. This is mainly found on mail from Rio de Janeiro and Bahia handed over at Jersey from ships bound for France. Most of this mail was addressed to London, and it was before being forwarded that this strike was applied. This handstamp remained in use until 1843 and is the most frequently found Jersey ship letter mark.

A similar type of handstamp, but with the wording transposed to read "SHIP LETTER/JERSEY" (Type **J13**), is known used in 1837. This mark in red is believed to have been applied in London as Jersey had no red ink pad at this time though they were in use in London. In addition it does not seem likely that the island would have used two different types at the same time. It is believed that letters from Brazil for the same addressee were bundled there and forwarded intact to London where they were separated and duly stamped by the Post Office before being delivered. Only two examples of this mark have so far been recorded.

(J11)

JERSEY SHIP LETTER

(J12)

SHIP LETTER JERSEY

(J13)

(J14)

(J15)

A step-type of marking (Type **J14**) was in use in 1840 and is known in red. It is extremely rare, only one example (on a letter from Gambia to the Wesleyan Missionary Society in London) having so far come to light.

A new handstamp was used from 1843 until 1853 (Type **J15**). This marking is normally found in black although it is known in blue and yellow, only one example being recorded in blue.

It also occurs used as a cancellation on the 1841 1d. red adhesive of Great Britain.

(*Price off cover* £300)

Cat. No.	Type No.	Dates of use	Colour	Price on cover
JC11	**J11**	1802	Black	—
JC12	**J12**	1834–43	Black	£350
JC13	**J13**	1837	Red	£3500
JC14	**J14**	1840	Red	£5000
JC15	**J15**	1843–53	Black	£500
JC16		1851	Blue	£8000
JC17		1852	Yellow	£5500

GUERNSEY

When the Guernsey Post Office was established in 1794 it was issued with a standard-type "SHIP-LRE" concave handstamp (Type **G3a**) for use on mail from private ships. The only known example, from March 1795, occurs on a letter from Vice-Admiral Cornwallis, with the Channel Fleet, to Edinburgh.

In 1802 the island was supplied with its standard crown-in-double-oval marking inscribed "SHIP-LETTER/GUERNSEY" (Type **G4**). This type was used from 1802 to 1815 and was brought back into use in 1844 until 1849. Examples of its usage during the earlier period are scarcer, only five or six examples having been recorded, than those of the period 1844–49.

The next type to come into use was a box inscribed "GUERNSEY/SHIP LETTER" (Type **G5**). This was received by Guernsey in 1834 and was used until 1842. As with Jersey a similar type, but with the wording transposed, exists, and it is probable that this was used in London for the same purpose as the Jersey mark. This type, of which seven or eight examples have been seen, (Type **G6**) was used from 1836 to 1840 and is only known in red.

In 1842 an unusual step-type of handstamp came into use (Type **G7**), though this marking remained in use for a very short time so that only seven examples have been found.

By far the rarest of all the ship letter handstamps used in Guernsey is the "INDIA LETTER/GUERNSEY" (Type **G8**). Only one example of this strike is known, used on a letter from Singapore to London in 1836.

Packet Stamp

An unusual type of handstamp to be found on mail from both Guernsey and Jersey is the straight line "FROM GUERNSEY" (Type **G9**). This marking was applied at Weymouth to packet letters from the islands to distinguish them from overseas ship letters for which a higher charge was levied. To avoid the trouble of having handstamps for each island the Weymouth authorities settled for this mark, bearing in mind that Guernsey was the last port of call for ships returning to Weymouth. It was used from 1810 to 1837 and has been found on letters from both islands. Somewhat earlier, a manuscript "From Guernsey" is known on a letter of January 1802, just before the second concave mark, No. GC2, was issued. The first version having, by that time, become almost indecipherable.

(G3a)

(G4)

```
GUERNSEY
SHIP  LETTER
```

(G5)

```
SHIP LETTER
GUERNSEY
```

(G6)

```
GUERNSEY
SHIP LETTER
```

(G7)

```
INDIA LETTER
GUERNSEY
```

(G8)

FROM GUERNSEY
(G9)

Cat. No.	Type No.	Dates of use	Colour	Price on cover
GC5a	**G3a**	1795	Black	
GC6	**G4**	1802–15	Black	£2750
GC7		1844–49	Black	£2500
GC8	**G5**	1834–42	Black	£450
GC9	**G6**	1836–40	Red	£1600
GC10	**G7**	1842	Black	£2500
GC11	**G8**	1836	Black	
GC12	**G9**	1810–37	Black	£950

Wrecks

Many ships have been wrecked on the rocky shores of the Channel Islands, but only one handstruck mark has so far been recorded as having been applied to recovered mail.

The Great Western Railways vessel S.S. *Ibex* left Weymouth on 4 January 1900 and struck a rock in the east channel on the Little Russel, near the Platte Fougère, at 6 a.m. on 5 January. Two seamen were lost, one a sailor on the *Ibex*, the other a R.N. rating coming home on leave, but all the passengers were saved. Forty-four bags of mail went down with the vessel, but as she rested on an even keel with masts, funnels and parts of the superstructure above water at low tide, divers were able to start work on her straight away and two parcel hampers were salvaged on the day of the sinking.

On 9 January the *Star*, a Guernsey newspaper, reported that the mail-bags were found to be floating under the poop deck. Five had been recovered by this date, three for Guernsey and two for Jersey. The letters were in fair condition, but the newspapers were reported to be pulp. The Guernsey letters were dried and delivered on the 9th, postmen being instructed to explain that they were from the *Ibex*. Salvage continued and by the 12th, thirty-three mail-bags had been recovered.

By 20 January all the mail-bags except two had been recovered. One was from London to Jersey and one from Dorchester to Guernsey. On 25 January the *Star* reported that a bag of mail from the *Ibex* had been washed ashore at St. Brelade's Bay, Jersey.

Letters for Jersey, Alderney and Sark recovered from the wreck were, after drying, tied up in bundles, or put into envelopes with a manuscript note to say where they had come from.

No handstamps were used at Guernsey to identify these letters. Nevertheless, two slightly different cachets reading "MAIL PER S.S. IBEX" are known. Both types are 40mm long with letters from printer's type, but one (Type **J16**) has all the letters 3mm high (except the "ER" of "PER" which are 2½mm) and full stops after the "S.S.", while the other (Type **J17**) has the words "MAIL" and "IBEX" in letters 3mm high, "PER S.S." in letters of 2½mm and no stops after "S S".

About nine covers are known with these cachets and all are addressed to Jersey; it would appear, therefore, that the cachets were applied by the Jersey Post Office after the letters were received from Guernsey, or possibly to letters washed up off Jersey.

A news-wrapper from the magazine *Commerce* addressed to Jersey has in manuscript "Recovered from wreck of G.W. Rly. S.S. Ibex lost off Guernsey about 28/12/99—received 14/1/1900". It bears the *Ibex* cachet Type **J16** with small "ER" of "PER" and stops after the "S.S.", and so do the other entires delivered around this date. One is known with the Jersey datestamp of 12 January 1900. The later covers, however, with Jersey datestamps of 30 July and 1 August 1900, have the cachet Type **J17** with small "PER S S" and no stops after the "S S". A possible explanation of this is that a further bag of letters was found in the *Ibex* after she had been taken into St. Peter Port on 21 July, having in some miraculous way been preserved from the ravages of the sea, and when these letters were delivered in Jersey a new cachet had to be made, the earlier one having been destroyed some months before when it was thought unlikely that any further letters would be recovered. Amongst the surviving items was one complete folded newspaper, which has never been opened.

One of the later covers is a piece of French postal stationery with impressed 5c. green Peace and Commerce stamp cancelled at Le Havre on 31 December 1899. It has an "officially sealed" label bearing the Jersey datestamp of 30 July 1900, and the *Ibex* cachet Type **J17**. Another cover with this cachet is recorded with Jersey arrival stamps of 1 and 2 August 1900.

A number of loose stamps—we have seen Canadian, Belgian and Dutch—have been found with cachet Type **J17** impressed diagonally. It is thought that these were found in the bottom of the mail-bag, cancelled, and handed over with the letters on delivery.

(Price on loose stamps £120 each)

MAIL P**ɛ**R S.S. IBEX
(J16)

MAIL PER S S IBEX
(J17)

Cat. No.	Type No.	Dates of use	Colour	Price on cover
JC18	**J16**	Jan. 1900	Black . . .	£1600
JC19	**J17**	July–Aug. 1900	Black . . .	£1800

Disinfected Maritime Mail

The fumigation of mail from the Mediterranean and Near East was prevalent in the eighteenth and nineteenth centuries and, very occasionally, a cover or letter to the Channel Islands is found treated by vinegar or smoke. Some of these letters bear slits made with chisels to facilitate the treatment. This would be carried out at Standgate Creek (on the Medway) if coming via London, the Mother Bank (Portsmouth), Milford Haven or on the ship itself.

(Price from £150)

5. Uniform Fourpenny Post

The experimental introduction of a uniform postal rate at 4d. commenced on 5 December 1839. It lasted until 9 January 1840, the uniform 1d. rate being introduced on 10 January.

Usually the fourpenny rate was marked in manuscript, but a few towns in Great Britain had a handstruck "4".

In Jersey and Guernsey the "4" was applied in manuscript and such letters are quite scarce.

(*Price on entire* £200)

6. Handstruck Numerals

JERSEY

These numerals, struck from wooden handstamps, were introduced to Jersey in the early 1840s. Prior to their introduction similar manuscript markings had been used by both islands. (*Price on entire* £110)

The first type of the 1d. known to have been used (Type **J18**) has been found on covers of 1843 to 1849 struck in red. The next type (Type **J19**) has been found on a number of covers which prove that it was in use from 1844 to 1850. This handstamp was also struck in red.

The 2d. handstamps date back to 1842 (Type **J20**), this type measures 17 × 28mm being used until 1850. It was struck in black. The next type to be recorded (Type **J21**) was used between 1849 and 1851 and generally struck in black, although examples of it have been found in blue on letters of 1851. A similar handstamp, measuring 11 × 24mm, has a very distinct round blob at the top end of the curve (Type **J21a**). In 1852 another type, although considerably thinner (Type **J22**), was used initially in blue and subsequently, to 1867, in black. In 1853 the authorities used another type (Type **J23**) for a while.

A figure "8" (Type **J24**) was used on mails in 1851 to collect ship letter charges. This type was struck in blue. An example is known on a ballon monté cover flown from Paris to Granville in 1870 and then forwarded by boat to Jersey where it received the octagonal Jersey–France M.B. mark in addition to Type **J24**. A further type (Type **J25**) is known to have been applied in 1868 on an unpaid letter to France. It was struck in black.

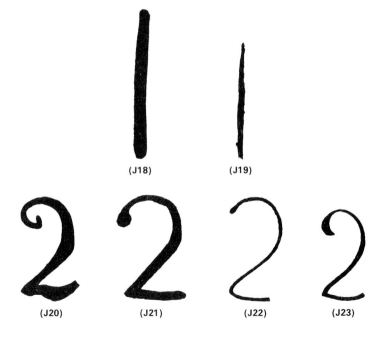

(J18) (J19)

(J20) (J21) (J22) (J23)

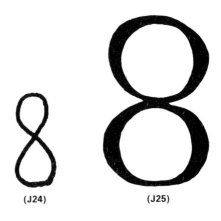

(J24)   (J25)

Cat. No.	Type No.	Dates of use	Colour	Price on cover
JC20	**J18**	1843–49	Red	£275
JC21	**J19**	1844–50	Red	£275
JC22	**J20**	1842–50	Black	£350
JC23	**J21**	1849–51	Black	£350
JC24		1851	Blue	£500
JC24a	**J21a**	1849	Black	£350
JC25	**J22**	1852	Blue	£600
JC26		1853–67	Black	£300
JC27	**J23**	1853	Black	£300
JC28	**J24**	1851–70	Blue	£600
JC29	**J25**	1868	Black	£1700

GUERNSEY

Guernsey had its own distinctive 1d. paid and 2d. unpaid handstamps. Two different forms of the 1d. version are known, Type **G10** between 1843 and 1848, and Type **G10a** between 1843 and 1849. Both were struck in red.

(G10)   (G10a)

There were four different types for the 2d. rate, Type **G11** used in 1842–43, Type **G11a** in 1843, Type **G11b** between 1843–47, and Type **G12** between 1843–49. All were struck in black, but Type **G11b** is also known in red on a letter of 1843 from Sark.

| (G11) | (G11a) | (G11b) | (G12) |

There is also a handstruck "8" (Type **G13**), which was used between 1844 and 1847 on mail from France arriving in the island unpaid.

(G13)

Cat. No.	Type No.	Dates of use	Colour	Price on cover
GC13	**G10**	1843–48	Red	£275
GC13a	**G10a**	1843–49	Red	£275
GC14	**G11**	1842–43	Black	£300
GC14a	**G11a**	1843	Black	£350
GC14b	**G11b**	1843–47	Black	£350
GC14c		1843	Red	£850
GC15	**G12**	1843–49	Black	£400
GC16	**G13**	1844–47	Black	£650

7. Use of First Adhesives and Mulreadys

Handstamps in the form of Maltese Crosses were distributed for use with the first adhesive postage stamps of Great Britain and the Mulready covers in 1840. Though mass-produced their hand manufacture led to small differences in detail in each handstamp and the more unusual ones are much sought by collectors. For further information refer to Stanley Gibbons *Great Britain Specialised Stamp Catalogue*, Volume 1.

From May 1840 a red ink was used with the Maltese Crosses and it was superseded by black in February 1841.

Jersey received Type **J26** and it was struck in red until February 1841. Covers are known, however, dated during November and December 1840 with it struck in black, but this was almost certainly by mistake.

The Guernsey Maltese Cross (Type **G14**) is distinctive in that the centre diamond is blunted at one side and the lower left-hand side of the inner cross has a blunted point.

References in philatelic literature are often made to a type of Maltese Cross for "the Channel Islands" in general. This is the "Alderney Cross". *See* Section 13.

The Mulready envelopes and lettersheets were used in Jersey and Guernsey as were the One Penny Black and Twopence Blue adhesives. All plates of the Penny Black can be found on covers from the Islands except for Plate 11, no example of which has yet been seen. The 1840 Twopence Blue (no lines) has not to date been found on cover from the islands.

Up to 1844, when numeral obliterators came into use, covers of the period would normally have had the stamps cancelled with the Maltese Cross and a Jersey or Guernsey datestamp would be struck elsewhere on the cover.

(J26)

(G14)

Mulready Envelope or Lettersheet

1d. with Jersey or Guernsey datestamp in addition to Maltese Cross .	*from*	£350
1d. with Southampton Ship Letter in addition to Maltese Cross	*from*	£500
2d. with Jersey or Guernsey datestamp in addition to Maltese Cross .	*from*	£1200

1840 1d. Black

Used in red on cover from Jersey or Guernsey		
Used in black on cover from Jersey or Guernsey	*from*	£300
Used on cover from Jersey with boxed handstamp		
No. 1, 2, 3 or 4 (Types **J7–J10**)	*from*	£450

1841 2d. Blue

Used on cover from Jersey or Guernsey £200

1841 1d. Red

Used on cover from Jersey or Guernsey .... 30·00
Used on cover from Jersey with boxed handstamp
   No. 1, 2, 3 or 4 (Types **J7**–**J10**) .... *from* £250
For 1d. red cancelled with Jersey datestamp Type **J33** *see* Section 9.

8. Numeral Obliterations

The Maltese Cross cancellation was replaced in 1844 by numeral obliterators. Guernsey and Jersey were given numbers in the series allotted to England and Wales, the former receiving the number 324 and the latter 409.

JERSEY

Several different types were in use in Jersey between 1844 and 1902. The first was sent out in April 1844, and had the number 409 with two curved lines on each side of it. An example of this handstamp used in September 1844 shows four bars above and below the numeral, but subsequent use shows the uppermost and lowest bars omitted as in Type **J27**.

No. JC31 (Type **J27a**) is very similar, but the cross bar of the 4 is 2mm from the base, the loop of the 4 is 3mm wide and the height of the figures is $6\frac{1}{2}$mm. The Type **J27** obliterator is $22\frac{1}{2}$mm wide but this is $21\frac{1}{2}$mm. No. JC31 appears to have been used from 1860 to 1864 and is mainly found on letters addressed to the Continent and on French stamps used on the Boîte Mobile Service.

No. JC32 (Type **J27b**) is again somewhat similar to Type **J27**, but the cross bar of the 4 is 3mm from the base. It appears to have been used from 1862 to 1870 and is often heavily struck so that the horizontal and vertical bars appear to form an unbroken oval. It is known on a number of letters addressed to France and on French stamps from the Boîte Mobile Service, but was not used exclusively for this purpose.

Type **J27c** was a recut of Type **J27** and came into use in July 1857. It can be distinguished by its figures, which are much smaller ($5\frac{1}{2}$mm high against 7mm of the original figures). The loop of the 4 is 4mm wide and the cross bar just under 2mm from the base. There is also a similar type with a blunt point to the 4 (Type **J27d**), issued later in the same year.

The next type (Type **J28**) is the first of the duplexes. It was dispatched from the G.P.O. on 22 April 1858 and the earliest date of use recorded is 3 May 1858 It was replaced at the end of 1863 by a very similar one (Type **J28a**) having a datestamp 19mm wide (1mm wider than the one it replaced).

With Type **J29** the numeral part of the duplex changed from horizontal to vertical format. The oval is 20–21mm in diameter and the loop of the 9 is oval. It was sent to Jersey on 15 October 1866 and the earliest recorded date of use is 4 November.

Type **J29a** is the largest of all the duplexes. The oval is 22–23mm in diameter and the loop of the 9 is rounder. It was dispatched from the G.P.O. on 17 January 1870 and the earliest date of use recorded is 7 February. It remained in use until 1884.

The last of the duplex types (**J30**) was taken into use in 1872 and remained in use until 1882. The datestamp has the name "JERSEY" around the circumference. There are two slightly different types of this cancellation. Type **J30** has a $19\frac{1}{2}$mm diameter datestamp with the "J" and "Y" level with the date and the obliterator is $18\frac{1}{2}$mm wide. Type **J30a**, issued 31 October 1873, has a $20\frac{1}{2}$mm datestamp, "J" and "Y" above the date and the obliterator is 20mm wide.

What appears to be a sub-type is dated 5 February 1881 and shows code B. On this cancellation, No. JC41, the numerals are shorter, the zero is rounder and the upright of the 4 leans over to the right. The lettering on the datestamp is also larger. With this exception, all types can be found lettered A, B or C. Additionally, Type **J29a** is known lettered O in 1874 and Type **J30** with a D.

The first single obliterator was sent on 12 December 1870 (Type **J31**). It is 22mm wide and the point of the 4 is blunted. A smaller version, (Type **J31a**), sent on 8 April 1873, is 21mm wide and has the figures more elongated. Type **J31b** is recorded as being sent on 8 October 1874 and **J31c** on 21 December 1875. These are seen used mainly on mail arriving from France on the Boîte Mobile Service between 1875 and 1881. They are 20mm wide and have three bars at top and bottom. Both have a full stop after the 9 but on Type **J31b** the tip of the 4 is 2mm from the upright. A later version (Type **J31d**), found on the French Peace and Commerce issues, has no stop after the 9, the tip of the 4 is 3mm from the upright and the 0 and the 9 almost touch each other.

Type **J32** is also a single obliterator 19–20mm in diameter. It was used almost exclusively on registered mail and is known used in conjunction with the oval registered stamp between 1872 and 1894. Type **J32a** has a wider oval (20mm) and the side bars are heavier. The figure 4 is also wider.

There is also a further type that should be mentioned although no examples of it have yet been seen. On 16 November 1881 the G.P.O. dispatched to Jersey a large oval obliterator (No. JC45a) and a separate datestamp. It was marked "For Stamping Machine 180504".

There are several single obliterators rather similar to Types **J31** to **J32a** but differing slightly in detail.

(J27)	(J27a)	(J27b)
(J27c)	(J27d)	
(J28)	(J28a)	
(J29)	(J29a)	

(J30)

(J30a)

(J31)

(J31a)

(J31b)

(J31c)

(J31d)

(J32)

(J32a)

No. JC45a

Cat. No.	Type No.		Dates of use	Price on cover from

All struck in black; No. JC30 also occurs in blue.

Barred Ovals

Cat. No.	Type No.		Dates of use	Price
JC29a	J27	(7mm figs. 4 bars)	1844	£120
JC30		(7mm figs. 3 bars)	1844–57 . .	30·00
JC31	J27a	(6½mm figures)	1860–64 . .	30·00
JC32	J27b	("unbroken" oval)	1862–70 . .	30·00
JC33	J27c	(recut; 5½mm figures)	1857	35·00
JC34	J27d	(blunt point to 4)	1857–61 . .	35·00

Duplexes

Cat. No.	Type No.		Dates of use	Price
JC35	J28	(18mm datestamp)	1858–63 . .	35·00
JC36	J28a	(19mm datestamp)	1863–72 . .	40·00
JC37	J29	(Vertical)	1866–86 . .	30·00
JC38	J29a	(larger oval)	1870–84 . .	30·00
JC39	J30	(19½mm datestamp)	1872–82 . .	28·00
JC40	J30a	(20½mm datestamp)	1873	28·00
JC41		(larger lettering, shorter numerals, code B)	1881–82 . .	28·00

Single Obliterators

Cat. No.	Type No.		Dates of use	Price
JC42	J31	(22mm wide)	1870	28·00
JC43	J31a	(21mm wide)	1873	28·00
JC44	J31b	(stop after 9)	1874	25·00
JC44a	J31c	(stop after 9)	1875–81 . .	25·00
JC45	J31d	(no stop after 9)	1878–81 . .	25·00
JC45a		(recorded by G.P.O. 1881)	—	—
JC46	J32	(19–20mm)	1872–94 . .	30·00
JC46a	J32a	(22mm)	1888–1904	30·00

GUERNSEY

Various types of numeral obliterator can be recorded for Guernsey between 1844 and the 1890s. The first was sent out in April 1844 and was put into use in May (Type **G15**). A similar version, but with a horizontal stroke in the centre of the "3", is known used between 1845 and 1852, but is not recorded in the G.P.O. Proof Book.

Type **G15a** was dispatched from the G.P.O. on 14 October 1853 and a similar mark followed in January 1858. The earliest date seen is 16 November 1853. It can be distinguished from the original by the figures, which are considerably smaller (5mm high against the 6½mm of Type **G15**). Type **G15b** is very similar to Type **G15**, but has the serif of the 2 pointing to the point of the 4 instead of being almost vertical. It is first known used in 1856. There is also a type (**G15c**), issued 2 July 1858, with the bottom loop of the 3 much flatter and the figures smaller.

A final type (**G15d**) is known from a cover of 1861. This has a serif at the end of the horizontal stroke on the 4, but otherwise resembles Type **G15a**.

Type **G16** is the first duplex. It was dispatched from the G.P.O. on 9 June 1858, and can be identified when off cover because it has a much rounder appearance that the single obliterator. The earliest date of use seen is 17 August 1858.

In July 1860 a further example of a duplex similar to Type **G16**, but having a datestamp closer to the numeral and with the figures of date more widely spaced, was dispatched from the G.P.O. (Type **G16a**). A similar handstamp followed on 18 May 1863, but this was preceded by a further variation, Type **G16b**, sent on 18 November 1862. In the numeral part of these two obliterators the centre point of the 3 is straight instead of pointing downwards as in the previous type, the serif of the 2 is well clear of the curve of the 2, the foot of the 2 and loop of the 4 are larger, the 4 having a flat top on Type **G16a**. Type **G16**, **16a** and **G16b** were in use until the autumn of 1868.

A new type with a vertical oval was sent out on 11 October 1867 (Type **G17**) which remained in use until replaced by a similar but heavier type in 1876 (Type **G17a**). These two types are very difficult to distinguish off cover, but **G17** has a smaller datestamp with smaller letters than **G17a**. The numeral parts differ in the following ways: **G17** has a short foot to the 2 and the serif points to the point of the 4; **G17a** has a longer foot to the 2 and the serif points inside the 4. The bars of **G17a** are heavier than **G17** and there is very little space between the bottom two.

Type **G17b** was put into use in 1880, and the earliest date recorded is 28 February. It is a much lighter type than the previous two, and the figure 4 is much narrower. It is known used up to 1888. An example used in 1887 appears to be much heavier and has the centre point of the 3 horizontal instead of sloping downwards, the serif of the 2 almost vertical, and the top of the 4 more pointed. This is possibly due to wear or else the stamp needed cleaning.

Vertical single obliterators are known used on newspapers from 1872, the first one (Type **G18**) being dispatched on 1 January. This has four bars at the top and bottom. Three bar types were sent on 15 January 1874 and 16 February 1874 (Types **G19** and **G19a**); these differ only in the tail of the 4 which is without serif on the Type **G19a**. In both types the 3 has a flat top. A version with two bars top and bottom was used in the 1890s.

(G15)   (G15a)   (G15b)

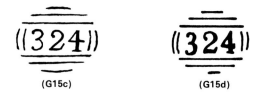

(G15c)   (G15d)

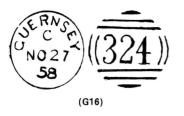

(G16)

(G16a)

(G16b)

(G17)

(G17a)

(G17b)

(G18)

(G19) (G19a) (G19b)

Cat. No.	Type No.		Dates of use	Price on cover from

All struck in black

Barred Ovals

GC17	**G15**	(6½mm figures; vertical serif)	1844–53 ..	30·00
GC18	**G15a**	(5mm figures)	1853–71 ..	30·00
GC19	**G15b**	(serif pointing to right)	1856–80 ..	30·00
GC20	**G15c**	(5mm figures, flatter loops to 3)	1858–71 ..	30·00
GC21	**G15d**	(as No. GC18, but 4 with serif)	1861	30·00

Duplexes

GC22	**G16**	(Horizontal)	1858–67 ..	30·00
GC23	**G16a**	(datestamp and obliterator closer) (blunt 4)	1860–68 ..	30·00
GC24	**G16b**	(pointed 4)	1862–67 ..	30·00
GC25	**G17**	(Vertical, 21mm wide)	1867–76 ..	28·00
GC26	**G17a**	(heavier bars, 22mm wide)	1875–80 ..	28·00
GC26a	**G17b**	(narrow 4)	1880–88 ..	28·00

Single Obliterators

GC27	**G18**	(four bars)	1872	40·00
GC28	**G19**	(three bars, upright serif)	1874	85·00
GC28a	**G19a**	(three bars, sloping serif)	1874–1905	85·00
GC28b	**G19b**	(two bars)	1890s.....	50·00

ALDERNEY

See Section 13 for details of postmarks used from May 1848 onwards.

9. Datestamps and Other Cancellations

JERSEY

First Type

Jersey's first datestamp was Type **J33** introduced in 1830. Known as "the improved steel datestamp with a double set of figures" it is recorded in the G.P.O. Proof Books as having been dispatched to Jersey on 31 May 1830. It was taken into use in June 1830 and is found struck in black up to 1845 and also in red from 1843 to 1845. It is interesting to note that it was used occasionally with some figures of the date missing, probably through carelessness. One example, used in 1830, has the date completely missing.

The datestamp having apparently become worn in use, a recut was provided and this was dispatched by the G.P.O. on 7 November 1845. This is Type **J33a**, distinguished by its sans-serif letters. The datestamp underwent another recut in 1848 and was dispatched to Jersey from the G.P.O. on 17 June 1848. It is known used up to 7 June 1849, but cannot be distinguished from the 1845 recut.

Red ink had continued in use from 1845 so that both recuts are struck in this colour.

Because the first datestamp was not normally used as a cancellation it is highly desirable when found on loose adhesives.

Travelling Types

The so-called "travelling" or "skeleton" handstamps were made up locally from movable letters in a skeleton frame. They were kept as standby for use when the permanent datestamps were unavailable for one reason or another.

Three types are known from Jersey at this period. Type **J34**, recorded struck in black in 1843, resembled the illustrated Type **J34a** with the addition of a cross as ornament below the date. Type **J34a** itself occurs in red in 1848 at the time of the second recutting of the first permanent datestamp.

The first recut, which had produced No. JC49, was covered by another travelling handstamp (Type **J35**). This latter is known struck in red dated between 29 October and 10 November 1845.

Double-arc Type

In 1849 the double-arc type was introduced (Type **J36**). It was dispatched from the G.P.O. in July 1849 and the earliest date of use seen is 4 October 1849. Three slightly different types exist: (a) with "J" and "Y" of "JERSEY" level with the top of the date (month); (b) with "J" below top of date and "Y" level with top; (c) with "J" and "Y" well above date line. This stamp had a somewhat colourful existence: it started with red in 1849, changed to blue in 1851, then to orange in December 1852, changed to black in 1854, went to a dirty green in 1855 and to grey-black in mid-1855, reverted to blue in 1857, and ended with black in 1858. Below the date appeared the letter "A", "B" or "C".

Early Single Circles

In 1858 a small single-circle datestamp (Type **J37**), 19mm in diameter, was introduced mainly for use as a backstamp. Further marks of this size were forwarded in 1860 and 1862. A 20mm diameter c.d.s. was dispatched on 31 December 1861 and was followed by a further example during 1862. These were replaced by 21mm diameter marks in 1869 and 1870. Such marks can be found lettered "A", "B", "C", "D", "E", "F", "P", "A2", "B2", "F2" and without any letters at all, and were in use up to 1896. The letters referred to the time of collection; stamps without letters were used for counter work.

Single-circle datestamps ranging from 19 to 24mm in diameter with the name "JERSEY" in short or tall letters around the top and the date in two lines across the centre were in use at various times between 1871 and 1926 (Type **J38**). They are known with the following letters above the date: "A", "B", "C", "D", "O" and "P" (telegraphic); also without any letters at all, or with letter and figure combinations such as "A1", "A2", "B1", "B2", "C1", "C2", "C8", "D1", "D2", "E1", "E2", "F2", "G2", "GF*A", "IF*A", "KC*A", "L*A", "LC*A", "M*P", "11*A" or with an asterisk. From about 1899 the letters were replaced by the time of the collection or the time the mail was made up.

Squared Circles

In 1881 what was officially called the "combined obliterator" (Type **J39**) was introduced to replace the duplex types. It was dispatched from the G.P.O. on 15 March 1881 and the earliest date of use seen is 23 March 1881. It can be found lettered "A", "B", "C", "D" and "E" and has four corner lines outside the circle. A similar type, but with only three corner lines outside the circle (Type **J39a**), was brought into use round about July 1883 and is known lettered "B", "C", "D", "E" and "F". On 9 December 1886 a slightly larger type (**J39b**), but with two long thin bars forming almost complete circles (except for four breaks of 5mm), one shorter thin bar and solid corners outside the circle, was dispatched from the G.P.O. The earliest date of use seen is 26 September 1887, and the latest 10 November 1896. This mark was lettered "A", "B" (reversed), "C", "D", "E", "F" or "G". A fourth type of the obliterator, with one line and a solid corner outside the circle, came into use early in 1892 and appears to have continued until about 1905 (Type **J39c**). It can be found lettered "B", "C", "D", "E", "F", "G", "H" and "L", and from about 1899 with the time instead of a letter. Several of these obliterators were in use at the same time and the sizes of the letters of "JERSEY" vary a lot. This cancellation is commonly known as the "squared circle".

Double Circles

From 1897 a double-circle datestamp with solid bars separated by a cross was put into service (Type **J40**). Eleven sub-types exist with different sizes of letters and cross and with bars of different thickness. It was used up to 1929. A similar type (**J41**) with a sans-serif figure 1 at the bottom instead of the cross was introduced in 1906. This can be found in seven sub-types with different sizes of letters and figures and with either thin or thick bars. Both types were used concurrently from 1906. Up to 1914 all the Jersey datestamps had the month preceding the day, but from then onwards the day preceded the month (This change was common throughout Britain).

About 1930 a double-ring circular datestamp reading "JERSEY (ST. HELIERS) CHANNEL ISLANDS" was introduced (Type **J42**). In 1938 a similar type (**J43**) was sent in which the words "CHANNEL ISLANDS" have been abbreviated to "CH. IS.". Although the correct postal name of the town has been St. Helier since 1947 Type **J43** is known used as late as 1962.

A double-circle cancellation (Type **J44**) reading "JERSEY. CHANNEL ISLANDS/1" (serifed), introduced about 1928, was joined about 1931 by "JERSEY/CHANNEL ISLANDS" (Type **J45**). The year 1945 saw the introduction of a new one reading "JERSEY C.I./1" (Type **J46**) and this has also been seen with a "2" at the bottom. Later versions of this mark, without the numeral at foot, were

inscribed "JERSEY CHANNEL ISLANDS" with or without a comma after "JERSEY".
The "JERSEY. CHANNEL ISLANDS" type was brought back in 1952 with a "3" at
the bottom. From the 1950s new versions with this wording and numbered "1", "2"
or "4" were introduced. This is Type **J44a**, recognisable by the thin arcs on each side
of the serial number.

Modern Single Circles

Several types of single circle have been used in recent times: one introduced in
1929 (Type **J47**) reads "JERSEY/CHANNEL ISLANDS", the space between the last
two words varying. A similar type with more condensed lettering was used from 1935
to 1943. It always has a "wavy" circle.

A type reading "JERSEY CHANNEL ISLANDS" (**J48**), with numbers between "1"
and "16" at the foot, was used from 1938. The cancellers show individual differences
in sizes of lettering and the presence or absence of a full stop after "JERSEY".

Above the date there is an asterisk or a code letter, of which "A", "B", "C", "D",
"E", "F", "G", "H", "O", "R", "S" and "W" have been noted. Number 12 has also
been seen without a code letter.

A 25mm cancel reading "JERSEY. CHANNEL ISLANDS 21" or "22" continuously
round the circle was used on letters posted "out of course" (Type **J48a**). It is
occasionally found as a normal cancel on stamps which had missed the machine
cancel.

Type **J49** is similar, but the words are abbreviated to "JERSEY. CHANNEL IS.".
Known in this type are an unnumbered datestamp, one numbered "3" without code
letter, one numbered "9" with code letter "Z", one numbered "10" with asterisk and
one numbered "11" without code letter.

Large circular datestamps of rubber are met with: these will be found below under
the "Cancellations for Small Packets".

Machine Cancellations

The first machine cancellation, a Krag type, was introduced in 1923. Up to 1928 it
had the word "JERSEY" measuring 18–19mm (Type **J50**), but after 1928 this
measured only 14–16mm (Type **J50a**). The datestamp occurs on both sides of the
wavy lines as it is a continuous impression. At Christmas time each year the time,
which normally appeared above the date, was removed. In some dies there was a
cross below the date.

The Krag machine was replaced in 1930 by a Universal type having a circular
datestamp and continuous wavy lines. It had six bars in 1930–31 (Type **J51**), five in
1931–35 (**J51a**) and seven from 1935 onwards (**J51b**). The continuous wavy lines
were in use until 1937 when a type with two breaks between the bars was used (Type
J51c). The removable centre-piece could be put into the machine either way up.

During 1942 continuous lines again appeared (No. JC84) but the segmented type
was again reverted to from 1943 (No. JC87). Between 1941 and 1945 the last two
figures of the date plug were cast by the *Evening Post* on its linotype machine. They
were then hand-shaped to fit the cancellation. From 1946 the correct figures were
again in use (No. JC86) and in 1948 the continuous-lines Type **J51b** was brought
back. Examples used from 1950 show one or two damaged bars.

In 1953 the bars with breaks were again used but with a new datestamp which
lacks the curved line at the bottom (Type **J52**). A new datestamp with larger letters
was introduced in 1960 (Type **J53**). A further type came into use in the 1960s with
small letters and a large curved arc. The time was sometimes replaced by a line (Type
J53a).

On 1 December 1969 new cancelling bars in the form of a box containing three
unevenly spaced horizontal lines was introduced by the Independent Postal
Administration (Type **J54**). The box is found either way up in relation to the
datestamp.

Slogans

Since 1931 Jersey has made use of machine cancellations to introduce slogans from time to time in place of the wavy lines. The first said "The Best Investment a Telephone" and this was followed in 1932 by one reading "The Telephone Makes Life Easier" which remained in use for about a year. *See* Section 15.

Crown Registered Marks

The first registration stamp used in Jersey was the Crown and "REGISTERED" marking. Two types are known. The first (Type **J55**) was used from 1855 to 1859 in black and is also known in red from 1858. Type **J56**, which shows a different crown, was used from 1859 to 1874 usually in red, but examples are known in black from 1864 and 1874.

Registration Cancellations

Circular datestamps were usually used for registration purposes on covers and often on parcels, although ovals also exist. The first oval bore only the name of the island (Type **J57**) and is recorded as being dispatched to Jersey on 19 August 1879. It is known lettered from "A" to "E" and without any letter at all. In 1930 it was replaced by one having "JERSEY CHANNEL ISLANDS" at foot (Type **J58**). In 1936 this appeared with the words "Channel Islands" in upper and lowercase letters. One used in 1938 has a serrated edge, due to wear. By 1939 another type with the words "JERSEY CHANNEL IS." in small capitals had been introduced (Type **J58a**), but from 1947 another one (**J58b**) with larger letters was used. Similar stamps in use at present read "REGISTERED" at the top, "JERSEY CHANNEL ISLANDS" at the bottom, and have a figure "2", "3" or "4" below the date (**J59**).

An example of a large "R" in oval with "FEE PAID" below (as Type **G47** of Guernsey) is known on a parcel post label of 1900. This was a general style of handstamp for use throughout Great Britain introduced in 1892.

Type **J60**, recorded as used on various occasions between 1939 and December 1946, bears no date and has the word "REGISTERED" across the middle.

Supplies of normal adhesive registration labels were exhausted in mid-1943 and a rubber unframed alphanumeric handstamp, e.g. A1583, was used from June 1943. Struck in blue, it consisted of a prefix letter, A, B or C, followed by a three or four digit number. The prefix C is by far the scarcest.

Express Post

An oval handstamp (Type **J60b**) for this service was supplied to Jersey on 11 April 1891. Examples of its use are rare.

Money Order Office Cancellation

The cancellation of the Money Order Office (Type **J61**) is occasionally seen on parcel post labels and is known cancelling stamps between 1900 and 1908.

Parcel Post Cancellations

The first cancellation for parcel post purposes (Type **J62**) was dispatched from the G.P.O. on 24 November 1886 and was made of rubber. Several examples of its use are known, the latest being on a parcel post label of 1911. The cancel consisted of a barred oval with "JERSEY" across the middle measuring 18mm. A second type (**J62a**), in which "JERSEY" measures 23mm, is known on a parcel post label used in 1890. The first oval measures 27mm across and the second 30mm, with the "J" and the "Y" much nearer to the sides.

More usually found is the double-ring rubber type with the name across the middle (Type **J63**). It was first sent to Jersey on 9 September 1892, others following in 1893, 1894, 1898 and 1904. These replacements differ in details. In one the inner arcs are above and below the first "E" and in another they come between the "J" and the "E".

The first label type appears to have been used in 1915 (Type **J64**). A replacement in similar design, but with the figure "1" incorporated was dispatched in 1917 (Type **J64a**).

A new label type (**J65**), the words "PARCEL/POST" appearing at the sides and reading upwards, came into use in the 1930s. It is noteworthy for having the words "CHANNEL ISLAND" in the singular.

This appears to have been altered later, the wording "CHANNEL ISLANDS" (plural) being recorded in 1960 (Type **J65a**).

Also in the 1930s there appeared a further large label type (**J66**), numbered either "1" or "2" at top right. Number "3" in this series followed in 1956.

In use for a short time in the 1950s was Type **J67**, a label type of smaller format and incorporating the name St. Heliers.

A single-circle parcel cancellation of 33mm diameter, with "PARCEL POST" round the top, "CHANNEL ISLANDS" round the bottom, and "JERSEY" and the date in two lines in the centre, was introduced in July 1970 (Type **J68**).

Cancellations for Small Packets

Type **J69** was a single-circle cancellation as **J70** but without "ST. HELIERS", dispatched to Jersey on 9 October 1893. Type **J70** (30mm) followed in 1905 and a number of minor variants are known. A larger type, 42mm in diameter, is known used in 1914 and as late as 1951.

A small rectangular cancel, reading "JERSEY (ST. HELIERS)/CHANNEL ISLANDS" (Type **J71**) with the date across the centre is known used in the 1930s. A further mark from this period is circular, 29mm diameter, inscribed "JERSEY/Channel Islands" in seriffed letters with the date across the centre (Type **J72**).

In 1938 a series of 30mm single circle marks (Type **J73**) was introduced which lasted for many years. Examples can be found with or without a time indication. Versions are known with the figures "1", "2" or "3" beneath "JERSEY" (Type **J73a**). "JERSEY 1" is unusual in that it also exists with "CH. IS." at foot (Type **J73b**). A later variation, from 1969, of the usual 30mm mark had bars either side of the date (Type **J73c**).

A further mute type (**J74**) is recorded from 1952. This is a single circle reading "JERSEY/CHANNEL ISLANDS" with five bars across the centre instead of a date. A roller type (**J75**) was used for a few weeks in 1957. This showed "JERSEY" set between double lines and was repeated continuously as the roller was applied.

The series of 30mm circular marks came to an end in 1990 with the appearance of a larger 38mm diameter type (**J76**).

Triangles

Cancellations of triangular shape are used on circulars and printed matter. They bear the figures or telegraphic code letters allotted to the post office by the G.P.O.

A small "409" in a triangle with base 17mm (Type **J77**), the figures being 2mm high, is known on King Edward VII ½d. stamps. It was dispatched on 4 August 1909 and subsequently appeared in 1934 with the wavy lines as part of a machine cancellation in place of the normal datestamp (Type **J77a**). A similar mark, but with 3mm figures, is known on the Postal Centenary and Occupation issues.

A further triangle with sides of 20mm and figures 5mm tall (Type **J78b**) was in use during the 1960s.

In the 1930s a larger version of the triangle, approximately 20mm at the base, was put into use (Type **J78**) and, again, a similar type was used with wavy lines as a machine cancellation, this time dating from 1952 (Type **J78a**).

The letters "JE" in a triangle (Type **J79**) are known cancelling a stamp of the 1897 issue. It is possible this is still in use.

Triangular cancellations with wavy lines are occasionally employed during a census or count of mail.

"Paid" Handstamps

Various "PAID" handstamps, applied in red, are to be found, usually on newswrappers or circulars.

On 26 June 1919 a handstamp Type **J80** (resembling **J81** but without "CHANNEL ISLANDS") was sent from the G.P.O. and this has a ½d. fixed value.

On the same day Type **J81** was dispatched which had a movable value. Its diameter was 29mm.

"PAID" handstamps had another useful role during the German Occupation. The 1d and 2½d. were put into service when postage stamps were not available, and as such were widely used from 1942 onwards. The 2d. value (postcard rate) is much scarcer, but is known used on various dates in 1942, 1944 and 1945. The 3d. and 5d. values are known used together on a parcel of 11 April 1945.

Some envelopes with this handstamp without date were sold in quantities of a dozen or more to residents of country districts, who posted them in pillar boxes. This avoided a journey into St. Helier for letters to be franked when stamps were unobtainable. The envelopes on arrival at the Head Post Office were given the normal machine cancellation.

A 1d. "PAID" handstamp was used in 1941 before the first Jersey 1d. stamp was ready and again later on. Another 1d. value (Type **J81a**) appears to have been made by removing the "2" from the ½d., but no examples of the original ½d. used properly are recorded.

The handstamp with movable values was supplemented in the 1950s by one in the larger size of 32mm (Type **J81b**).

Machine "Paid" Stamps

The first type of "PAID" marking applied by machine (**J82**) is believed to have consisted of the words "JERSEY/PAID ½d./date" in three lines. It was in use from about 1926 to 1929 and in the latter year the words "GREAT BRITAIN" were added, giving Type **J83**. These were used in conjunction with the wavy lines of the Krag cancelling machine.

A boxed type (**J84**) followed in 1932. This had an inner square containing "½D." and the date in two lines above; the outer square read "JERSEY/PAID" (top and bottom) and "GREAT BRITAIN" (left and right, both reading upwards).

Type **J85** came into use about 1937. This consists of a circular datestamp inscribed "JERSEY/GT. BRITAIN" and with date in two lines across the centre. Beside the datestamp is "(value)/PAID", on each side of which are seven wavy lines.

The value in 1937 had been ½d. When postage was raised in 1940 a "1D/PAID" die was introduced; similarly in 1951 a "1½D." die was brought in for the new printed paper rate. Since then higher values have made their appearance to cope with increasing postal rates (values noted have been 2d., 2½d., 3d., 4d., 4½d., 5d., 6d. and 7d.) and the c.d.s. no longer contains "GT. BRITAIN" (Type **J85a**). A new cancel used in 1955 had the curved line absent from the c.d.s. (Type **J85b**).

Like the "PAID" handstamps, the "1D/PAID" machine version found an additional use during the Occupation, serving in lieu of adhesives when these ran out from time to time.

When the two-tier service began in 1968 the values in Type **J85** were replaced by "1ST PAID" or "2ND PAID" (Type **J86**). In its turn this was abandoned in February

1971, giving rise to Type **J87** which reads "POSTAGE PAID". Type **J88** has "POSTAGE R PAID" between the wavy lines, the "R" signifying Rebate (bulk postings of circulars).

The children who each year send letters to Father Christmas have (if they include their address) received a reply in recent times through special arrangements made by the Post Office. Type **J89**, struck in red, is "SANTALAND/POSTAGE PAID" in a circular datestamp with a boxed slogan showing Father Christmas and "MERRY CHRISTMAS". It was used in 1974 and 1975. In 1976 it was replaced by a similar stamp, but with Santa in a sleigh.

Postal Administration "Paid" Marking

Since 1969 the Jersey Postal Administration has been using a 31mm single-circle handstamp reading "POSTAL ADMINISTRATION/JERSEY CHANNEL ISLANDS" (Type **J90**). Across the centre is "POSTAGE/date/PAID".

Meter Stamp

Various official and private organisations use meter postage in Jersey, but their numerous markings are outside the scope of this Catalogue.

During the German Occupation the Head Post Office at St. Helier commandeered Neopost No. 8 from the Airport and it was used from time to time in lieu of adhesives. The machine is known to have franked covers in the denominations of $\frac{1}{2}$d., 1d., 1$\frac{1}{2}$d., 2$\frac{1}{2}$d or 4$\frac{1}{2}$d. plus 1d. (registered cover of 6 July 1942). It was operated by the P.O. clerks on prepayment of cash by the public.

During its first use as a $\frac{1}{2}$d. stamp the die appears with a vertical crack down the centre, but this seems to have been repaired later.

Philatelic Bureau Cancellations

Jersey has a Philatelic Bureau (address P.O. Box 304, St. Helier) offering many services to collectors.

For its own mail the Bureau uses Type **J90** or Type **J91**. This latter is inscribed "PHILATELIC BUREAU" with the lettering in various sizes.

A similar type (**J92**), containing the words "PHILATELIC SERVICE", has been in use since 1 January 1970 but this is solely for the cancelling-to-order of loose adhesives.

The various "First Day of Issue" markings are dealt with in Section 15.

(J33)

(J33a)

(J34a)

(J35)

(J36)

(J37)

(J38)

(J39)

(J39a)

(J39c)

(J40)

(J41)

(J42)

(J44)

(J44a)

(J45)

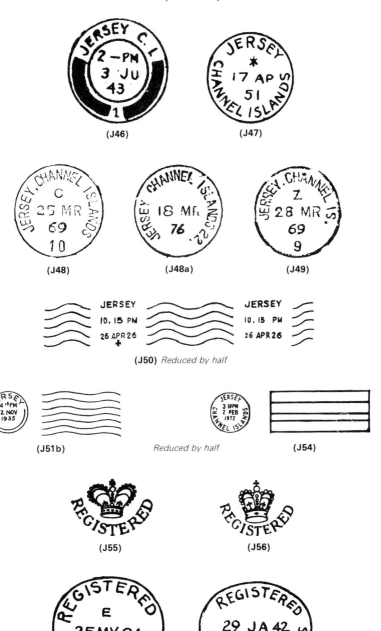

(J46)

(J47)

(J48)

(J48a)

(J49)

(J50) *Reduced by half*

(J51b)

Reduced by half

(J54)

(J55)

(J56)

(J57)

(J58a)

(J59)

(J60)

(J60b)

(J61)

(J62)

(J63)

(J64)

Reduced by half

(J66)

(J67)

Reduced by half

(J68)

(J70)

(J72)

(J73)

(J73a)

(J73c)

(J74)

(J75)

(J76)

(J77)

(J78)

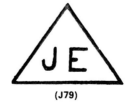

(J79)

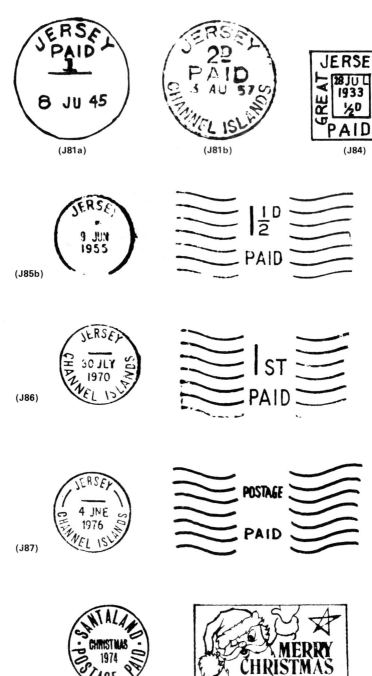

(J81a)

(J81b)

(J84)

(J85b)

(J86)

(J87)

(J89)

(J90)

(J91)

(J92)

Cat. No.	Type No.		Dates of use	Colour	Price on cover from
First Type					
JC47	**J33**		1830–45	Black	20·00
	On 1841 1d. red adhesive, dated 1841			*(off cover)*	£600
JC48			1843–45	Red	20·00
	On 1841 1d. red adhesive, dated 1845			*(off cover)*	£850
JC49	**J33a**	(recut, sans-serif)	1845–49	Red	20·00
Travelling Types					
JC51	**J34**	(with ornament)	1843	Black	£400
JC52	**J34a**	(no ornament)	1848	Red	£500
JC53	**J35**		1845	Red	£600
Double-arc Type					
JC54	**J36**		1849–58	Various	25·00
Early Single Circles					
JC55	**J37**	(name straight)	1858–96	Black	2·00
JC56	**J38**	(name curved)	1871–1926	Blue	3·00
				Black	1·00
Squared Circles					
JC57	**J39**	(4 corner lines)	1881–84	Black	12·00
JC58	**J39a**	(3 corner lines)	1883–91	Black	9·00
JC59	**J39b**	("second circle")	1887–96	Black	6·00
JC60	**J39c**	(1 line, solid corner)	1892–1905	Black	3·00

Cat. No.	Type No.		Dates of use	Colour	Price on cover from
Double Circles					
JC61	**J40**	(cross at foot)	1897–1929	Black	2·00
JC62	**J41**	(sans-serif 1)	1906–30	Black	1·00
JC63	**J42**	JERSEY ST. HELIERS CHANNEL ISLANDS	1930–45	Black or red . .	1·00
JC64	**J43**	JERSEY ST. HELIERS CH. IS.	1938–62	Black	50
JC65	**J44**	JERSEY. CHANNEL ISLANDS/1	1927–38	Black	5·00
JC66		JERSEY. CHANNEL ISLANDS/3	1952–	Black	30
JC67	**J44a**	JERSEY. CHANNEL ISLANDS/1	1950s–70s	Black	30
JC68		JERSEY. CHANNEL ISLANDS/2	1961	Black	30
JC69		JERSEY. CHANNEL ISLANDS/4	1950s–	Black	30
JC70	**J45**	JERSEY CHANNEL ISLANDS	1931–48	Black	2·00
JC71	**J46**	JERSEY C.I./1	1945–54	Black	30
JC72		JERSEY C.I./2	1945–54	Black	30
JC72a		JERSEY CHANNEL ISLANDS	1970s	Black	30
JC72b		JERSEY, CHANNEL ISLANDS	1980s	Black	30
Modern Single Circles					
JC73	**J47**	JERSEY/CHANNEL ISLANDS	1929–58	Black	30
JC73a	**J47a**	Ditto, but with condensed lettering	1935–43	Black	50
JC74	**J48**	JERSEY CHANNEL ISLANDS, 1–16	1938–69	Black or red . .	30
JC75	**J48a**	JERSEY CHANNEL ISLANDS, 21 or 22	1952–76	Black	50
JC76	**J49**	JERSEY CHANNEL IS.	1950s	Black	50
Machine Cancellations					
JC77	**J50**	JERSEY 18–19mm	1923–28	Black	4·00
JC78		(time omitted)	1923–28	Black	8·00
JC79	**J50a**	JERSEY 14–16mm	1928–30	Black	4·00
JC80	**J51**	(6 wavy lines)	1930–31	Black	1·00
JC81	**J51a**	(5 wavy lines)	1931–35	Black	80
JC82	**J51b**	(7 wavy lines)	1935–37	Black	50
JC83		(re-use)	1948–53	Black	35
JC84		(locally made figures)	1942–43	Black	3·00
JC85	**J51c**	(7 wavy lines segmented)	1937–41	Black	50
JC86		(re-use)	1946–59	Black	35
JC87		(locally made figures)	1941–45	Black	3·00
JC88	**J52**	(datestamp, with or without arc)	1953–60	Black	15
JC89	**J53**	(larger letters)	1960–69	Black	15
JC90	**J53a**	(small letters)	1960s	Black	15
JC91	**J54**	(straight-lined box)	1969–	Black	10
Crown Registered Mark					
JC92	**J55**		1855–59	Black	£220
JC92a			1858	Red	£300
JC93	**J56**	(different crown)	1859–70	Red	£200
JC94			1864–74	Black	£180
Registration Cancellations					
JC95	**J57**	JERSEY	1879–1936	Black	4·00
JC95a	**G47**	R in oval/FEE PAID	1900	Black	20·00
JC95b	**J58**	JERSEY, CHANNEL ISLANDS	1930–38	Black	3·00
JC96		JERSEY Channel Islands	1936	Black	3·00
JC97	**J58a**	JERSEY CHANNEL IS.	1939–47	Black or violet.	3·00
JC98	**J58b**	(larger letters)	1947–55	Black or violet.	3·00
JC99	**J59**	JERSEY CHANNEL ISLANDS 2	1954–	Black	3·00
JC100		JERSEY CHANNEL ISLANDS 3	1954–	Black	3·00

Cat. No.	Type No.		Dates of use	Colour	Price on cover from
JC101		JERSEY CHANNEL ISLANDS 4	1954–	Black	3·00
JC102	**J60**	REGISTERED, no date	1939–46	Black	5·00
JC102a	**J60a**	Local rubber handstamp (prefix A or B)	1943	Blue	20·00
JC102b		Prefix C		Blue	60·00

Express Post Cancellation

JC102c	**J60b**		1891	Black	60·00

Money Order Office Cancellation

JC103	**J61**		1900–08	Black	30·00

Parcel Post Cancellations

JC104	**J62**	Barred oval 27mm	1886–1911	Black	30·00
JC105	**J62a**	(larger, 30mm)	1890	Black	40·00
JC106	**J63**	Double ring	1892–1916	Black or violet.	8·00
JC107	**J64**	PARCEL JE POST/JERSEY	1915–17	Black	12·00
JC108	**J64a**	PARCEL JE POST/JERSEY/1	1917	Black	12·00
JC109	**J65**	JERSEY/date/CHANNEL ISLAND	1930s–	Black	2·00
JC110	**J65a**	Ditto, but ISLANDS (plural)	1960	Black	2·00
JC111	**J66**	JERSEY/CHANNEL ISLANDS/1	1930s–	Black	2·00
JC112		JERSEY/CHANNEL ISLANDS/2	1930s–	Black	2·00
JC113		JERSEY/CHANNEL ISLANDS/3	1952–	Black	1·00
JC114	**J67**	JERSEY/(ST. HELIERS)	1950s	Violet	5·00
JC115	**J68**	Single circle	1970–75	Black	50
JC115a	**J68a**	Ditto, but without JERSEY	1972–75	Black	50
JC115b	**J68b**	Ditto, but JERSEY below date	1972–	Black	50

Cancellations for Small Packets

JC116	**J69**	F/JERSEY	1893	Black	40·00
JC117	**J70**	F/JERSEY (ST. HELIERS) (36mm)	1905	Black	40·00
JC117a		Ditto, but 42mm	1914	Black	12·00
JC118	**J71**	Rectangular cancel	1930	Black	20·00
JC119	**J72**	JERSEY/Channel Islands (serifs)	1938	Black	12·00
JC120	**J73**	JERSEY/CHANNEL ISLANDS (30mm) (with or without time)	1938–	Black	10·00
JC121	**J73a**	JERSEY 1/CHANNEL ISLANDS (with or without time)	1938–60	Black or violet.	50
JC121a		JERSEY 2/CHANNEL ISLANDS (with or without time)	1938–52	Black or violet.	50
JC121b		JERSEY 3/CHANNEL ISLANDS (with or without time)	1958–79	Black or violet.	
JC121c	**J73b**	JERSEY 1/CH. IS.	1938	Black	50
JC121d	**J73c**	JERSEY/CHANNEL ISLANDS (30mm) (with bars either side of date)	1969–86	Black or violet.	50
JC122	**J74**	JERSEY/bars/CHANNEL ISLANDS	1952	Black	5·00
JC123	**J75**	Roller cancel	1957	Black	35·00
JC124	**J76**	JERSEY/CHANNEL ISLANDS (38mm)	1990	Black	1·00

Triangles

JC127	**J77**	409 (2mm high) in small triangle	1909–30s	Black	15·00
JC128	**J77a**	(with wavy lines)	1934–	Black	10·00
JC128a	**J77b**	409 (3mm high) in small triangle	1940–41	Black	20·00

Cat. No.	Type No.		Dates of use	Colour	Price on cover from
JC129	**J78**	409 in larger triangle	1930s–70s	Black	2·00
JC130	**J78a**	(with wavy lines)	1952–	Black	3·00
JC130a	**J78b**	409 in triangle with 20mm sides	1960s	Black	3·00
JC131	**J79**	JE in triangle	1897–1970	Black	2·00

"Paid" Handstamps

JC132	**J80**	$\frac{1}{2}$d., without CHANNEL ISLANDS	1919–	Red	12·00
JC133	**J81**	Various values with CHANNEL ISLANDS, 29mm	1919–55	Red	1·00
		Used in lieu of adhesives			
JC133a		1d. or 2$\frac{1}{2}$d.		Red	25·00
JC133b		2d.		Red	70·00
JC133c		3d. or 5d.		Red	£150
JC134	**J81a**	$\frac{1}{2}$d. modified as 1d.	1944–45	Black or red . .	40·00
JC135	**J81b**	As Type **J81**, but 32mm	1956–	Red	1·00

Machine "Paid" Markings

JC136	**J82**	JERSEY/PAID $\frac{1}{2}$d./date	1926–29	Red	8·00
JC137	**J83**	GREAT BRITAIN added	1929	Red	8·00
JC138	**J84**	$\frac{1}{2}$d. boxed type	1932	Red	5·00
JC138a		With telephone slogan	1930s	Red	6·00
JC139	**J85**	(Value)/PAID between wavy lines	1937–68	Red	50
		1D/PAID used in lieu of adhesive	1942–45	Red	20·00
JC140		As No. JC139	1958	Black	1·00
JC141	**J85a**	GT. BRITAIN removed; with arc	1951	Red	50
JC142	**J85b**	New c.d.s., no arc	1955	Red	50
JC143	**J86**	1ST PAID between wavy lines	1968–71	Red	30
JC144		2ND PAID between wavy lines	1968–71	Red	30
JC145	**J87**	POSTAGE PAID between wavy lines	1971–	Red	30
JC146	**J88**	POSTAGE R PAID between wavy lines	1972–	Red	80
JC147	**J89**	SANTALAND/POSTAGE PAID	1974–75	Red	4·00
JC148		(Santa in sleigh)	1976–	Red	2·00

Postal Administration "Paid" Marking

JC149	**J90**	POSTAL ADMINISTRATION POSTAGE PAID	1969–	Black	10
JC149a		PHILATELIC BUREAU POSTAGE PAID	1973–	Black	20

Meter Stamp Neopost No. 8

		Used in lieu of adhesives	1941–45		
JC150		$\frac{1}{2}$d., 1d. or 2$\frac{1}{2}$d.		—	40·00
JC150a		other values		—	60·00
JC150b		on registered cover	1942	—	£400

Philatelic Bureau Cancellations

JC151	**J91**	PHILATELIC BUREAU	1970–	Black	30
JC152	**J91a**	PHILATELIC BUREAU/JERSEY CHANNEL ISLANDS (arranged as Type **J90**)	1980s	Black	30
	J92	PHILATELIC SERVICE: (c.t.o. on adhesives only)			

"First Day of Issue": *see* Section 15.

Prices for Nos. JC104–124 refer to markings *on piece*.

GUERNSEY

Guernsey datestamps show many similarities to the Jersey types and can be considered under the same headings.

First Type

The first Guernsey datestamp (Type **G20**) is recorded in the P.O. Proof Books as having been dispatched on 31 May 1830 and it was in use in June. It was recut, a new stamp (Type **G20a**) being dispatched on 29 July 1843: the letter "N" appears to have been repaired and a new set of figures supplied with the 4's sans-serif. The Postmaster faced a problem in 1844 with this datestamp, through shortage of numerals. When a "4" occurred in the day of the month he had to substitute an inverted "7" for the first "4" of "1844" (Type **G20b**).

Travelling Types

While the datestamp Type **G20** was away for its recut in 1843 a "skeleton" or "travelling" type was evidently put into use, since a strike is recorded on 28 July 1843 (Type **G21**).

In 1847 Type **G20a** finally gave out. For the period from the end of July until mid-August another "travelling" type saw service (Type **G22**). Dates between 29 July and 13 August 1847 have been recorded.

Double-arc Type

On 15 August 1847 the G.P.O. dispatched a double-arc datestamp (Type **G23**) lettered "A", "B" or "C". It appears to have been in use till 1854, although a replacement was supplied on 27 December 1851 (Type **G23a**). In turn a new datestamp (Type **G23b**) was sent on 14 October 1853.

Type **G23** had arcs less than 3mm apart. The other types (arcs 3mm apart) are distinguished by the position of the letters "G" and "Y" of "GUERNSEY" in relation to a line drawn across the bottom of the date (month and day). In Type **G23a**, "G–Y" falls below the base of the date; in Type **G23b** "G–Y" stands above the base of the date.

Numerous colours are found in strikes of this stamp. It started with black in 1847, changed to blue in 1849, then to various shades of yellow from January 1853, reverted to black via a rust colour in 1854, went to a dirty green in 1856, and ended in blue-black in 1858.

Early Single Circles

A small circular datestamp 19mm in diameter (Type **G24**) was introduced in 1858. An example is recorded in the Proof Books as having been dispatched on 2 June. It was mainly used as a backstamp on letters arriving in the island and is found lettered "A", "B", "C", "D" or "P". Three slightly different types were used between 1858 and 1882 and again between 1902 and 1907. The letters signify time of arrival—morning, afternoon or evening.

Other single-circle datestamps (Type **G25**), ranging from 19 to 26mm in diameter with the name "GUERNSEY" in small or large letters round the top and the date in two lines across the centre, were used between 1872 and the 1930s. They are known with the following letters above the date: "A", "B" or "C"; also with an asterisk or without any letters at all. From 1898 the letters were replaced by the actual time of the collection. Many different sub-types exist.

Squared Circles

The "combined obliterator", often termed the "squared circle" by collectors, was introduced in 1887 (Type **G26**). It started with four lines outside the circle and was lettered "A", "B", "C" or "D". In 1896 the letters were replaced by the time of posting. In 1899 a slightly smaller type (**G26a**) was taken into use, having only three corner lines, and this continued until 1905.

Double Circles

A double-circle datestamp (Type **G27**) with solid bars separated by a cross was put into service in 1905 (earliest date recorded 24 March). There are five sub-types with different sizes of letters and cross, and with bars of different thickness. Type **G27** remained in use up to 1928. Up to 1914 all Guernsey datestamps had the month preceding the day, but from then onwards the day precedes the month.

In 1929 a double-circle datestamp worded "GUERNSEY (ST. PETER PORT)/CHANNEL IS." was introduced (Type **G28**), the earliest recorded date of use being 20 December. It was replaced in 1937 by a similar type in which "CHANNEL IS." has been abbreviated to "CH. IS." (Type **G28a**) and this remained in use until 30 September 1969 along with with one having "CHAN. IS." at the bottom (Type **G28b**).

Other double-circle datestamps seen (Type **G29**) are "GUERNSEY C.I./1" and "GUERNSEY C.I./2" with black bars each side of the numeral, which is at the foot. They are believed to date from 1945 and were supplied in case the cancelling machine broke down.

A new type of double-circle, inscribed "GUERNSEY POST OFFICE" and with only a thin arc at foot (Type **G30**), has been in use since 1984.

Modern Single Circles

The early 1930s saw the introduction of new single-circle cancellations and they remained in use until 30 September 1969. They were 23–24mm in diameter and had "GUERNSEY" at the top and "CHANNEL ISLANDS" at the bottom (Type **G31**). An asterisk appears above the date. A variety occurs between 1939 and 1941 showing a stop between "CHANNEL" and "ISLANDS".

In 1945 numbers from "5" to "11" are found inserted in place of the asterisk and such cancellers were for use at the counter on registered mail and postal orders. In 1953 the numbers were replaced by letters running from "E" to "M" (except "I").

In contrast to Type **G31** there is a single-circle cancellation, Type **G32**, in which the words "GUERNSEY CHANNEL ISLANDS" read right round the circumference. This is also known with figure "1" or "N" at the foot (Type **G33**).

A rare type (**G34**), used for short periods in 1945 and 1946 as a cancelling stamp, has "GUERNSEY CH. IS." at the top and "PARCEL DEPOT" at the bottom. It was probably meant for internal use on dockets.

From 1952, and mainly at peak times such as Christmas, a canceller numbered "12" and reading "GUERNSEY (ST. PETER PORT) CHAN. IS." has seen service (Type **G35**).

When the Bailiwick of Guernsey became postally independent on 1 October 1969 there was a complete revision of all datestamps then in use.

The Head Office counter received the single-circle Type **G36** (inscription in capitals and lower case letters), diameter 26½mm, the individual cancellers being lettered "E" to "N" (less "I") to which one letter "P" was later added. The Sorting Office was issued with the same style of datestamp; this shows no identifying letter, but sometimes has the time or an asterisk above the date.

Very similar cancellers, which show an island or town name at the foot, are from sub-offices and these are listed in Section 14.

A further series with "GUERNSEY POST OFFICE" in capitals (Type **G36a**) was introduced in 1987. There were several slightly different handstamps in this series and examples can be found without code or with "E" above the date.

At its opening on 2 June 1971 the Postal Museum was provided with a special single-circle datestamp and this is still in use (Type **G37**). It features the Guernsey scroll marking of pre-adhesive days (*see* Section 3).

Machine Cancellations

A Krag machine was introduced in Guernsey in June 1923, giving a cancellation of five wavy lines in conjunction with square datestamps reading "GUERNSEY" and (below) the date in one line. This Type **G38** is a continuous impression of datestamps and lines.

A Universal machine replaced it in December 1931 (Type **G39**) and this consisted of a circular datestamp flanked by five wavy lines.

In 1936 Type **G39a** was put into use, the wavy lines increased to seven in number and now broken in two places so that the centre portion was removable. This type saw service until 1939.

In 1939 another type (**G39b**) was introduced in which the seven wavy lines were continuous and this remained in service throughout the German Occupation. In 1941 the figure "0" was split by Lionel Le Huray, a Post Office engineer, to make the final 1 of the year. Between 1942 and 1945 the last two figures in the date were cut in lead by the Guernsey Press.

In May 1945 the machine was refitted with a new datestamp lacking the lower arc below "GUERNSEY" and having seven wavy lines in the segmented style (Type **G40**). However, in mid-1947 the wavy lines were changed to the continuous form (Type **G40a**).

A new datestamp came into use in May 1948 (Type **G41**). This had tall thin letters occupying half the circle and the other half filled with an arc; it developed a crack in November. The seven wavy lines were segmented. From February 1949 until 1958 the old datestamp first used for Type **G39a** in 1936 was pressed into service again.

During November 1954 datestamp Type **G39** was reused temporarily in conjunction with the seven continuous wavy lines.

A completely new datestamp (Type **G42**) took its place in 1954 and it was in turn replaced in 1955 (Type **G42a**) and again in 1960 (Type **G43**). The seven segmented wavy lines were still employed. The time is sometimes replaced by a line.

Postal independence in 1969 saw the wording of the datestamp altered to "GUERNSEY POST OFFICE" with an arc at the foot. This single circle of 22mm diameter (Type **G44**) has the time and date in three lines (the time sometimes replaced by a line) and the seven segmented wavy lines continue as before. As from 1972 the wavy lines have given way to two parallel thin bars 50mm long and 8mm apart (Type **G45**), although slogans are usually used. During two weeks in April/May 1982 and in January/February 1986 Type **G44** was reused by mistake.

Slogans

The wavy lines of the machine cancellations have been replaced from time to time by slogans. The first was the "EP" and "lover's knot" used extensively in the British Isles to celebrate the Wedding of (the then) Princess Elizabeth in 1947. *See* Section 15.

Crown Registered Mark

A mark showing a crown above the word "REGISTERED" (Type **G46**) is known used in Guernsey struck in blue (1852) or black (1884).

Registration Cancellations

The first registration cancellation known for Guernsey is the large "R" in oval type (Type **G46a**), issued throughout Great Britain from 1885 onwards. An example was sent to Guernsey in 1891 and the mark is known used from 1893. This was replaced by a smaller "R" in oval with "FEE PAID" beneath (Type **G47**). Exmples are known on mail between 1898 and 1905.

Oval registered cancellations were introduced in 1938. The two pre-war versions were inscribed "GUERNSEY, CHANNEL ISLANDS" (Type **G48**) or "GUERNSEY, CH. IS." (Type **G48a**).

During the Occupation a rubber stamp was made locally (Type **G49**), a

30 × 19mm box inscribed "GUERNSEY" struck in violet. In the centre the registration number is added by numbering machine in red.

An undated marking (Type **G50**) was put into use in 1945. It measures 38 × 25mm and reads "GUERNSEY" at the top and "CHANNEL ISLANDS" at the bottom. The word "REGISTERED" occurs across the centre between parallel lines and the whole stamp is in the shape of a flattened oval.

The pre-war version, Type **G48a**, appears again in 1948 and was used until two new ovals were issued in 1962. One of these was similar to Type **G48**, but had no comma after "GUERNSEY". The other was inscribed "GUERNSEY ST. PETER PORT C.I." (Type **G51**). A further variant of Type **G48**, recorded in 1969, shows "GUERNSEY CHANNEL ISLANDS", again without the comma.

The coming of postal independence led to a different design of oval handstamp, namely Type **G52**. This is inscribed "Guernsey Post Office/Registered" in upper and lowercase letters and was for use in the Sorting Office. Type **G53**, in which the words are transposed so that "Registered" is at the top, was the handstamp employed at the Head Office counter. It has "GUERNSEY POST OFFICE" in capitals.

In 1990 the Sorting Office mark was changed to a circular style which showed, most unusually, the telephone number of the office at foot (Type **G53a**)

Express Post

An oval handstamp (Type **G53b**) for this service was supplied to Guernsey on 11 April 1891. Examples of its use are rare.

Money Order Office Cancellation

A datestamp of the Money Order Office, reading "GUERNSEY" at the top and "M.O.O." at the bottom, is known cancelling stamps at various dates between 1884 and 1936 (Type **G54**).

Parcel Post Cancellations

The first parcel post cancellation (Type **G55**), issued in 1886, is a single oval inscribed "GUERNSEY" in the centre and the circle filled with three lines above and three below. In the autumn of 1889 the more familiar double-ring rubber cancel (Type **G56**) superseded it, again inscribed simply "GUERNSEY". Between 1889 and 1905 seventeen cancellers in this design were supplied. It remained in use until 1915 when it was replaced by the large "label" design. It has been recorded used on postage stamps, though this was obviously not its proper function.

Of the seventeen cancellers of Type **G56** one had serifed letters amd all the others were sans-serif. Variations in the sizes of the letters and the disposition of the inner arc can be distinguished.

About 1910 Type **G57** is recorded, in which the wording within the double ring is now "GUERNSEY/ST. PETER PORT" in two lines.

Type **G56** and **G57** remained in concurrent use until the introduction of the first of the large "label" types in 1915. This was Type **G58**, the right-hand third of which shows the letters "GU" in a background of diagonal lines. The remaining space is divided horizontally in three and worded "PARCEL GU POST/GUERNSEY/date". In 1925 the wording was altered to give Type **G59**. In this, "GU" in the right-hand third now reads "PARCEL POST" while the left-hand space is filled with "GUERNSEY/CHANNEL ISLANDS" in two lines in the upper part and the date below.

Further label types are known after the Second World War, but as mentioned above under "Modern Single Circles" an internal marking saw a rare usage in 1945–46 cancelling *letters*. This is the "GUERNSEY CH. IS./PARCEL DEPOT" c.d.s. (Type **G34**).

Dating from 1948 is Type **G60**, a label cancellation copiously worded and elaborately subdivided. The right-hand third is in three parts, the bottom one being shaded, the middle reading "PARCEL POST" and the top either blank or (Type

G60a) containing a numeral. The left-hand space has "GUERNSEY/(ST. PETER PORT)/CHAN. IS. (SMITH STREET) filling the upper two-thirds with the lower third consisting of more shading and a box for the date.

A somewhat smaller and less elaborate rectangular cancel came into use in the 1950s (Type **G61**). The main area is filled with "GUERNSEY/CHANNEL ISLANDS", but above this is a narrow box enclosing "PARCEL POST" and a numeral.

The large-label design came back into use in 1956 and persisted until the newly independent Guernsey Post Office reorganised all cancellations in 1969–70. The layout of the "label" has again been altered with Type **G62**. In three of the corners (top and bottom left and bottom right) are diagonal lines of shading. At the left and right are panels with "PARCEL" reading upwards at the left and "POST" reading upwards at the right. The centre is divided into three panels, the middle one showing the date. The top and bottom panels have the variant wordings which distinguish the cancellers.

Type **G62**, issued in 1956, read "SMITH STREET" (above) and "GUERNSEY/(ST. PETER PORT) CHAN. IS." (below). It was soon withdrawn, perhaps because the emphasis on "SMITH STREET" was a mistake. Early in 1957 the words were redistributed (Type **G62a**) to read: "GUERNSEY" (above) and "(ST. PETER PORT)/CHAN. IS. (SMITH ST.)" (below).

A rare mark from 1958 shows "(SMITH ST.)/CHANNEL ISLANDS" at foot, but the final version, introduced in 1961, had "ST. PETER PORT" (above) and "GUERNSEY/CHANNEL ISLANDS" (below). This is Type **G63**.

Completely new cancellations were put into use in Guernsey in 1970 for the parcel post. The box-type marking (Type **G64**) reads "GUERNSEY POST OFFICE/PARCEL POST" above the date and "HEAD OFFICE" below. The initial version was introduced on 20 July 1970 and there were a number of different sizes of this style during the following years. A version reported between 1984 and 1988 shows the lowest line altered to read "SORTING OFFICE".

From mid-1986 circular postmarks were used (Type **G64a**) inscribed either "PARCELS" or "FOREIGN PARCEL SECTION" at foot.

Cancellations for Small Packets

Various rubber stamps have seen service in cancelling small packets and they tend to be short-lived. The following are noted from 1932.

Type **G65** is a circular stamp, diameter 30mm. It reads "GUERNSEY" at the top and either "CHANNEL ISLES" (No. GC109) or "CHANNEL ISLANDS" (No. GC110) at the bottom with the date (and sometimes the time) across the centre. A similar version, but with "Channel Islands" at foot was struck in purple on telegrams during 1941.

Type **G66** is a similar circle but the wording is "GUERNSEY ST. PETER PORT" round the top and "CHANNEL IS." round the bottom.

Type **G67** is a 50 × 20mm rectangle with "GUERNSEY/date/CHANNEL ISLANDS" in three lines.

A marking from 1949 is a single circle worded "GUERNSEY/CHANNEL ISLANDS" in two lines across the centre (Type **G68**).

A roller cancel (Type **G69**) was introduced in 1957, reading "GUERNSEY/(ST. PETER PORT)/CHAN. ISLES (SMITH ST.) between double lines and repeated endlessly.

A new rubber handstamp for small packets was part of the complete revision of cancellations at the time of postal independence in 1969. This is Type **G70** in which "Guernsey Post Office" appears (in upper and lowercase) at the top, with a star between dashes at the foot. The date and time are shown in two lines in the centre. By 1971 this datestamp had been modified so that "GUERNSEY POST OFFICE" is now in capital letters (Type **G71**). There were bars above and below the date from 1975, and this version also exists with the star as shown in Type **G70** or a small square at foot.

Triangles

The triangular cancellations are for use on bulk postings of circulars. Type **G72** is "GU" in a large triangle and began to be used in 1939. In 1940 Type **G73** was introduced, namely "324" in a smaller triangle. It replaced the datestamp in the cancelling machine and the centre section of the wavy lines was simultaneously replaced by 1D (1940–42) or 2D "PAID". This "324" in a triangle began to be used from 1950 with the wavy lines of the machine cancellation but omitting the inserted "PAID" (Type **G73a**).

"Paid" Handstamps

Two "PAID" handstamps were sent to Guernsey on 10 August 1920. One had a fixed $\frac{1}{2}$d. (Type **G74**) and the other had movable values (Type **G75**). They were single circles with "GUERNSEY" around the top and the value, the word "PAID" and the date in three lines below.

The "PAID" handstamps were struck in red. The $\frac{1}{2}$d. saw use till 1940 when rising postal rates made it obsolete. During the Occupation the year figures were made locally and, as they did not fit well, are sometimes printed poorly or do not show at all. From 1942 the "PAID" handstamps were pressed into service if adhesives ran short, when letters prepaid in cash at Head Office were franked by this method.

In the 1950s a new movable type, 32mm diameter, reading "GUERNSEY/GREAT BRITAIN" with the "value/PAID/date" across the middle came into use (Type **G75a**).

The independent Postal Administration introduced the single-circle Type **G76** in 1969, reading "Guernsey Post Office/ PAID/date" and of 32mm diameter. A 30mm type (**G76a**) had "GUERNSEY POST OFFICE" in capitals and an ornament at the bottom.

On Type **G76a** "PAID" is across the centre, above the date, but a further variant, introduced in 1982, has a curved "PAID" at foot (Type **G76b**). Parcels posted under this service were franked with Type **G76c**.

Machine "Paid" Markings

A new die for use in the Krag cancelling machine (Type **G38**) was introduced in 1925. This is Type **G77** in which the words "GUERNSEY/PAID $\frac{1}{2}$D./date" appear in three lines flanked by five wavy lines. In 1929 the words "GREAT BRITAIN" were added to the die in a line below "GUERNSEY" (Type **G78**).

A different die was fitted in 1931, to give Type **G79**. In this boxed type there was an inner square containing "$\frac{1}{2}$D" with the date in two lines below. The outer square read "GUERNSEY/PAID" (top and bottom) and "GREAT BRITAIN" (left and right, both reading upwards).

The Universal machine came into use in 1937 with segmented wavy lines, seven in number. The centre part could be fitted with the "PAID" indication (Type **G80**) as, for example, "$\frac{1}{2}$D/PAID". The circular datestamps read either "GUERNSEY/GT. BRITAIN" or had "GT. BRITAIN" omitted (Type **G80a**), both with the date in two lines across the centre.

During the German Occupation the machine "PAID" marking was used in a similar way to the "PAID" handstamps to denote prepayment of postage in cash at various times of shortage of adhesives from 1942 to 1945.

When two-tier postage was instituted in 1968 value figures were taken out and dies reading "1ST PAID", "2ND PAID" or "R PAID" (for rebate postings) used instead (Type **G81**).

With postal independence in 1969 the datestamp was modified to read "GUERNSEY POST OFFICE" (Type **G82**). Then with decimalisation on 15 February 1971 the two-tier system was abandoned and in consequence the "1ST PAID" and "2ND PAID" became simply "PAID".

From 1973 various slogan postmarks were used. These showed circular datestamps reading "GUERNSEY POSTAGE PAID" (Type **G83**).

Philatelic Bureau Cancellations

In June 1971 a new States Philatelic Bureau with adjacent offices was opened in St. Peter Port next to the Head Post Office.

For its own mail the Bureau uses single-circle handstamps (Type **G84**) which read (upper and lowercase) "Guernsey Post Office/Philatelic Bureau" around the circumference and the date (in capitals) in two lines (Type **G84**) or one line (Type **G84a**) across the centre. A smaller type, diameter 23mm, is known from 1969. A new mark, with similar wording, introduced in 1986, had a double outer ring (Type **G85**).

Mail returned to the Bureau was marked with a large single circle inscribed "RECEIVED AT GUERNSEY PHILATELIC BUREAU" and centre date (Type **G86**).

In September 1978 the Guernsey Post Office Board announced that it would supply, when requested, stamps cancelled to order ("that is, stamps cancelled without being affixed to envelopes so that the gum is retained"). The cancellation is Type **G87**, also reading "GUERNSEY POST OFFICE/PHILATELIC BUREAU".

"First Day of Issue" markings are dealt with in Section 15.

(G20a)	(G20b)	(G22)
(G23a)	(G25)	(G26)
(G27)	(G28a)	(G28b)

(G30)

(G31)

(G32)

(G34)

(G36) No. GC60

(G36a)

(G37)

GUERNSEY

8. 15 AM

14 JAN 24

(G38)

(G39b) c.d.s.

(G40) c.d.s.

(G41) c.d.s.

(G42a) c.d.s.

(G43) c.d.s.

(G44-45) c.d.s.

(G47)

(G48a)

(G49)

(G51)

(G52)

(G53a)

(G53b)

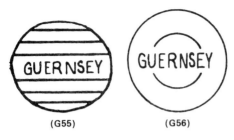

(G55)   (G56)

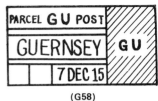

(G58)
Reduced by half

(G60) *Reduced by half*

(G62) *Reduced by half*

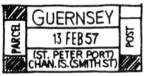

(G62a) *Reduced by half*

(G64)

(G64a)

(G67)

(G70)

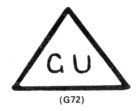

(G72)

(G73a) *Die*

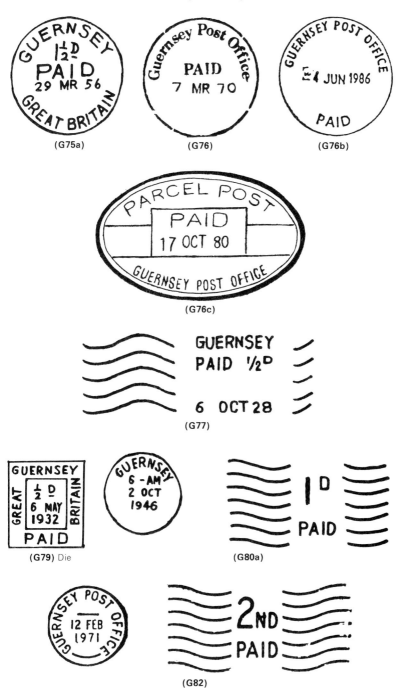

(G75a)

(G76)

(G76b)

(G76c)

(G77)

(G79) Die

(G80a)

(G82)

(G83)

(G85)

(G86)

Cat. No.	Type No.		Dates of use	Colour	Price on cover from
First Type					
GC29	**G20**		1830–47	Black	35·00
GC29a		(without date)	1830	Black	55·00
GC30	**G20a**	(recut)	1843–47	Black	45·00
GC31	**G20b**	(inverted 7 in year)	1844	Black	£120
Travelling Types					
GC32	**G21**		1843	Black	£550
GC33	**G22**		1847	Black	£450
Double-arc Type					
GC34	**G23**		1847–54	Black or blue .	25·00
GC35	**G23a**		1852–58	Various	25·00
GC36	**G23b**		1853–58	Various	25·00
Early Single Circles					
GC37	**G24**	(19mm diameter)	1858–1907	Black or blue .	12·00
GC38	**G25**	(19–26mm diameter)	1872–1930s	Black	2·00
Squared Circles					
GC40	**G26**	(four lines)	1887–1902	Black	8·00
GC41	**G26a**	(three lines)	1899–1905	Black	8·00
Double Circles					
GC42	**G27**	(cross at foot)	1905–28	Black	1·00
GC43	**G28**	GUERNSEY (ST. PETER PORT)/ CHANNEL IS.	1929–37	Black	1·00
GC44	**G28a**	GUERNSEY (ST. PETER PORT) CH. IS.	1937–69	Black	1·00
GC45	**G28b**	GUERNSEY (ST. PETER PORT)/ CHAN. IS.	1962–69	Black	1·00

Cat. No.	Type No.		Dates of use	Colour	Price on cover from
GC47	**G29**	GUERNSEY C.I./1	1945–64	Black	1·00
GC48		GUERNSEY C.I./2	1945–63	Black	1·00
GC48a	**G30**	GUERNSEY POST OFFICE	1984–	Black	30

Modern Single Circles

Cat. No.	Type No.		Dates of use	Colour	Price on cover from
GC49	**G31**	GUERNSEY/CHANNEL ISLANDS	1931–69	Black	2·00
GC50		same, numbered 5–11	1945–54	Black	1·50
GC51		same, lettered E–M	1953–69	Black	1·50
GC51a		stop between CHANNEL and ISLANDS and larger letters	1939–41	Black	2·00
GC52		locally made year figures	1942–45	Black	2·00
GC53	**G32**	GUERNSEY CHANNEL ISLANDS	1930s–69	Black	1·00
GC54	**G33**	GUERNSEY CHANNEL ISLANDS /1	1937–69	Black	1·50
GC54a		GUERNSEY CHANNEL ISLANDS /N.	1958	Black	2·00
GC55	**G34**	PARCEL DEPOT	1945–46	Black	35·00
GC56	**G35**	GUERNSEY (ST. PETER PORT)	1952–69	Black	2·00
GC57	**G36**	Guernsey Post Office, E–H, J–N, P	1969–	Black	30
GC58		same, no letter	1969–	Black	30
GC59		same, with time	1969–	Black	30
GC60		same, with asterisk	1969–	Black	30
GC60a	**G36a**	GUERNSEY POST OFFICE	1987	Black	30
GC60b		Same, with R	1988	Black	30
GC61	**G37**	POSTAL MUSEUM	1971–82	Black	20

Machine Cancellations

Cat. No.	Type No.		Dates of use	Colour	Price on cover from
GC62	**G38**	Square datestamp	1923–31	Black	3·00
GC63	**G39**	(5 wavy lines and c.d.s.)	1931–36	Black	50
GC64	**G39a**	(7 wavy lines segmented)	1936–39	Black	30
GC65		(datestamp re-used)	1949–58	Black	30
GC66	**G39b**	(7 wavy lines continuous)	1939–45	Black	30
GC67		(split 0 for 1)	1941	Black	3·00
GC68		(locally made figures)	1942–45	Black	3·00
GC69	**G40**	(c.d.s. no arc, segmented lines)	1945–48	Black	50
GC70	**G40a**	(c.d.s. no arc, continuous lines)	1947–48	Black	1·00
GC71	**G41**	(c.d.s. tall letters, segmented lines)	1948–49	Black	1·00
GC72	**G42**	(c.d.s. short arc, segmented lines)	1955–69	Black	50
GC73	**G42a**	(c.d.s. small letters, arc exceeds semicircle)	1958–59	Black	50
GC74	**G43**	(c.d.s. shorter arc, segmented lines)	1960–69	Black	30
GC75	**G44**	GUERNSEY POST OFFICE	1969–72, 1982, 1986	Black	50
GC76	**G45**	(two parallel bars	1972–81	Black	20

Crown Registered Mark

Cat. No.	Type No.		Dates of use	Colour	Price on cover from
GC77	**G46**		1852	Blue	£600
GC77a			1884	Black	£600

Registration Cancellations

Cat. No.	Type No.		Dates of use	Colour	Price on cover from
GC78	**G46a**	Large R in oval	1893	Black	40·00
GC79	**G47**	R in oval/FEE PAID	1898–1905	Black	30·00
GC80	**G48**	Oval REGISTERED/GUERNSEY, CHANNEL ISLANDS	1938–39	Black	3·00
GC81	**G48a**	REGISTERED/GUERNSEY, CH. IS.	1938–40, 1948–69	Black	2·00

Cat. No.	Type No.		Dates of use	Colour	Price on cover from
GC82	**G49**	Local rubber stamp	1944	Violet with red	25·00
GC82a			1944	Black with red.	£175
GC82b		Frame only	1944	Black or violet.	90·00
GC82c		Number only	1944	Red	£120
GC83	**G50**	REGISTERED between lines	1945–46	Black or violet.	2·00
GC84	**G48**	Oval REGISTERED/GUERNSEY CHANNEL ISLNDS (no comma)	1962–66	Black	4·00
GC84a	**G51**	Oval REGISTERED/GUERNSEY ST. PETER PORT C.I.	1962–65	Black	3·00
GC84b	**G48**	Oval REGISTERED/GUERNSEY CHANNEL IS. (no comma)	1969	Black	5·00
GC85	**G52**	Oval Guernsey Post Office/Registered	1969–80	Black	3·00
GC86	**G53**	Oval REGISTERED/GUERNSEY POST OFFICE	1969–88	Black	2·00
GC87	**G53a**	Circular (with telephone no. at foot) GUERNSEY REGISTERED	1990	Black	1·00

Express Post Cancellation

GC88	**G53b**		1891	Black or red ..	80·00

Money Order Cancellation

GC89	**G54**		1884–1936	Black	45·00

Parcel Post Cancellations*

GC90	**G55**	Barred oval	1886–89	Black	30·00
GC91	**G56**	GUERNSEY sans-serif	1889–1915	Black or red ..	3·00
GC92		GUERNSEY serifed	1890	Black	15·00
GC92a	**G57**	GUERNSEY/ST. PETER PORT	1910–15	Black	10·00
GC93	**G58**	PARCEL GU POST/GUERNSEY	1915–25	Black	25·00
GC94	**G59**	GUERNSEY/CHANNEL ISLANDS	1925–45	Black	6·00
GC95	**G60**	GUERNSEY/(ST. PETER PORT)	1948–52	Black	2·00
GC95a	**G60a**	(with numeral)	1948–52	Black	3·00
GC96	**G61**	PARCEL POST/GUERNSEY	1950s	Violet	4·00
GC97	**G62**	SMITH STREET	1956	Black	10·00
GC98	**G62a**	(ST. PETER PORT)/CHAN. IS. (SMITH ST) at foot	1957–61	Black	2·00
GC98a	**G62b**	(SMITH ST.)/CHANNEL ISLANDS at foot	1958	Black	3·00
GC99	**G63**	ST. PETER PORT at top	1961–70	Black	1·00
GC100	**G64**	GUERNSEY POST OFFICE/HEAD OFFICE (53 × 36mm)	1970	Black	3·00
GC101		Ditto, but 54 × 31mm	1973	Black	1·00
GC102		Ditto, but 52 × 32mm	1975–76	Black or violet.	30
GC103		Ditto, but 57 × 9mm	1977–80	Black	30
GC104		Ditto, but 50 × 38mm	1980–83	Black	30
GC105		Ditto, but 47 × 34mm	1984–87	Black	30
GC106		GUERNSEY POST OFFICE/SORTING OFFICE (47 × 34mm)	1984–88	Black	40
GC107	**G64a**	Circular GUERNSEY POST OFFICE/PARCELS	1986–	Black	40
GC108		Ditto, but GUERNSEY POST OFFICE / FOREIGN PARCEL SECTION	1986–	Black	40

Cat. No.	Type No.		Dates of use	Colour	Price on cover from

Cancellations for Small Packets*

GC109	**G65**	GUERNSEY / CHANNEL ISLES c.d.s.	1932–39	Black	4·00
GC110		GUERNSEY/CHANNEL ISLANDS c.d.s.	1938–79	Black or violet.	50
GC111		Ditto, but inscr. Channel Islands	1940–49	Purple	4·00
GC112	**G66**	GUERNSEY ST. PETER PORT/ CHANNEL IS.	1938–53	Black or violet.	1·00
GC113	**G67**	Rectangular cancel	1938–52	Black or violet.	1·00
GC114	**G68**	GUERNSEY/CHANNEL ISLANDS s.c.	1949–61	Black or violet.	2·50
GC115	**G69**	Roller cancel	1957	Black	35·00
GC116	**G70**	Guernsey Post Office c.d.s.	1969–72	Black	30
GC117	**G71**	GUERNSEY POST OFFICE c.d.s.	1971–	Black	30
GC117a		Date between bars, star and arcs at foot	1975–76	Black	30
GC117b		Ditto, blank at foot	1975–76	Black	30
GC117c		Ditto, small space at foot	1987–	Black	30

Triangles

GC119	**G72**	GU in triangle	1939–69	Black or red . .	25·00
GC120	**G73**	324, wavy lines and PAID	1940–60s	Red	5·00
GC121	**G73a**	324 and wavy lines	1950–69	Black	2·00

"Paid" Handstamps

GC122	**G74**	½d.	1920–40	Red	3·00
GC123		½d. modified for use as 1d.	1945	Red-brown . . .	6·00
GC124	**G79**	1d.	1921–48	Red	1·00
GC125		1½d.	1922–52	Red	1·00
GC126		2d.	1946	Red	1·00
GC127		2½d.	1942–44	Red	25·00
GC128	**G75a**	GUERNSEY/GREAT BRITAIN 1½D.	1956	Red	1·00
GC129		Ditto, 2½D.	1963	Red	1·00
GC130		Ditto, 4½D.	1967	Red	1·00
GC131		Ditto, 7D. (with date)	1959	Red	2·00
GC132		Ditto, 7D. (without date)	1959	Red	2·00
GC133		Ditto, no value	1966–67	Red	2·00
GC134		GUERNSEY/GT. BRITAIN (no value)	1964	Red	1·00
GC135		GUERNSEY/CHANNEL ISLANDS	1969–70	Red	1·00
GC136	**G76**	Guernsey Post Office/PAID	1969–71	Red	30
GC137	**G76a**	GUERNSEY POST OFFICE (PAID across centre)	1969–80	Red	30
GC138	**G76b**	Ditto, but PAID at foot	1982–	Red	50
GC139	**G76c**	Oval PARCEL POST/PAID	1980–	Red	1·00

Machine "Paid" Markings

GC140	**G77**	GUERNSEY/PAID ½d/date	1925–29	Red	8·00
GC141	**G78**	GREAT BRITAIN added	1929–32	Red	6·00
GC141a		Date omitted	1930	Red	12·00
GC142	**G79**	½d. boxed type (5 wavy lines)	1931–36	Red	5·00
GC142a		Ditto, but 7 wavy lines	1936	Red	10·00
GC143	**G80**	½D/PAID between wavy lines	1937–40	Red	2·00
GC144		Ditto, but 1D	1940–48	Red	3·00
GC145		Ditto, but 1½D	1938, 1953–55	Red	2·00

Cat. No.	Type No.		Dates of use	Colour	Price on cover from
GC146	**G80**	Ditto, but 2D	1956	Red	2·00
GC147		Ditto, but 2½D	1940–56, 1961	Red	4·00
GC148		½D PAID between wavy lines (GREAT BRITAIN omitted)	1937–40	Red	3·00
GC149		Ditto, but 1D	1941–51	Red	3·00
GC150		Ditto, but 1½D	1951–54	Red	2·00
GC151		Ditto, but 2D	1956–60	Red	2·00
GC152		Ditto, but 2½D	1941–57, 1961–65	Red	3·00
GC153		Ditto, but 3D	1965–68	Red	1·00
GC154		Ditto, but 4D	1967–68	Red	1·00
GC155		Ditto, but 4½D	1960	Red	1·00
GC156	**G81**	1ST PAID between wavy lines	1968–69	Red	1·00
GC156a		Ditto, but 2ND	1968–69	Red	1·00
GC156b		Ditto, but R (rebate postings)	1969	Red	1·00
GC158	**G82**	GUERNSEY POST OFFICE 1ST PAID	1969–71	Red	50
GC159		Ditto, but 2ND	1969–71	Red	50
GC160		Ditto, but R (rebate postings)	1969–71	Red	2·00
GC161		Ditto, but without value	1971–	Red	20
GC162		As No. GC161, but used as canceller in error	1974	Black	2·00
GC163	**G83**	GUERNSEY POSTAGE PAID c.d.s. plus various slogans	1973–74	Red	1·00

Philatelic Bureau Cancellations

GC164	**G84**	26½mm c.d.s., no asterisk	1969–	Black	30
GC165		23mm c.d.s.	1969	Black	40
GC166	**G84a**	27½mm c.d.s. (smaller letters, asterisk code)	1970	Black	30
GC167		29mm c.d.s. (smaller asterisk)	1984	Black	50
GC168	**G85**	Double outer circle	1986	Black	1·00
GC169	**G86**	RECEIVED AT (returned mail)	1973	Black	50
	(G87)	PHILATELIC BUREAU: c.t.o. on adhesives)			

"First Day of Isue": *see* Section 15
*Prices for Nos. GC90–117c refer to markings *on piece*.

10. Postage Due and Instructional Marks

Instructional marks may be separated into three groups:
(1) Marks which indicate that a certain amount of postage due is to be collected;
(2) Marks explaining the reason for a charge and which often include the amount due;
(3) Marks detailing some irregularity in transmission which does not involve an extra charge.

Instructional markings have been in use generally throughout the British Isles and so can only be allocated to a particular office where a cover bears other identifying features.

As mentioned in Section 8, the replacement of the Maltese Cross cancellation in 1844 led to offices receiving an identifying number. In the course of this, Jersey was given 409 and Guernsey 324. These numerals will be found in some of the instructional marks.

Colours of Strikes. There was a procedure for the colour of ink to be used, but it was by no means always adhered to. The office of dispatch should normally impress on underpaid letters a mark in red indicating the charge to be collected and the reason for it. If an underpayment was first noticed at the office of arrival the mark should have been applied in black.

Jersey (409) usually did this correctly, but Guernsey (324) nearly always used black ink only.

Marks in the third group, where no charge is involved, were usually struck in violet or green, though black is very common, too.

Manuscript Marks. A number of early letters from Jersey and Guernsey have manuscript endorsements and the following are recorded:
1. "Missent to (Jersey datestamp of 1848)".
2. "Not found" in red on a Jersey letter of 1842.
3. "Not known" in red on a letter from the Isle of Wight to Guernsey in 1857.
4. "Now residing in London/Address not known" in red on a letter from Newark to Guernsey in 1841.
5. "Left for St. Malow from (Guernsey datestamp of 1855)".
6. "More to pay" and large figure 2 in black on letter from Guernsey to Jersey of 1856.

(*Prices of manuscript markings on entire*: simple charge marks, £15–£25; instructions—Not known, etc., £30–£50; instructions plus a datestamp, £125–£150)

Weymouth Marking. One of the consequences of postal independence for Jersey and Guernsey was the action taken in the Islands to deal with mail continuing to be prepaid with withdrawn British stamps. This is outlined in the sub-sections following.

But the converse of this problem existed. Many people arriving back in Weymouth after a holiday on the Islands mistakenly affixed Jersey or Guernsey stamps to letters posted on the mainland, where they had no validity.

From 1972 Weymouth Post Office (number 873) applied a 60 × 25mm postage due marking inscribed "CHANNEL ISLAND/STAMPS NOT/ADMISSABLE WHEN/POSTED ON UK/MAINLAND" in black or green. The surcharge at top left was completed in manuscript. The problem persisted and by 1983 this mark had been replaced by a boxed oblong "CHANNEL ISLANDS STAMPS NOT VALID IN U.K.".

Price on cover £2

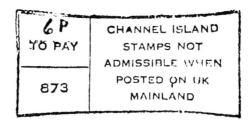

CHANNEL ISLANDS STAMPS
NOT VALID IN U.K.

Postage due markings of Weymouth

It should be noted, however, that, until their withdrawal at the end of June 1971, the reply halves of Reply Paid Postcards posted in England could be legitimately used in Jersey or Guernsey and the Islands' stamps could also be used elsewhere if affixed to such a card.

The various marks in this Section are classified as follows:
(1) Postage Due indicators
    (a) Due marks on Inland mail (JD or GD numbers)
    (b) Due marks on Overseas mail (JE or GE numbers)
(2) Explanatory Charge marks
    (a) Stamps Invalid (JI or GI numbers)
    (b) Liable to Letter or Postcard Rate (JL or GL numbers)
    (c) More to Pay (JM or GM numbers)
    (d) Return to Sender (JS or GS numbers)
(3) Irregularities in transmission (JT or GT numbers)

JERSEY

(1) Postage Due
(a) On inland mail
(i) To 1969
    The earliest charge marks recorded in the G.P.O. Proof Books are for ½d. and 1d. of a type common to many provincial towns. The date recorded is December 1880, but as they had no identifying number, they are excluded here.
    A stamp specifically for Jersey was dispatched in February 1883 and, although in use until 1900, it is rare on cover. The mark has a large 2d. with 409 below, all enclosed by an oval (Type **J100**).
    From 1902 a new style of handstamp was introduced showing a large figure together with the number 409, but without the enclosing oval (Type **J101**). The 1d.

appeared in 1902 and was usually applied in black, although a few examples from the 1930s are in red. Other values followed in 1914 and 1921.

A revised 1d. handstamp was issued in 1919, incorporating the words "TO PAY" (Type **J102**). A similar 4d. marking (Type **J104**) was introduced in 1921 and a 1½d. (Type **J103**) followed a year later. Both the 1d. (Type **J102**) and the 2d. (Type **J101**) are known with "½d." added in manuscript. A 2½d. marking, similar to Type **J103**, has been seen used in 1923.

A new type of unpaid marking appeared during the 1940s. This was a boxed type with the words "TO PAY/POSTED/UNPAID" on the right-hand side and the surcharge on the left. Four sub-types are known for Jersey. The first (Type **J105**) has a space in the surcharge box for the amount to be inserted in manuscript. Type **J106** is a smaller version of this marking which is also known, struck in red or green, with fixed denominations of 5d. (1952–63), 6d. (1964) or 8d. (1966).

(ii) 1969 onwards

Although Types **J105** and **J106** were used for a time after postal independence two new forms of marking were introduced from 1971, relating to mail which was unpaid or to items which were underpaid.

A simple rectangular handstamp (Type **J107**) inscribed "POSTED/UNPAID" entered service in 1971, the amount due being indicated by the figure 4 shown beneath a P. This mark exists struck in blue or violet.

Increases in postage rates extended the range over the years: 5p and 6p in 1972, 7p in 1974, 8p and 10p in 1975, 2p and 14p in 1976 and 12p in 1978. The 7p version had the old British numeral "409" in the bottom right corner. Handstamps in this series from 1978 onwards were in a larger size, 48 × 22mm instead of 44 × 21mm. The 16p in this size appeared in 1978, 14p and 18p in 1980, 20p in 1981 and, finally, 22p in 1982.

A new style of unpaid handstamp, including the additional inscription "TO PAY", was introduced in 1984 (Type **J108**). The initial value was 18p, but as postage rates rose further handstamps in this type were produced: 24p in 1984, 20p and 26p in 1985, 28p in 1986, 22p and 30p in 1987, 32p in 1988, and 34p in 1989.

A further blank mark appeared in 1989. This was a black oblong inscribed "POSTED UNPAID/TO PAY" with a box at lower left for the amount to be added in manuscript (Type **J109**).

The first marking for underpaid mail was introduced in 1971. This was a simple rectangular handstamp (Type **J110**) inscribed "1p/TO PAY" and struck in violet. It was withdrawn in 1975. A larger box type (Type **J111**), inscribed "TO PAY/UNDERPAID", was also introduced in 1971. This has a space in the left-hand box for the surcharge to be inserted in manuscript. Fixed amount handstamps in the same design were subsequently introduced: the 1p and 2p in 1975, the 4p in 1976, and 6p in 1981.

A new style underpaid handstamp (Type **J112**), measuring 41 × 16mm, was introduced in 1984 in a similar design to the contemporary unpaid mark. This showed a space at bottom left for the surcharge amount to be added in manuscript. Subsequently fixed amount handstamps in the same design, 6p in 1984 and 8p in 1985, were used. A further version, measuring 41 × 21mm, appeared in 1985.

(J100)   (J101)   (J101a)   (J102)

(J103)

(J104)

(J105)

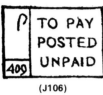

(J106)

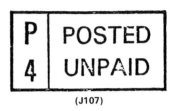

(J107)

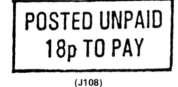

(J108)

(J109)

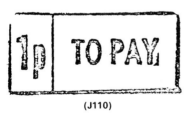

(J110)

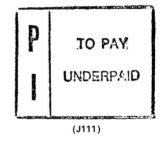

(J111)

(J112)

Cat. No.	Type No.		Dates of use	Colour	Price on cover
JD1	**J100**		1883–1900	Black	£300
JD2	**J101**	(1d.)	1902–38	Black	10·00
JD2a		(1d.)	1930s	Red	30·00
JD2b	**J101a**	(1d.)	1903–05	Black	15·00
JD2c		(1d.) (409 omitted)	1904	Black	40·00
JD3	**J102**	(1d.)	1919–69	Black, red, green .	10·00
JD4	**J103**	(1½d.)	1922–28	Black, red, green .	18·00
JD5	**J101**	(2d.)	1914–1950s	Black, red, green .	8·00
JD5a	**J103**	(2½d.)	1923	Black	£200
JD6	**J101**	(3d.)	1914–1950s	Black, red, green .	8·00
JD7	**J104**	(4d.)	1921–1950s	Black, red, green .	18·00
JD8	**J101**	(5d.)	1921	Black, red	20·00
JD9	**J105**	(blank)	1940s–1970	Black, red, violet .	3·00
JD10	**J106**	(blank)	1958–	Black, red, violet, blue, green	1·00
JD10a		(5d.)	1952–63	Black, red, green .	15·00
JD11		(6d.)	1964–	Green	12·00
JD11a		(8d.)	1966	Green	
JD11b	**J107**	(2p)	1976	Blue, violet	3·00
JD12		(4p)	1971–80	Blue, violet	1·00
JD13		(5p)	1972–74	Violet	2·00
JD14		(6p)	1972–75	Violet	2·00
JD15		(7p)	1974–75	Violet	3·00
JD16		(8p)	1975–76	Violet	2·00
JD17		(10p)	1975–78	Blue, violet	2·00
JD18		(12p)	1978–80	Violet	2·00
JD19		(14p) (44 × 21mm)	1976–78	Blue, violet	2·00
JD19a		(14p) (48 × 22mm)	1980–82	Blue, violet	2·00
JD20		(16p)	1978–82	Violet	1·00
JD21		(18p)	1980	Violet	1·00
JD22		(20p)	1981	Violet-blue	1·00
JD23		(22p)	1982	Violet	4·00
JD24	**J108**	(18p)	1984–85	Violet	2·00
JD25		(20p)	1985–86	Violet	2·00
JD26		(22p)	1987	Violet	3·00
JD27		(24p)	1984–89	Violet	3·00
JD28		(26p)	1985–86	Violet	2·00
JD29		(28p)	1986–90	Violet, black	2·00
JD30		(30p)	1987–88	Violet	2·00
JD31		(32p)	1988–89	Violet	2·00
JD32		(34p)	1989–90	Black	2·00
JD33	**J109**	(blank)	1989	Violet, black	1·00
JD34	**J110**	(1p)	1971–75	Violet	2·00
JD35	**J111**	(blank)	1971–	Black, green, violet	2·00
JD36		(1p)	1975–77	Black, violet	4·00
JD37		(2p)	1975–	Violet, black, blue.	2·00
JD38		(4p)	1976–80	Violet, blue	1·00
JD39		(6p)	1981–83	Violet	2·00
JD40	**J112**	(blank) (41 × 16mm)	1984–85	Violet	2·00
JD41		(blank) (41 × 21mm)	1985	Violet	1·00
JD42		(6p)	1984–86	Violet	2·00
JD43		(8p)	1986	Violet	1·00

(*b*) *On Overseas Mail*
Postage Due markings on Overseas mail, both incoming and outgoing, have always formed a separate series to conform to the demands of international postal regulations.

(i) Outwards
A very early marking, found on letters to the Continent in the late 1860s, is an unframed "INSUFFICIENTLY/STAMPED" (Type **J150**).
The Universal Postal Union decided in 1875 that underpayment on mail passing from one country to another should be indicated by striking a large letter "T" (for Taxe) on the item.
Under this system Jersey introduced a series of four hexagonal markings for underpaid mail to France (Type **J151**). These show within the hexagon a figure beneath the T and carry below the frame the letters JE for Jersey. The initial handstamps showed the figures 5, 10, 15 or 25 denoting the deficiency (*not* the surcharge) in centimes, 5c being equal to $\frac{1}{2}$d. Four further values in this range were introduced in 1907, 20, 30, 40 and 50.
Two postcards have been seen, dated 1912 and 1913, without any figure beneath the T.
When the scheme for assessing postage due on underpaid mail was initially agreed by the UPU countries, the currency standard adopted was a franc of 100 centimes. This was replaced, after the First World War, by a gold franc, but general monetary instability and constantly revised postage rates continued to make calculations connected with postage due complicated.
An easier system was adopted in 1967 under which amounts in centimes were replaced by a fractional indicator. The originating country showed in its Taxe marking a fraction whose denominator was the basic foreign letter rate in its own currency. From 1967 to 1976, the numerator figure was equivalent to twice the deficiency in postage, again in national currency. The receiving administration then multiplied the resulting fraction by its own foreign rate and collected this sum from the addressee.
The first of these fractional markings for Jersey (Type **J152**) appeared in 1971. The denominator "5" is contained in a large box with T for Taxe. The figure below the fraction bar became 8 in 1974, 10 in 1076, 10.5 in 1977, 11.5 in 1978, 13.5 in 1980, 18 in 1981, 19.5 in 1982 and 20.5 in 1983. A redesigned fractional mark without a frame (Type **J153**) appeared in 1985 with 22 below the bar.

(ii) Inwards
1976 saw a further change in the procedure for surcharging overseas mail. The total postage due is now compounded as a single rate deficiency plus standard surcharge so that the numerator in the Taxe marks indicates a single rate deficiency.
To accommodate this change Jersey introduced a large box mark to be applied to incoming underpaid overseas mail (Type **J154**). This contains three compartments "TO PAY UNDERPAID/+SURCHARGE FEE/TOTAL TO PAY", the amounts being written in by hand.

INSUFFICIENTLY
STAMPED
(J150)

(J151)

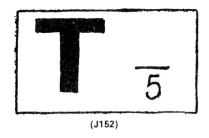

(J152)

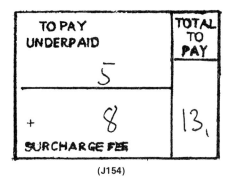

(J154)

Cat. No.	Type No.		Dates of use	Colour	Price on cover
JE1	**J150**	INSUFFICIENTLY/ STAMPED	1860s	Black, red . .	£250
JE2	**J151**	T 5	1890–1903	Black	£180
JE3		T 10	1890–1906	Black	£180
JE4		T 15	1890	Black	£180
JE5		T 20	1907	Black	£180
JE6		T 25	1890	Black	£200
JE7		T 30	1907	Black	£180
JE8		T 40	1907	Black	£180
JF9		T 50	1907–10	Black	£200
JE10		T blank	1913	Black	£200
JE11	**J152**	T 5	1971–76	Violet	5·00
JE12		T 8	1974	Violet	5·00
JE13		T 10	1976	Violet	5·00
JE14		T 10.5	1977–79	Violet	4·00
JE15		T 11.5	1978	Violet	4·00
JE16		T 13.5	1980	Violet	4·00
JE17		T 18	1981	Violet	3·00
JE18		T 19.5	1982–83	Violet	3·00
JE19		T 20.5	1983–85	Violet	3·00
JE20	**J153**	T 22	1985–	Violet	1·00
JE21	**J154**		1976–	Violet, blue .	1·00

(2) Explanatory Charge Marks
(*a*) *Stamps Invalid*

After Postal Independence in 1969 stamps of Great Britain and of Guernsey were no longer valid for the payment of postage from Jersey. Special "STAMPS INVALID" handstamps were introduced to cover cases of such incorrect usage.

The first Jersey handstamp in this series (Type **J160**) was unframed and inscribed "STAMP VOID". The length of the mark varies suggesting that the two words may have been applied separately. Some examples have been seen with a space between the two words; whilst in others the "P" and "V" are almost touching. It was brought into use in October 1969, possibly as a temporary measure, and exists in violet or green. This handstamp was withdrawn in 1970, being replaced by a framed version (Type **J161**), 6.3cm long, which can be found in blue, black, violet or green. A similar marking, but in smaller size (Type **J162**) followed in 1985.

Type **J163** appeared in 1970 and included the value of the surcharge, 8d. After decimalisation in 1971 it was replaced by Types **J164** and **J165**. Type **J164** has a space for the surcharge to be added by hand and Type **J165** includes the Post Office number, 409. A 6p mark similar to Type **J165** followed in 1972. Increasing postage rates necessitated the uprating of these surcharge marks at regular intervals. A 7p handstamp (Type **J166**) was used in 1974, followed by 8p (1975), 10p (1975), 14p (1976) and 16p (Type **J167**) (1978). A replacement 16p (Type **J168**), with heavier lettering, was introduced in 1982, and was followed by 18p (1984), 20p (1985), 22p (1982), 24p (1984), 26p (1985), 28p (1986), 30p (1987) and 32p (1988) marks in the same style. In 1990 the size of the mark was increased and the 36p value was as Type **J169**.

STAMP VO·I D
(J160)

STAMP INVALID
(J161)

STAMP INVALID
(J162)

STAMP INVALID
8d TO PAY
(J163)

STAMP INVALID
__. TO PAY
(J164)

```
┌─────────────────────────┐
│  STAMP  INVALID         │
│    5p TO PAY            │
│                  ┌─────┐│
│                  │ 409 ││
└──────────────────┴─────┴┘
```
(J165)

```
┌─────────────────────────┐
│   STAMP INVALID         │
│    7p TO PAY            │
└─────────────────────────┘
```
(J166)

```
┌─────────────────────────┐
│  STAMP  INVALID         │
│   16p TO PAY            │
└─────────────────────────┘
```
(J167)

```
┌─────────────────────────┐
│  STAMP INVALID          │
│   16p TO PAY            │
└─────────────────────────┘
```
(J168)

```
┌─────────────────────────┐
│  STAMP INVALID          │
│  36p TO PAY             │
└─────────────────────────┘
```
(J169)

Cat. No.	Type No.		Dates of use	Colour	Price on cover
JI1	**J160**	STAMP VOID	1969–70	Violet, green	4·00
JI2	**J161**	STAMP INVALID	1970–83	Violet, green, blue, black	1·00
JI3	**J162**	STAMP INVALID	1983–	Violet	1·00
JI4	**J163**	8d.	1970–71	Violet, green	5·00
JI5	**J164**	Blank	1971–78	Violet	6·00
JI6	**J165**	5p	1971–73	Violet	5·00
JI7		6p	1972–74	Violet, black	5·00
JI8	**J166**	7p	1974–75	Violet	4·00
JI9		8p	1975–76	Violet	4·00
JI10		10p	1975–76	Violet	3·00
JI11		14p	1976–81	Violet, blue	2·00
JI12	**J167**	16p	1978–79	Violet, blue	2·00
JI13	**J168**	16p	1982	Violet	2·00
JI14		18p	1984	Violet	2·00
JI15		20p	1985–86	Violet	2·00
JI16		22p	1982	Violet	3·00
JI17		24p	1984	Violet	2·00
JI18		26p	1985	Violet	2·00
JI19		28p	1986	Violet	2·00
JI20		30p	1987	Violet	2·00
JI21		32p	1988	Violet	1·00
JI22	**J169**	36p	1990	Black	2·00

(*b*) *Liable to Letter or Postcard Rate*

A "Liable to Letter Rate/409" handstamp (Type **J170**) was introduced in 1895 for use on postcards which did not conform to regulations. A larger handstamp appeared during the 1930s (Type **J171**), which incorporated the 1d. surcharge. Both these marks continued in use until the 1960s. A boxed handstamp (Type **J172**), inscribed "TO PAY/LIABLE TO/LETTER/RATE" with a space on the left for the surcharge to be added by hand, also dates from the 1930s.

Two other boxed types are known. The first (**J173**), inscribed "TO PAY/ CONTRARY TO/REGULATIONS/LIABLE TO/...... RATE" with a space on the left for the surcharge to be added in manuscript, is known from a single example, dated 1957, the word "letter" also being added by hand. The second type (**J174**), inscribed "TO PAY/LIABLE TO/LETTER RATE/ABOVE ..... OZ" is only known from a Post Office proof sheet of 1971.

A similar mark inscribed "TO PAY/LIABLE TO SECOND/CLASS LETTER RATE/...../INSUFFICIENTLY PREPAID" (Type **J175**) was used from 1973 onwards.

A framed marking (Type **J176**) in similar format to Type **J171** but inscribed "TO PAY/LIABLE TO/POSTCARD RATE/409" was brought into use during the 1930s. This was applied to postcards mailed at the cheaper printed matter rate.

A "Contrary to Regulations" handstamp (Type **J177**) was used in Jersey from 1880. It was intended primarily for postcards which contravened Post Office Regulations. At the same time a boxed mark, inscribed "Closed contrary/to regulations/409" (Type **J178**), was also introduced.

A boxed "TO PAY/POSTED/OUT OF/COURSE" in the "409" series (Type **J179**) is known in red from 1948 used on registered letters not correctly posted.

The need for a general handstamp of this type persisted into the Jersey Post Office period and an oblong mark inscribed "CONTRARY TO/REGULATIONS/LIABLE TO/SURCHARGE" appeared in 1986 (Type **J180**).

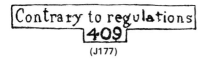

(J177)

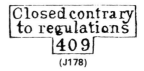

(J178)

Contrary to regulations 409

(J179)

CONTRARY TO REGULATIONS LIABLE TO SURCHARGE

(J180)

Cat. No.	Type No.		Dates of use	Colour	Price on cover
JL1	J170	Liable to Letter Rate	1895–1960s	Black	15·00
JL2	J171	1d./TO PAY/LIABLE TO LETTER RATE	1930–60s	Black, red, green	20·00
JL3	J172	TO PAY/LIABLE TO/ LETTER RATE	1930s–60s	Black, red	15·00
JL4	J173	TO PAY/CONTRARY TO/REGULATIONS /LIABLE TO/...... RATE	1957	Green	40·00
JL5	J174	TO PAY/LIABLE TO/ LETTER RATE/ ABOVE .... OZ.	1971	Black	
JL6	J175	TO PAY/LIABLE TO SECOND/CLASS LETTER RATE/..../ INSUFFICIENTLY PREPAID	1973	Violet	2·00
JL7	J176	1d./TO PAY/LIABLE TO/POSTCARD RATE	1930s–60s	Black, red	20·00
JL8	J177	Contrary to regulations	1880	Black	25·00
JL9	J178	Closed contrary to regulations/409	1880–1957	Black, green	50·00
JL10	J179	9d./TO PAY/ POSTED/OUT OF/COURSE/409	1948	Red	20·00
JL11	J180	CONTRARY TO/ REGULATIONS/ LIABLE TO/ SURCHARGE	1986	Violet	2·00

(*c*) *More to Pay*

Two different types of "More to Pay" marks are known. The first, a stepped type (**J180**), was dispatched to Jersey in 1878 and is inscribed "More to pay/above ..... oz/409". Originally struck in black, a single example in green is known from 1957. A similar style mark, but with larger figures, was supplied in 1882.

The second type (**J181**) is a boxed marking, inscribed "MORE TO/PAY/LETTER RATE/ABOVE ..... OZ", with a space at the left for the addition of the surcharge in manuscript. Examples are known used between 1962 and 1971.

A marking with a similar purpose has been seen from 1968. This was used in connection with a rise in postage rates and is the familiar "409" oblong type inscribed "SURCHARGE DUE/TO INCREASED/POSTAL CHARGES" (Type **J182**).

(J180)

(J181)

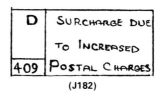

(J182)

Cat. No.	Type No.	Dates of use	Colour	Price on cover
JM1	**J180**	1878–1960	Black, green	50·00
JM1a		1882	Black	50·00
JM2	**J181**	1962–71	Black, violet	15·00
JM3	**J182**	1968	Green......	35·00

(*d*) *Postage Due for Return to Sender*

After 1895 letters mailed at the printed matter rate and then returned to sender, were charged for the return postage by the Post Office. The amount paid was equivalent to the single printed matter rate, originally $\frac{1}{2}$d. Such mail received a large rectangular handstamp inscribed "POSTAGE/DUE/FOR/RETURN/TO/SENDER" (Type **J185**). This type was common to all British Post Offices, including Jersey and Guernsey, and was struck in black.

It was replaced in 1930 by Type **J186**, inscribed "Undelivered for/reason stated/POSTAGE/DUE FOR/RETURN/TO/SENDER". Such marks were also common to all Post Offices, there being no identifying number within the handstamp. This version was supplemented in 1932 by a double-framed marking, Type **J187**, which included the Jersey Post Office number in the bottom left-hand corner.

A 1d. postage due for return to sender handstamp (Type **J188**) was introduced in May 1940, following rises in postage rates. This was very similar to Type **J186**, and was common to all Post Offices. It is only found struck in violet.

A 1½d. handstamp (as Type **J187**) followed in June 1951. This was replaced by a 2d. marking in identical format in 1956. Further postage rises necessitated a 2½d. handstamp in 1961 and a 3d. in 1965. Examples of these recent Jersey marks are scarce.

This series of handstamps was withdrawn in 1968, following the introduction of the two-tier system.

(J185)

(J186)

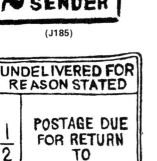

(J187)

(J188)

Cat. No.	Type No.		Dates of use	Colour	Price on cover
JS1	**J185**	(½d.)	1895–1930	Black	50·00
JS2	**J186**	(½d.)	1930–39	Black	50·00
JS3	**J187**	(½d.)	1932–39	Black	50·00
JS4	**J188**	(1d.)	1940–51	Violet	30·00
JS5	**J187**	(1½d.)	1951–56	Violet	30·00
JS6		(2d.)	1956–61	Violet	30·00
JS7		(2½d.)	1961–65	Violet	30·00
JS8		(3d.)	1965–68	Violet	30·00

(3) Irregularities in Transmission

The first in this series of markings dates from the pre-adhesive era when letters, posted too late to catch the mailboat, were handstamped "too late" in small lower case letters (Type **J190**). This mark is known from 1831, being replaced by a script version (Type **J191**) in 1846. This was originally struck in green, but is later known in red from 1849 and in black between 1900 and 1905. A second copy of the handstamp was supplied in 1875.

A group of markings was introduced in 1879–80 to cover the regulations which stated that mail sent at any rate lower than that for letters was to be left open at the ends and must not contain any enclosures. The marks involved, Types **J192/3**, each included the Jersey numeral, 409. The first, dating from 1879, reads "Contains a communication/ of the nature of a Letter/409". The other, issued November 1880, is inscribed "Prohibited enclosure/409". Both handstamps were of the boxed and stepped type.

The G.P.O. proof books for February 1882 show two similar style markings, but these have not been seen on covers before 1900. They were "Not Known/409" (Type **J194**) and "Gone Away/409", (Type **J195**).

A bilingual "Inconnu/Not Known" boxed mark (Type **J194a**) is known from 1945.

Another marking, "POSTED OUT/OF COURSE", was used on registered mail irregularly posted (Type **J196**). This handstamp was unframed.

Three general missent marks have been recorded. A "Missent to Jersey" (5 × 32mm) is known from 1958 and a larger type from 1975. A boxed mark "Missent to", with a blank for "Jersey" to be added in manuscript, exists on a 1971 proof sheet of Post Office markings.

The 11 × 46mm handstamp GOREY, recorded on a card in 1960 wrongly addressed to St. Martin's, was replaced in 1967 by a large boxed mark "YOUR CORRECT POSTAL ADDRESS IS/GOREY, JERSEY./ANY OTHER FORM OF ADDRESS/MAY LEAD TO DELAY." (Type **J201**). Such marks were required because of confusion over whether certain addresses were in Gorey or St. Martin's.

A somewhat similar handstamp, seen used in 1971, is inscribed "YOUR CORRECT POSTAL ADDRESS IS/   /ANY OTHER FORM OF ADDRESS MAY LEAD/TO DELAY. PLEASE ADVISE SENDER", the correct address being inserted in manuscript (Type **J202**).

A framed two line handstamp, inscribed "UNDELIVERED FOR REASON STATED/ RETURN TO SENDER", was introduced during the 1940s. On this original version, Type **J203**, the frame is 63mm long and the lower phrase 45mm. A similar, but larger, type (**J204**), with a frame 69mm and the lower phrase 49mm, came into use during 1975.

In 1960 the Post Office introduced a large boxed stamp, headed "RETURN TO SENDER", with eight reasons listed as to why the envelope had not been delivered. The Jersey number, 409, appeared at the foot. This was replaced in 1969 by a similar type (**J206**) which had "409" omitted.

Letters marked "Airmail", but insufficiently prepaid for transmission by air, received a boxed handstamp (Type **J207**), introduced in 1974, inscribed "Insufficient postage paid for/Transmission by air./Diverted to surface route". The system was changed in 1976 when underpaid airmail letters were returned to sender for additional postage. Such mail was marked by an unframed handstamp (Type **J208**) with a space for the additional amount in manuscript.

Where meter-franked letters were posted showing an incomplete impression a special marking was applied. Two different types are known. Type **J209** is worded "TO PAY / POSTAGE CANNOT BE / PREPAID BY MEANS / OF AN INCOMPLETE / FRANKING IMPRESSION / LIABLE TO .... RATE" with a box to the left for the surcharge to be inserted by hand. This was modified at decimalisation in 1971. The "D" was amended to "P" and the final sentence removed from the inscription (Type **J210**).

Letters charged postage due on which the charge was not collected at the first attempt are returned to the sorting office where a handstamp inscribed "CHARGE NOT COLLECTED/FRESH LABEL REQUIRED" was applied (Type **J211**). Its use is first recorded in 1923, but becomes much more frequent after 1969.

Surcharged mail not accepted by the addressee has, since 1986, been handstamped with an unboxed "REFUSED" (Type **J212**) before being returned to sender.

Mail sent to Jersey Poste Restante and unclaimed was marked, as early as 1909, with a small framed "Non Reclamé/Not Called for" in italic fount. In 1975 this was replaced by a similar worded handstamp, but in capitals (Type **J214**). Since 1971 such mail has been stamped "NOT/CALLED FOR" (Type **J215**). Mail to Post Office boxes which had been discontinued was marked "BOX CANCELLED/RETURN TO SENDER" (Type **J216**).

The "RETURNED LETTER BRANCH" datestamp has been used since 1975 on letters returned to sender.

too late
(J190)

Too Late
(J191)

Contains a communication
of the nature of a Letter
409
(J192)

Prohibited enclosure
409
(J193)

Not Known
409
(J194)

Inconnu
Not Known
(J194a)

Gone Away
409
(J195)

**POSTED OUT
OF COURSE**
(J196)

YOUR CORRECT POSTAL ADDRESS IS
GOREY, JERSEY.
ANY OTHER FORM OF ADDRESS
MAY LEAD TO DELAY
(J201)

```
┌─────────────────────────────────────────┐
│ YOUR CORRECT POSTAL ADDRESS IS           │
│                                          │
│                                          │
│ ANY OTHER FORM OF ADDRESS MAY LEAD       │
│ TO DELAY.      PLEASE ADVISE SENDER.     │
└─────────────────────────────────────────┘
```
(J202)

```
┌─────────────────────────────────────────┐
│   UNDELIVERED FOR REASON STATED          │
├─────────────────────────────────────────┤
│     RETURN TO SENDER                     │
└─────────────────────────────────────────┘
```
(J203)

```
┌─────────────────────────────────────────┐
│ UNDELIVERED FOR REASON STATED            │
├─────────────────────────────────────────┤
│     RETURN TO SENDER                     │
└─────────────────────────────────────────┘
```
(J204)

```
┌─────────────────────────────────────────┐
│          RETURN TO SENDER                │
│   Undelivered For Reason Stated          │
│   Gone Away............  Deceased.......  │
│   Not Known........     Refused.......    │
│   Not Occupied.......   Not Called For   │
│   No Such Address       Insufficiently   │
│   In..................  Address ......    │
└─────────────────────────────────────────┘
```
(J206)

```
┌─────────────────────────────────────────┐
│  Insufficient postage paid for           │
│  Transmission by air.                    │
│  Diverted to surface route.              │
└─────────────────────────────────────────┘
```
(J207)

Underpaid for Airmail Service.
Returned for   Additional
Postage. When remailing, cross
out this notice or paste stamps
over i'

(J208)

| D | TO PAY
POSTAGE CANNOT BE
PREPAID BY MEANS
OF AN INCOMPLETE
FRANKING IMPRESSION
LIABLE TO............RATE |

(J209)

| p

409 | TO PAY
POSTAGE CANNOT BE
PREPAID BY MEANS
OF AN INCOMPLETE
FRANKING IMPRESSION |

(J210)

CHARGE NOT COLLECTED

FRESH LABEL REQUIRED

(J211)

REFUSED

(J212)

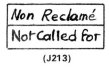

Non Reclamé
Not Called for

(J213)

NON RECLAME
NOT CALLED FOR

(J214)

NOT
CALLED FOR

(J215)

BOX CANCELLED

RETURN TO SENDER

(J216)

(J217)

Cat. No.	Type No.		Dates of use	Colour	Price on cover from
JT1	**J190**	too late	1831	Black	£300
JT2	**J191**	Too Late	1846	Green.	£200
JT3			1849	Red	£250
JT4			1900–05	Black	£100
JT5	**J192**	Contains a communication	1879	Black	£120
JT6	**J193**	Prohibited enclosure	1880	Black	£120
JT7	**J194**	Not Known	1900–59	Black, violet	30·00
JT7a	**J194a**	Inconnu/Not Known	1945	Violet	10·00
JT8	**J195**	Gone Away	1900–59	Black, violet	25·00
JT9	**J196**	POSTED OUT OF COURSE	1950s	Violet	15·00
JT10	**J197**	Missent to Jersey	1958	Violet	20·00
JT11	**J198**	Missent to Jersey	1975	Violet	8·00
JT12	**J199**	Missent to	1970s	Violet	
JT13	**J200**	GOREY	1960–67	Black	15·00
JT14	**J201**	YOUR CORRECT POSTAL ADDRESS IS GOREY	1967	Violet	20·00
JT15	**J202**	YOUR CORRECT POSTAL ADDRESS IS	1971	Violet	15·00
JT16	**J203**	UNDELIVERED	1940s	Violet	1·00
JT17	**J204**	UNDELIVERED	1975–	Violet	1·00
JT18	**J205**	RETURN TO SENDER 409	1960	Violet	5·00
JT19	**J206**	RETURN TO SENDER	1969–	Violet, blue	1·00
JT20	**J207**	Insufficient postage	1974	Violet	4·00

Cat. No.	Type No.		Dates of use	Colour	Price on cover from
JT21	**J208**	Underpaid for Airmail Service	1976	Violet	3·00
JT22	**J209**	INCOMPLETE FRANKING	1960–71	Violet	10·00
JT23	**J210**	INCOMPLETE FRANKING	1971–	Violet	5·00
JT24	**J211**	CHARGE NOT COLLECTED	1923–68	Violet	25·00
JT25	**J212**	REFUSED	1986	Violet	3·00
JT26	**J213**	Non Reclamé/Not Called for	1909	Black	10·00
JT27	**J214**	NON RECLAME/NOT CALLED FOR	1975	Violet	5·00
JT28	**J215**	NOT/CALLED FOR	1981	Black, violet	3·00
JT29	**J216**	BOX CANCELLED	1977	Violet	4·00
JT30	**J217**	RETURNED LETTER BRANCH	1975	Violet	5·00

GUERNSEY

(1) Postage Due

(a) On Inland Mail

(i) To 1969

A large 1d. with the numeral 324 below (Type **G100**) was introduced towards the end of the nineteenth century, with a similar 2d. marking following a short time later. Both continued in use until 1969. A 3d. marking (Type **G101**), including the words "TO PAY", dates from 1919 with a 4d. version in the same format being used from the 1920s.

As in Jersey a new boxed type instructional marking was issued to Guernsey in 1939. Type **G102** was inscribed "TO PAY/POSTED/UNPAID" and a blank space was left in the surcharge box for the value to be inserted in manuscript. A revised type (**G103**) appeared during the early 1950s, showing a single frame line and a fixed denomination; 5d. in 1950 and 6d. in 1964. A larger version of this fixed value mark is also known with "D" immediately above the 6d. (1958) or 8d. (1968) value (Type **G104**). From 1960, however, the island reverted to the previous version with a blank box, but now with a single frame line.

(ii) 1969 onwards

A new range of instructional markings was introduced by Guernsey in 1969. As for Jersey there were two series, one for unpaid and the other for underpaid mail.

A large rectangular marking (Type **G105**), inscribed "TO PAY/POSTED/UNPAID" with a space at the left for the surcharge to be added, was used from 1969. This was withdrawn after decimalisation in 1971 and replaced by an elongated box type (**G106**), again with a space for the surcharge to be inserted in manuscript. Due to damage this was superseded in 1977 by a further boxed type (**G107**) measuring 46 × 15mm. A replacement mark issued in 1982 (Type **G108**) had larger lettering and measured 40 × 18mm.

The first marking in the underpaid series was also introduced in 1969. This boxed type (**G109**) is very similar to the contemporary unpaid marking. An elongated type (**G110**) followed in 1971 and was, in turn, replaced by an unframed marking (Type **G111**) in 1977. Five years later a replacement mark, also unframed, showed "POSTED" ranged right (Type **G112**).

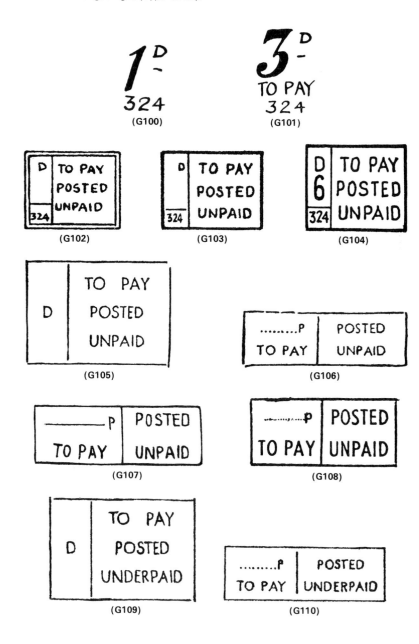

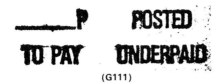

(G111)

(G112)

Cat. No.	Type No.		Dates of use	Colour	Price on cover from
GD1	**G100**	(1d.)	1897–1969	Black, red, green .	12·00
GD1a		("324") omitted)	1904	Black, red, green .	40·00
GD2		(2d.)	1900–69	Black, red, green .	12·00
GD3	**G101**	(3d.)	1919–62	Black, red, green .	18·00
GD4		(4d.)	1920–62	Black, red, green .	20·00
GD5	**G102**	(blank)	1939–69	Black, red	10·00
GD6	**G103**	(5d.)	1950–69	Black, violet, green	10·00
GD7		(6d.)	1964–65	Green.	10·00
GD8		(blank)	1960–69	Black, violet, red .	6·00
GD9	**G104**	(6d.)	1958–60	Green.	
GD10		(8d.)	1968–70	Green.	
GD11	**G105**	(blank)	1969–71	Black, violet, green	2·50
GD12	**G106**	(blank)	1971–77	Violet, blue	1·00
GD13	**G107**	(blank)	1977–81	Violet, blue, green	1·00
GD14	**G108**	(blank)	1982–	Green, black	1·00
GD15	**G109**	(blank)	1969–71	Black, violet, green	3·00
GD16	**G110**	(blank)	1971–76	Violet, blue, green	2·00
GD17	**G111**	(blank)	1977–82	Violet, blue, green, black	1·50
GD18	**G112**	(blank)	1982–	Black, blue	1·00

(*b*) *On Overseas Mail*
(i) Outwards
   A series of Taxe markings (Type **G150**), identical to the Jersey handstamps, but with the letters GU replacing JE beneath the frame, was introduced into Guernsey during the nineteenth century. The initial markings showed the figures 5, 10, 15 or 25. Examples showing 20 or 40 followed in 1907.
   A fractional type (**G151**) was used by Guernsey from 1971. This was a small boxed handstamp showing the letter "T", but without any figures; the actual fractions being added in manuscript. This was replaced by a similar plain, but larger, type (**G152**) in 1981. In 1986 another mark, similar in size to the 1971 version, was introduced. This had the line of dots level with the centre of the "T" (Type **G153**).

(ii) Inwards

Guernsey also introduced a large boxed handstamp (Type **G154**) in 1976, this being applied to underpaid mail from abroad. It consisted of four compartments inscribed "SURCHARGED, ITEM POSTED/UNDERPAID BY/   P.   /PLUS P. /SURCHARGE FEE" and "TOTAL/TO PAY", the relevant figures being inserted in the boxes by hand.

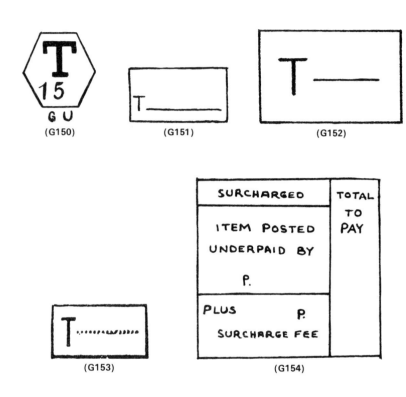

(G150)   (G151)   (G152)

(G153)   (G154)

Cat. No.	Type No.		Dates of use	Colour	Price on cover from
GE1	**G150**	T 5	1890–1905	Black	£250
GE2		T 10	1890	Black	£200
GE3		T 15	1890–93	Black	£200
GE4		T 20	1907	Black	£250
GE5		T 25	1890	Black	£250
GE6		T 40	1907	Black	£250
GE7	**G151**	T blank	1971–81	Violet	4·00
GE8	**G152**	T blank	1981–83	Violet	1·00
GE9	**G153**	T blank	1986	Violet	1·00
GE10	**G154**		1976–	Violet	2·00

(2) Explanatory Charge Marks
(*a*) *Stamps Invalid*
    To date, only three types of invalid handstamps have been used in Guernsey. The first (Type **G160**) was unframed and contained the words "STAMP INVALID" 44mm in length. This was replaced in 1971 by a cachet, 21mm square, (Type **G161**) inscribed "STAMP(S) INVALID/.......P/TO PAY"; the surcharge being inserted in manuscript. Type **G161** was lost during 1980 and was replaced by a larger cachet, 30 × 32mm, with similar wording (Type **G162**).

STAMP INVALID
(G160)

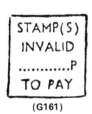

(G161)

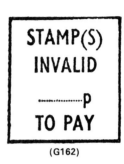

(G162)

Cat. No.	Type No.		Dates of use	Colour	Price on cover
GI1	**G160**	STAMP INVALID	1969–71	Violet, blue, black.	3·00
GI2	**G161**	Blank	1972–80	Violet, green	1·00
GI3	**G162**		1981	Violet, black	1·00

(*b*) *Liable to Letter or Postcard Rate*
    A "Liable to Letter Rate" handstamp was first used in Guernsey in 1895. This was of a similar stepped design to Jersey Type **J170**, except that the Guernsey numeral 324 was shown. This continued in use until 1960.
    A new handstamp (Type **G170**), which included the 1d. surcharge, was introduced during the 1930s.
    A modern style boxed marking with a double frame (as Jersey Type **J172**), inscribed "TO PAY/LIABLE TO/LETTER/RATE" and with a space on the left for the surcharge to be added, appeared during the 1930s. This was replaced by a single framed boxed type (Type **G171**) in 1964. A further version, identical to Type **G171**, is known with "1d." in the surcharge box.
    Two different "Liable to Postcard Rate" types are known. The first is a stepped marking (Type **G172**) similar to that issued for Jersey. This was replaced by a boxed mark (Type **G173**), inscribed "TO PAY/LIABLE TO/POSTCARD/RATE" with a space for the insertion of the surcharge, issued in 1960.

A "Contrary to Regulations" handstamp, similar to Jersey Type **J177** but containing the numeral 324, was introduced into Guernsey in 1880. Only one example has been seen to date.

(G170)

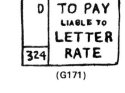
(G171)

(G172)

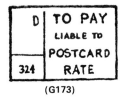
(G173)

Cat. No.	Type No.		Dates of use	Colour	Price on cover
GL1	**J170**	Liable to Letter Rate	1895–1960	Black, green	14·00
GL2	**G170**	1d. TO PAY/LIABLE TO/LETTER RATE	1930–60	Black, red, green	20·00
GL3	**J172**	TO PAY/LIABLE TO LETTER RATE	1930	Black, red	12·00
GL4	**G171**	TO PAY/LIABLE TO/LETTER RATE	1964–67	Black, blue, violet, green	12·00
GL5		1d. TO PAY/LIABLE TO/LETTER RATE	1964–65	Green, blue, black, violet	12·00
GL6	**G172**	1d. TO PAY/LIABLE TO/POSTCARD RATE	1930–60	Black, violet, green	20·00
GL7	**G173**	TO PAY/LIABLE TO/POSTCARD/RATE	1960	Black	15·00
GL8	**J177**	Contrary to regulations	1880	Black	80·00

(c) More to Pay

Three types of "More to Pay" marks are recognised for Guernsey. A stepped handstamp, similar to Jersey Type **J180**, was brought to Guernsey during the 1870s, but only three examples (1921, 1922 and 1935) have so far been recorded on cover.

A circular "MORE TO PAY" with a cross paté at each side has been seen on an 1871 letter from Lannion to Guernsey with a manuscript "4". It has not yet been traced in the G.P.O. proof book.

Two boxed marks (Types **G180/1**) have been seen on Guernsey mail. These are both inscribed "MORE TO/PAY/LETTER RATE/ABOVE ....OZ". Type **G180** has two thin frame lines and Type **G181** one thick line. The lettering of Type **G180** is larger than that of its replacement. The first type is known in black during the Occupation (1943–44) and in black or green between 1952 and 1965. It was replaced by Type **G181**, which has only been recorded in green, during 1965.

A marking with a similar purpose has been seen from 1968. This was used in connection with a rise in postage rates and is the usual type of "324" oblong inscribed "SURCHARGE DUE TO INCREASED POSTAL CHARGES" (Type **G182**).

(G180)

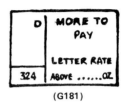

(G181)

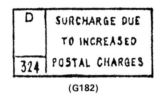

(G182)

Cat. No.	Type No.	Dates of use	Colour	Price on cover
GM1	**J180**	1878–1960	Black	50·00
GM2	**G180**	1943–44	Black	£150
GM2a		1952–65	Black, green	25·00
GM3	**G181**	1965–70	Green.	12·00
GM4	**G182**	1968	Green.	30·00

(d) Postage Due for Return to Sender

As described under Jersey three different ½d./POSTAGE/DUE/FOR/ RETURN/TO/SENDER/ handstamps were used on Guernsey. The first two are identical to Jersey Types **J185/6** and the third is similar to Type **J187**, except that the Post Office number shown is 324. A 1d. handstamp, identical to Jersey Type **J188**, appeared in 1940 and can be found on covers sent to Guernsey inhabitants evacuated to the mainland. Such covers are usually endorsed in manuscript "Evacuated" or "Gone Away" with the initials or signature of the postman.

After the liberation, a new postage due for return to sender handstamp appeared. This type (**G185**) had no value in the left-hand surcharge box, the postage due being inserted in manuscript. This was replaced during the 1960s by a similar marking

(Type **G188**), again without value. The main difference between Types **G185** and **G188** is in the position of the "D" within the surcharge box.

1½d., 2d., 2½d. amd 3d. markings (as Types **G186/7**) also appeared for Guernsey and are more common than their Jersey counterparts.

UNDELIVERED FOR REASON STATED	UNDELIVERED FOR REASON STATED
D — POSTAGE DUE FOR RETURN TO SENDER — 324	D 1½ — POSTAGE DUE FOR RETURN TO SENDER — 324
(G185)	(G186)
UNDELIVERED FOR REASON STATED	UNDELIVERED FOR REASON STATED
D 2½ — POSTAGE DUE FOR RETURN TO SENDER — 314	D — POSTAGE DUE FOR RETURN TO SENDER — 324
(G187)	(G188)

Cat. No.	Type No.		Dates of use	Colour	Price on cover from
GS1	**J185**	(½d.)	1895–1930	Black	40·00
GS2	**J186**	(½d.)	1930–39	Black	40·00
GS3	**J187**	(324) (½d.)	1932–39	Black	40·00
GS4	**J188**	(1d.)	1940–45	Violet	45·00
GS4a			1945–51	Violet	15·00
GS5	**G185**	(blank)	1945–60	Violet	20·00
GS6	**G186**	(1½d.)	1951–57	Violet, green	12·00
GS7	**G187**	(2d.)	1956–61	Violet, green	18·00
GS8	**G188**	(blank)	1960–68	Violet	15·00
GS9	**G187**	(2½d.)	1961–65	Violet	15·00
GS10		(3d.)	1965–68	Violet	25·00

(3) Irregularities in Transmission

Two types of missent mark are known. The first, recorded from 1954, is boxed and inscribed "MISSENT TO GUERNSEY" (Type **G190**). The other mark, dating from 1975, is a similar inscription, but unboxed and in upper and lower case letters (Type **G191**).

Letters on which a late fee had been paid were handstamped with an unboxed "LATE FEE PAID" (Type **G192**) recorded in 1937. A mark with a similar use was introduced in 1988 and read "ACCEPTED AFTER/LAST COLLECTION/AT SENDERS REQUEST" within a box (Type **G193**).

Mail franked with incomplete meter marks received special handstamps. The first, dating from the 1960s, is similar to the contemporary mark from Jersey but shows the Guernsey number, 324, at bottom left (Type **G194**). On decimalisation this was replaced by a mark in a similar size, but inscribed, in five lines ".....P TO PAY/Postage cannot be/paid by means of/an incomplete/franking impression" (Type **G195**). This lasted until 1978 when an oblong replacement, with similar wording, but all in capitals, extending over four lines only, was used (Type **G196**).

Mail misdirected or letters lacking their envelopes received an unboxed "Found in course/of sorting" mark (Type **G197**) known from the 1950s. A similar purpose was served by a large cachet, including space for a c.d.s., which read "STATES OF GUERNSEY/POST OFFICE BOARD/FOUND OPEN OR DAMAGED/AND OFFICIALLY SECURED/INITIALS ....." introduced in 1969 (Type **G198**).

There are a considerable number of marks associated with mail which, for one reason or another, could not be delivered. The first, known as early as 1916 was a boxed mark reading "Undelivered for reason stated/To be returned to Sender/at the address shown on cover" (Type **G199**). Later versions of this oblong mark were as Type **J203** of Jersey and at least two different sizes exist.

Handstamps were also supplied to give the reasons for non-delivery. A stepped "Gone Away" with "324" beneath is known from 1900 (Type **G200**) and a bi-lingual boxed "PARTI/GONE AWAY" from 1973 (Type **G201**). Other marks in French made their appearance during the 1960s and 1970s, "ADRESSE INSUFFISANTE" (Type **G202**) and "RETOUR" (Type **G203**).

As the amount of returned mail increased Guernsey adopted the "check box" type of mark which provided a list of reasons for the postman to indicate. The first such mark dates from 1956 and is identified by the word "INITIALS" at top right (Type **G204**). In 1960 this was replaced by a further horizontal mark headed "RETURN TO SENDER" and with the Guernsey number, 324, at foot (Type **G205**). When the States postal administration took over the mark was redesigned to a square format (Type **G206**) and then, in 1982, to a vertical shape with a bi-lingual heading (Type **G207**).

Letters on which postage due had been charged, but the fee not collected were stamped with a boxed oblong inscribed "CHARGE NOT COLLECTED/FRESH LABEL REQUIRED" with a diagonal cross between the two lines (Type **G208**).

From 1969 mail sent to a Guernsey post office box and not collected was returned marked "NON RECLAME/NOT CALLED FOR" within a box (Type **G209**). A later mark "BOX CANCELLED RETURN TO SENDER" (Type **G210**) served a similar purpose.

In the drive to speed the mail a boxed mark reading "YOUR CORRECT POSTAL ADDRESS IS/....../ANY OTHER FORM OF ADDRESS MAY LEAD TO DELAY. PLEASE ADVISE SENDER" was introduced in 1960 (Type **G211**). By 1982 this had been replaced by an unboxed "PLEASE HELP US TO SPEED YOUR MAIL/BY ENSURING THAT THE SENDER KNOWS/YOUR P.O. BOX NO. FULL POSTAL ADDRESS" (Type **G212**). After postal independence mail returned to Guernsey sometimes had a circular "RECEIVED AT/GUERNSEY POST OFFICE" applied (Type **G213**).

Official letters from the postal administration often carry "ON POSTAL SERVICE" (Type **G214**) or "SERVICE DES POSTES" (Type **G215**) boxed straight-line marks.

MISSENT TO GUERNSEY

(G190)

LATE FEE PAID

(G192)

ACCEPTED AFTER
LAST COLLECTION
AT SENDERS REQUEST

(G193)

D	TO PAY
	POSTAGE CANNOT BE PREPAID BY MEANS OF AN INCOMPLETE FRANKING IMPRESSION
324	LIABLE TO .... RATE

(G194)

..............P TO PAY
Postage cannot be
paid by means of
an incomplete
franking impression

(G195)

.... P TO PAY
POSTAGE CANNOT BE PAID
BY MEAN OF AN INCOMPLETE
FRANKING IMPRESSION

(G196)

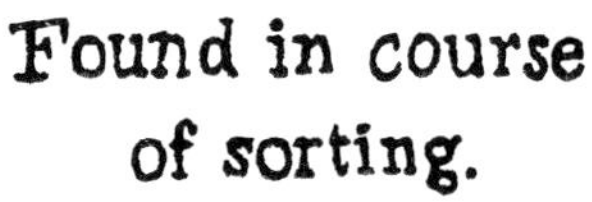

Found in course
of sorting.
(G197)

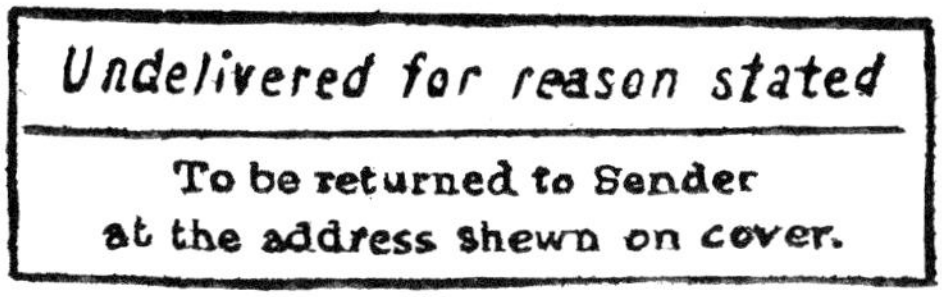

Undelivered for reason stated

To be returned to Sender
at the address shewn on cover.

(G199)

Gone Away
324

(G200)

PARTI

GONE AWAY

(G201)

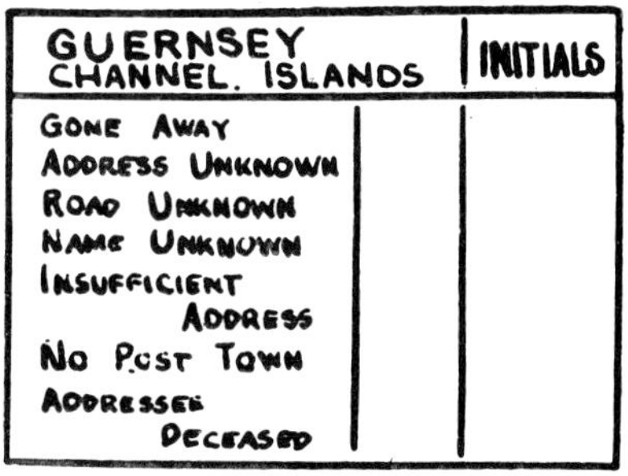

GUERNSEY CHANNEL. ISLANDS	INITIALS
GONE AWAY	
ADDRESS UNKNOWN	
ROAD UNKNOWN	
NAME UNKNOWN	
INSUFFICIENT ADDRESS	
No POST TOWN	
ADDRESSEE DECEASED	

(G204)

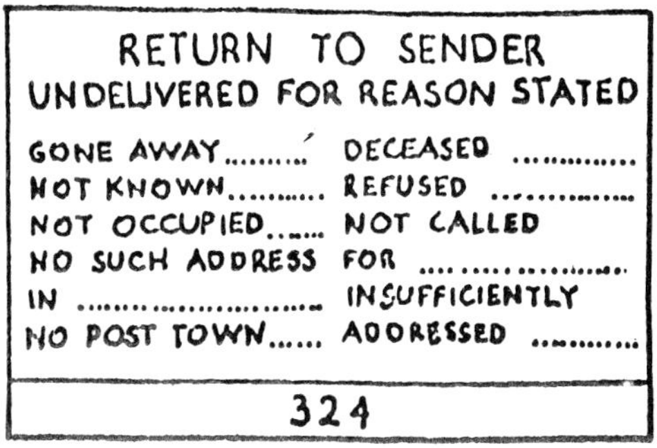

RETURN TO SENDER	
UNDELIVERED FOR REASON STATED	
GONE AWAY.........´	DECEASED ....
NOT KNOWN...........	REFUSED ....
NOT OCCUPIED.......	NOT CALLED
NO SUCH ADDRESS	FOR ....
IN	INSUFFICIENTLY
NO POST TOWN......	ADDRESSED ....
324	

(G205)

RETURN TO SENDER UNDELIVERED FOR REASON STATED	TICK	INITIALS
NOT KNOWN AT THIS ADDRESS		
INSUFFICIENT ADDRESS		
DECEASED		
GONE AWAY ADDRESS		
NOT CALLED FOR		
NOT KNOWN AT NO.		
NOT TO BE FOUND		
REFUSED		

(G206)

RETURN TO SENDER
RENVOI A L'EXPÉDITEUR

☐ Gone away
Parti sans laisser d'adresse

☐ No such address
Adresse inexistente

☐ Address incomplete
Adresse incomplète

☐ Address illegible
Adresse illisible

☐ Refused   ☐ Undelimed
Reiusé   Nonreclinc

☐ Decessed   ☐ Unknown
Decода   Inconniuc

(G207)

NON RECLAME

NOT CALLED FOR

(G209)

RECEIVED AT
- 2 OCT 1974
GUERNSEY POST OFFICE

(G213)

ON POSTAL SERVICE

(G214)

Cat. No.	Type No.		Dates of use	Colour	Price on cover from
GT1	**G190**	MISSENT TO GUERNSEY (60 × 10mm)	1954	Violet	40·00
GT2		MISSENT TO GUERNSEY (75 × 13mm)	1973	Violet	35·00
GT3		MISSENT TO GUERNSEY (74 × 9mm)	1984	Blue-black	10·00

Cat. No.	Type No.		Dates of use	Colour	Price on cover from
GT4	**G191**	Missent to Guernsey	1975	Violet	10·00
GT5	**G192**	LATE FEE PAID	1937	Black	
GT6	**G193**	ACCEPTED AFTER LAST COLLECTION	1988	Black	2·00
GT7	**G194**	INCOMPLETE FRANKING	1960s	Green, violet	12·00
GT8	**G195**	Incomplete franking	1971	Violet	8·00
GT9	**G196**	INCOMPLETE FRANKING	1978–	Blue	5·00
GT10	**G197**	Found in course of sorting	1950s	Black, green	18·00
GT11	**G198**	FOUND OPENED OR DAMAGED	1969	Black	2·00
GT12	**G199**	Undelivered for reason stated	1916	Violet	20·00
GT13	**J203**	UNDELIVERED . . . . . . (63mm long)	1940s	Violet	2·00
GT14		UNDELIVERED . . . . . . (60mm long)	1970s	Violet, red, green .	2·00
GT15	**G200**	Gone Away 324	1900	Black, green	20·00
GT16	**G201**	PARTI/GONE AWAY	1973	Black	5·00
GT17	**G202**	ADRESSE INSUFFISANTE (38 × 7mm)	1975	Black	5·00
GT18		ADRESSE INSUFFISANTE (60 × 7mm)	1975	Black	5·00
GT19	**G203**	RETOUR (38 × 11mm)	1968–75	Black	5·00
GT20		RETOUR (34 × 9mm)	1980–	Black	4·00
GT21	**G204**	INITIALS	1956–59	Violet	3·00
GT22	**G205**	RETURN TO SENDER 324	1960–70	Violet	2·00
GT23	**G206**	RETURN TO SENDER	1971	Black	1·00
GT24	**G207**	RETURN TO SENDER /RENVOI A L'EXPÉDITEUR	1982	Black	1·00
GT25	**G208**	CHARGE NOT COLLECTED	1940–	Violet	2·00
GT26	**G209**	NON RECLAME/NOT CALLED FOR	1969	Violet	5·00
GT27	**G210**	BOX CANCELLED RETURN TO SENDER	1979	Black	2·00
GT28	**G211**	YOUR CORRECT POSTAL ADDRESS IS	1960–75	Black	2·00
GT29	**G212**	HELP US SPEED YOUR MAIL	1982	Black	2·00
GT30	**G213**	RECEIVED AT GUERNSEY POST OFFICE	1969	Violet	2·00
GT31	**G214**	ON POSTAL SERVICE (50 × 9mm)	1971–79	Black	2·00
GT32		ON POSTAL SERVICE (55 × 12mm)	1987	Black	2·00
GT33	**G215**	SERVICE DES POSTES	1971–	Black	2·00

11. Military Mail

Guernsey Militia
During the Napoleonic Wars letters from the Guernsey Militia Headquarters and the replies were carried round the island by the chasseurs of the Militia. They are quite rare and no more than thirty examples have been recorded, most of these being endorsed "On Service" in manuscript. One is illustrated. Similar letters probably exist for Jersey, but we have not seen any.

Guernsey Militia letter of 1795

Soldiers and Sailors Letters
Covers exhibiting the correct 1d. rate granted to soldiers and sailors by the Act of 1795 are sought after.

Similarly, letters written from Fort Regent in Jersey and Fort George in Guernsey during the times that they contained military garrisons are collectable, commanding a small premium. During the period 1854–70 such letters, although bearing adhesives, were often marked "On Her Majesty's Service".

Royal Jersey Militia Camp
Mail posted at a summer camp of the Royal Jersey Militia in 1908 was marked with a violet cachet consisting of a large double-circle inscribed "MEDICAL CORPS/THE ROYAL MILITIA OF JERSEY", with a large cross in the centre. The postage stamps were cancelled at the head office.

Liberation 1945
After the islands were liberated from German Occupation British Field Post Offices were established in Guernsey and Jersey. That for Guernsey was F.P.O. 138 and that for Jersey F.P.O. 302. They functioned from 9 May to 10 November 1945.

In Guernsey a circular rubber stamp with "ARMY/POST OFFICE" in the centre and six vertical bars at top and bottom was also used on parcels and small packets. This can only be identified as coming from Guernsey if the F.P.O. number is also used on the wrapper. A registration label then in use had 138 struck in violet after the printed "F.P.O. No."

Force Headquarters

The Military Headquarters in Jersey used a special boxed handstamp (50 × 18mm) on mail and an example is illustrated on a postcard sent on 8 June 1945. The card also shows the temporary 1d. Paid handstamp (Type **J81a**) made up from the ½d. value.

The card illustrated is now in the Occupation Museum at St. Peter's. The message on the reverse is interesting historically and reads: "Please cause the captured GERMAN horse loaned to you to be at St. Mary's Arsenal on 12th June 1945 at 11.30 a.m." This is under signature of an Army Officer.

Force Headquarters handstamp

Field Post Office markings

	Dates of use	Colour		Price
Guernsey Militia letters	1790–1815	—	*from*	£150
Soldiers and Sailors Letters at 1d. rate	1795–1820	—	*from*	£200
Royal Jersey Militia cachet	1908	Violet . .	*on cover*	£180
F.P.O. 138 c.d.s. (Guernsey)	1945	Black. . .	*on cover*	£100
F.P.O. 302 c.d.s. (Jersey)	1945	Black. . .	*on cover*	£150
F.P.O. 138 on censored cover	1945	Black. . .	*on cover*	£200
F.P.O. 302 on censored cover	1945	Black. . .	*on cover*	£300
Guernsey registered cover with F.P.O. 138 on registration label and ARMY/POST OFFICE handstamp	1945	Violet . .	*on cover*	£500
ARMY POST OFFICE handstamp	1945	Violet . .	*on piece*	£100
FORCE HEADQUARTERS handstamp	1945	Black. . .	*on card*	£250

For Prisoner of War mail *see* Section 21.

12. Paquebot Marks

Paquebot marks have been used in both Islands on mail landed from ships calling there. The letters or postcards were either handed to the purser for delivery to the nearest post office, or posted in a special box provided on board. On arrival at the post office the stamps, usually foreign ones and mainly French, were cancelled with a Jersey or Guernsey postmark with a "PAQUEBOT" mark also applied.

During Hovercraft trials in 1976 between the islands and France, various items of mail were landed at Guernsey or Jersey and received the appropriate Paquebot mark. 203 items had the Jersey mark impressed and 170 the Guernsey one. Further mail was carried in 1977 and 1978. (*See also Section* 16).

Measurement of Paquebot marks are made from the middle of the base of the "P" to the middle of the base of the "T". All Guernsey marks are scarcer than their Jersey counterparts.

JERSEY

The earliest example (Type **P1**) recorded for Jersey has the word "PAQUEBOT" in sloping serifed letters measuring $32\frac{1}{2} \times 5$mm. It is known struck in violet on covers dated 1895, 1896 and 1898, but a further example from 1902 shows that the handstamp was breaking up and spreading, as the impression measures almost 36mm.

The next type used (**P2**) was similar, but measured 38×6mm, being found struck in black between 1901 and 1909, but with examples also known in violet during 1904 and 1905. A further handstamp (**P3**), measuring $33 \times 4\frac{1}{2}$mm, with sloping letters is known, struck in violet or black, from 1905. This was an omnibus type issued to nineteen ports in the British Isles, including both Jersey and Guernsey.

The early years of this century were the heyday of the picture postcard era and many cards from this period exist with paquebot markings.

We have not seen any paquebot marks used after 1911 until a new handstamp was prepared for Jersey in 1973. This has sans-serif letters measuring $32 \times 4\frac{1}{2}$mm and is still in use (Type **P4**).

Other Jersey marks with a maritime flavour were those used on board the Swedish-America Line's vessels *Kungsholm* and *Gripsholm* when they visited the island in 1970, 1971, 1972 and 1973. Special handstamps were used and are listed in Section 15.

GUERNSEY

The only early paquebot mark recorded for Guernsey is found struck in violet or red between 1902 and 1910. It is of the same omnibus type (**P3**) as Jersey and is also known in black on a single 1922 card from Cherbourg to Guernsey. The next recorded mark (Type **P6**) is slightly larger ($36\frac{1}{2} \times 5$mm) and has a curly top to the "T". Only three examples are known, all on French cards of 1928. A sans-serif PAQUEBOT (Type **P7**), $35\frac{1}{2} \times 6$mm, is known struck in black on a small number of French reply-paid cards of 1969.

In 1972 the Guernsey Post Office Board introduced a new Paquebot mark in upper and lower case letters (Type **P8**); this is found struck in violet on Hovercraft covers and other items.

From 1980 a smaller mark, 23mm in length (Type **P9**) was used.

PAQUEBOT
(P1)

PAQUEBOT
(P2)

PAQUEBOT
(P3)

PAQUEBOT
(P4)

PAQUEBOT
(P6)

PAQUEBOT
(P7)

Paquebot
(P8)

Paquebot
(P9)

Cat. No.	Type No.	Dates of use	Colour	Measurements	Price on cover
Jersey					
JP1	**P1**	1895–1905	Violet	$32\frac{1}{2}$ × 5mm (sloping) .	£350
JP2	**P2**	1901–09	Black	38 × 6mm (sloping) . .	£150
JP2a		1904–05	Violet	ditto	£150
JP3	**P3**	1905–11	Violet	33 × $4\frac{1}{2}$mm (sloping) .	£150
JP3a		1905	Black	ditto	£175
JP4	**P4**	1973–	Violet	30 × $4\frac{1}{2}$mm (upright) .	3·00
Guernsey					
GP1	**P3**	1903–10	Violet	33 × $4\frac{1}{2}$mm (sloping) .	£350
GP1a		1902–10	Red	ditto	£400
GP1b		1922	Black	ditto	£400
GP2	**P6**	1928	Black	$36\frac{1}{2}$ × 5mm (sloping) .	£400
GP3	**P7**	1969	Black	$35\frac{1}{2}$ × $6\frac{1}{2}$mm (upright)	50·00
GP4	**P8**	1972–80	Violet	28 × $6\frac{1}{2}$mm (upright) .	5·00
GP5	**P9**	1980–	Violet	23 × 3mm (upright) . .	3·00

See also: "Hovermail flights" in Section 16 (Airmails and Hovercraft Mail) and details of French Paquebot marks from Carteret in Section 17 (Mails between the Channel Islands and France).

13. The Smaller Islands

The smaller islands dealt with in this section are: Alderney, Sark, Herm, Jethou, Brecqhou and Lihou.

ALDERNEY

When post offices were established in Guernsey and Jersey in 1794 no provision was made for Alderney and mail for that island was carried privately until 1812. In that year Sir John Doyle, Governor of Guernsey, wrote to Francis Freeling, Secretary of the Post Office, and offered to arrange carriage of mails by his "scouts". Freeling accepted this and instructed the Guernsey Postmistress to make up an Alderney bag whenever required. Some kind of post office was set up on Alderney by Le Mesurier, whose family were the hereditary governors.

The arrangement between Doyle and Freeling held good until 1815 when peace was signed between Britain and France, and the carriage of letters reverted to private ships. A private post office is thought to have survived on Alderney after this, but no postal markings were used.

In August 1823 the States of Guernsey passed an Ordinance which set up a special office, known as the Foreign Post Office and run by George S. Syvret and Matthieu Barbet, to handle all mail addressed to or from Alderney and the neighbouring French coast. The masters of all ships were instructed to deliver their letters there and call for mail before sailing. The Ordinance was strengthened later in 1823 and again in 1833. Its purpose appears to have been to give a monopoly of letters for France and Alderney to one of the private offices still existing and to provide official sanction to the payment of 1d. to the master of the ship carrying the letter and to the agent at the port. The Ordinance was finally repealed in 1841, but the private post office apparently continued to function for several years afterwards.

On 21 July 1840 a Memorial from the inhabitants of Alderney praying for the establishment of a Government Post Office there was forwarded by the Hon. Fox Maule; also an application from Mr. Brown complaining of the extra charge on letters from Guernsey. The Postmaster General replied on 5 August saying that he could not consent, at present, to make any alterations to the existing arrangements for sending letters to Alderney. It was not until March 1848 that a post office was established on the island.

For some considerable time it was thought that the first cancellation used on Alderney was a distinctive Maltese Cross. There is, however, no direct evidence of its use on the island. Of the eleven known entires and thirty-odd examples on pieces and loose stamps with this cancellation only one entire shows a Guernsey backstamp and two others were written on Jersey. More recently an entire of 1845, originating in Amsterdam and addressed to London, has been found, showing a "PD" mark and oval "Paid London Ship Letter" handstamp under an example of the so-called Alderney Maltese Cross. This suggests that the mark was, at that time, in use at the London Ship Letter Office.

With the opening of the sub-post office in 1848 the G.P.O. in London despatched an undated double arc handstamp (Type **1**) on 8 January. This was struck on the face of the cover or entire beside the postage stamp which was cancelled by a "965" numeral obliterator (Type **3**) sent to the island on 8 May. This obliterator had four bars at top and at foot, and was used until the mid-1860s. An additional double arc handstamp with slightly larger lettering was despatched on 17 May 1855.

A further double arc handstamp (Type **2**), now with date and code A, was despatched to the island on 2 April 1851. Normally struck in black examples are known in orange-yellow on covers to Jersey in 1852 and 1854. Additional dated double arc marks were sent on 15 June 1855 (code A), 9 September 1857 and 23 October 1857 (both code C). These marks are very scarce on complete cover as most mail came from a solicitor's archives from which the addresses were removed.

The double arc handstamps were replaced by a 20mm single circle datestamp (Type **4**) with code A. This was despatched on 24 April 1860 and was in use by 24 May. A similar mark, but with code C, was sent on 31 December of the same year.

During the mid-1860s the "965" numeral obliterator was replaced by a smaller version (Type **3a**) which had only three bars at top and bottom. This was much more thickly cut than the original and soon showed considerable wear.

A 21mm single circle with code A was despatched by the G.P.O., London, on 8 November 1872 (Type **4a**) to be followed by a further 20mm single circle with code C (Type **4b**).

These marks were used to cancel the stamps. Type **4a** survived in use until 1934. An example is known, from 1910 without date or code, struck on a Type **RL1** registration label. The different 20mm datestamps can be identified by the relative positions of the "A" and "Y".

The first of the double-circle datestamps (Type **9**) appeared in 1895, initially with code A, but without a code after 1914. A 28mm "skeleton" mark (Type **5**) is known used on 13 October 1922 and seems to have been replaced by a further double-circle (Type **9a**) which had much thinner bars and no code. The earliest known use of the replacement is 20 July 1923. In 1935 yet another mark in this series appeared with much thicker bars, an asterisk code and "CH. IS." at foot (Type **10**). Just before the mark was withdrawn, between 1 and 10 August 1966, it showed code A for the morning despatch and B for the afternoon.

A 24mm single circle datestamp (Type **6**) was introduced in 1936 and remained in use until 1955 when a replacement 24mm single circle inscribed "ALDERNEY/GUERNSEY. CHANNEL ISLANDS" appeared (Type **7**).

The replacement for Type **10** in August 1966 was a fresh design of double circle datestamp without bars (Type **11**).

When the Guernsey postal service became independent on 1 October 1969 the British-style datestamps were replaced by the standard format 23½mm single circle (Type **8**) with asterisk code and a similar 26½mm single circle used with codes A, B, asterisk or without code.

From 9 December 1975 a new double circle (Type **12**) was issued for counter work and this exists with A, B or asterisk codes. A replacement, issued 13 February 1979 had larger letters and a short line either side of "ALDERNEY". The same three codes were employed with the asterisk used for the morning mail despatch and "B" for the afternoon, but later this was changed so that the asterisk code was used for all counter transactions, "B" for mail posted between 9 am and 4 pm and "A" for mail posted before 9 am and after 4 pm.

In September 1985 a new 24mm single circle datestamp (codes A or B) (Type **8a**) and a double circle as Type **12a**, but with longer lines either side of "ALDERNEY" (codes A or asterisk) were issued as replacements.

The Winchfield Error

A vertical 965 is known as part of a duplex, but this was never issued to Alderney. It was made in error for 963 and sent to Winchfield in Hampshire.

A registered cover of 1882 and a postal stationery card of 1897 are known showing this postmark error.

(Price on cover £500; *on piece from* £50)

Parcel Post Cancellations

The first parcel post cancellation was a double-ring rubber type (**13**) with the name "ALDERNEY" across the centre. It was dispatched from the G.P.O. on 13 July 1911.

The similar Type **14**, reading "ALDERNEY/CHANNEL ISLANDS", is also known on Edwardian stamps, but its date of introduction cannot be traced. It was probably about 1912 and seems to have been needed because Type **13** had quickly disintegrated in use. Both are scarce markings.

A large label type of parcel post cancellation (Type **15**) was issued to the island about 1947. The earliest date of use seen is 1949. In 1958 a new parcel stamp in the large label type was introduced and this is Type **16**. It has "ALDERNEY" at the top, the date across the centre and "CHANNEL ISLANDS" at the bottom; there are the words "PARCEL" at the left and "POST" at the right, both reading upwards.

A somewhat simpler label type (**17**) dates from 20 July 1970, in the period of independence. This reads "GUERNSEY POST OFFICE/PARCEL POST/date/ ALDERNEY" and measures 53 × 36mm. A smaller type face was fitted in 1975, measuring 51 × 30mm (**17a**) and the mark replaced in 1978 by a larger version (59 × 36mm) (**17b**). A slightly smaller mark (57 × 35mm) appeared in 1980 and the series reverted to a smaller size in 1982 with one measuring 48 × 35mm.

Cancellations for Small Packets

Three single-circle cancellations for use on packets and small parcels are recorded. Type **18**, in use from 1955 to 1958, reads "ALDERNEY GUERNSEY" at the top and the unusual abbreviation "CHAN. ISLES" at the bottom. Between 1958 and 1970 a new rubber stamp was used (Type **19**) with the words "ALDERNEY" at the top and "CHANNEL ISLANDS" at the bottom. A similar stamp, but with the words in seriffed letters, is known used in 1969. On independence Type **20** was introduced, the wording being "GUERNSEY POST OFFICE/ALDERNEY". This was issued on 16 June 1970 and is a rubber stamp of 30mm diameter. It was replaced by a similar 33mm cancellation in 1989.

Special Cancellations

A small First Day of Issue cancellation was used on 11 November 1970 when the first Christmas stamps were issued by Guernsey, the 4d. denomination of which featured St. Anne's Church, Alderney.

On 28 May 1975 a special cancellation was used to mark the visit of the Queen Mother and other special handstamps appeared regularly from 1981 onwards.

Following the introduction of stamps for Alderney in 1983 pictorial "FIRST DAY OF ISSUE" marks were applied at the Guernsey Philatelic Bureau. For current prices of complete sets with such postmarks see the current issue of *Collect Channel Islands and Isle of Man Stamps*.

Military Cachet

An unusual stamp made of rubber and sent to Alderney on 30 January 1907 is oval in shape and reads "POST OFFICE" at the top, "R.E. OFFICE" across the centre and "ALDERNEY" at the bottom. The R.E. probably stands for Royal Engineers and it seems likely that the cachet was intended to mark military mail posted by the garrison, but not to cancel postage stamps. An example is known on an Edward VII $\frac{1}{2}$d. on piece.

Occupation and Liberation Mail

During the German Occupation Alderney was virtually evacuated of its civilian population, most of whom came to Britain just before the Germans arrived, and was heavily fortified by the Nazis. Russian P.O.W. labour was used.

Letters for Guernsey civilians employed on the Island during 1942–43 were accepted by Guernsey Post Office at normal rates and handled by the Germans.

In August 1943 750 French Jews were taken to the Island and a concentration camp was established at Camp No. 2 which was called "Norderney". The inmates of the camp were allowed to send and receive two letters per month, but this privilege was sometimes withdrawn.

Letters were inscribed on the back with the internee's name, personal reference, registered number, hut number, and nature of employment. Some had the large red cachet of the *Insel Frontführer* of the Todt Organisation applied. They then had a 1f.50 Pétain stamp affixed and were handed in at the island office where they were put into sacks and sent by ship to France.

On arrival at Cherbourg the letters were taken to Paris where they arrived at St. Lazare station and were sent to the chief receiving office to be cancelled with the single-line obliterator "PARIS CENTRALISATEUR".

Sometimes the mails went via St. Malo or Granville and were taken to Montparnasse station from where, after receiving the circular datestamp of the station, they were delivered in the normal way.

All the letters were censored by the Germans, but it is not known if this was done in Paris or on Alderney. Very few letters have survived.

Covers to or from the German Occupation forces are known between 1940 and 1944. These were normally carried by the *Feldpost* via Guernsey and show *Feldpost* datestamps carrying the Guernsey code letters b, d or e. Single covers have, however, been found with code letter m or n. Two covers are known which were received by soldiers in Alderney and then turned inside-out and re-used back to Germany.

The British Post Office in Alderney was closed from 22 June 1940 to 21 September 1945. The Army Postal Service provided postal facilities from May to September 1945 and from that date until 30 September 1946 an officer of the Guernsey Post Office was sent to Alderney and postal services were provided in the sub-office building. Colonel Marriette resumed his appointment as Sub-Postmaster on 1 October 1946.

Submarine Cover

On 16 May 1947 the submarine H.M.S. *Alderney* made a voyage to Portsmouth carrying six covers. They bear the Alderney single-circle datestamp of 16 May and the rectangular datestamp "COMMANDING OFFICER/16 MAY 1947/H.M.S. ALDERNEY". The 2½d. postage stamp is cancelled with the Gosport, Hants, datestamp of 17 May 1947.

Local Carriage Labels

The Commodore Shipping Company and the Alderney Shipping Company Ltd. have issued adhesive labels for prepayment of fees for carriage of parcels on their vessels plying between Guernsey and Alderney. The Alderney Parcel Delivery Service also issues adhesives for internal delivery of parcels. These, while interesting when properly used on pieces of parcel wrappings, are outside the scope of this Catalogue.

(1)

(2)

(3)

(3a)

(4)

(4a)

(4b)

(5)

(6)

(7)

(8)

(8a)

(9)

(9a)

(10)

(11)

(12)

(12a)

(13)

(14)

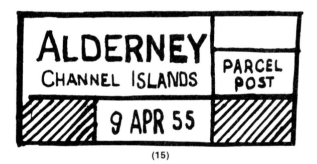
(15)

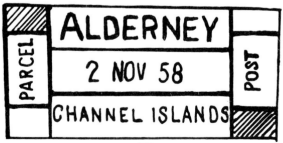
(16)

```
GUERNSEY POST OFFICE
   PARCEL POST

   19 AUG 1971

   ALDERNEY
```

(17)

```
GUERNSEY POST OFFICE
    PARCEL POST

   28 AUG 1975

  A L D E R N E Y
```

(17a)

(18)

(19)

(20)

1907 cachet

Cat. No.	Type No.		Dates of use	Price on cover

Nos. AC1–36: All normally struck in black

Prices for Nos. AC19–26 are for markings on piece

AC1	**1**	ALDERNEY undated double arc	1848–55	£1400
			(*on piece*)	£250
AC2	**2**	ALDERNEY dated double arc (code A)	1851–60	£300
			(*on piece*)	60·00
AC2a		Struck in orange-yellow	1852–54	
AC2b		Code C	1857	£300
			(*on piece*)	60·00
AC3	**3**	Numeral obliterator (4 bars)	1848–60s	£175
			(*on piece*)	25·00
AC4	**3a**	Numeral obliterator (3 bars)	1862–97	£125
			(*on piece*)	15·00

Single circles

AC5	**4**	ALDERNEY (20mm) (code A or C)	1860–71	£150
AC6	**4a**	ALDERNEY (21mm)	1872–1934	90·00
AC6a		On Type RL1 registration label	—	25·00
AC7	**4b**	ALDERNEY (20mm)	1884–98	£125
AC8	**5**	ALDERNEY skeleton (28mm)	1922	£600
AC9	**6**	ALDERNEY/CH. IS.	1936–55	10·00
AC10	**7**	ALDERNEY/GUERNSEY CHANNEL ISLANDS	1955–70	10·00
AC11	**8**	GUERNSEY POST OFFICE/ Alderney (23½mm) (asterisk code)	1969–	3·00
AC12		ditto, but 26½ mm. (code A, B, asterisk or none)	1970–85	3·00
AC13	**8a**	GUERNSEY POST OFFICE/ ALDERNEY (24mm) (code A or B)	1985–	3·00

Double circles

AC14	**9**	ALDERNEY, thick bars, cross at foot (code A or none)	1895–1932	10·00
AC14a	**9a**	same, thinner bars	1923–35	15·00
AC15	**10**	ALDERNEY/CH. IS., thick bars, (code asterisk)	1935–66	5·00
AC15a		Code A or B	1966 (1–10.8)	15·00
AC16	**11**	ALDERNEY/GUERNSEY CHANNEL ISLANDS (code A or B)	1966–69	5·00
AC17	**12**	GUERNSEY POST OFFICE/ ALDERNEY (code A, B or asterisk)	1975–79	5·00
AC18	**12a**	GUERNSEY POST OFFICE/ —ALDERNEY— (code A, B or asterisk)	1979–85	3·00
AC18a	**12b**	ditto, but longer lines each side of ALDERNEY (code A or asterisk)	1985–	3·00

Parcel Post cancellations

AC19	**13**	ALDERNEY double ring	1911	75·00
AC20	**14**	ALDERNEY/CHANNEL ISLANDS	1912–	60·00
AC21	**15**	Label, date at foot	1947–58	25·00

Cat. No.	Type No.		Dates of use	Price on cover
AC22	**16**	Label, date in centre	1958–70	15·00
AC23	**17**	Box type (53 × 36mm)	1970–75	10·00
AC23a	**17a**	Box type (51 × 30mm)	1975–78	8·00
AC23b	**17b**	Box type (59 × 36mm)	1978–80	6·00
AC23c	**17c**	Box type (57 × 35mm)	1980–82	6·00
AC23d	**17d**	Box type (48 × 35mm)	1982–	3·00

Single circles (Small Packets)

AC24	**18**	ALDERNEY GUERNSEY/CHAN. ISLES	1955–58	15·00
AC25	**19**	ALDERNEY/CHANNEL ISLANDS	1958–70	10·00
AC25a	**19a**	ALDERNEY/CHANNEL ISLANDS (seriffed letters)	1960s–70	20·00
AC26	**20**	GUERNSEY POST OFFICE/ ALDERNEY (30mm)	1970–89	5·00
AC26a		ditto, but 35mm	1989–	3·00

Special handstamps

AC27	–	First Day of Issue	11.11.70	3·00
AC28	–	Visit of H. M. Queen Elizabeth THE QUEEN MOTHER	29.5.75	3·00
AC29	–	SALVATION ARMY ALDERNEY CENTENARY	5.8.81	1·00
AC30	–	INTER-ISLAND TRANSPORT (aircraft)	25.8.81	1·00
AC31	–	INTER-ISLAND TRANSPORT (ship)	25.8.81	1·00
AC32	–	50TH ANNIVERSARY OF AIRPORT		
AC33	–	THIRTY-FIVE C.I.S.S.	13.4.85	1·00
AC34	–	INAUGURATION OF LIFEBOAT STATION	10.5.85	1·00
AC35	–	30TH SIGNAL REGIMENT	24.9.85	1·00
AC36	–	Royal Visit	24.5.89	1·00

Dates of use	*Price on cover*

CACHETS, ETC.

Struck in colours indicated

1907	Oval POST OFFICE/R.E. OFFICE/ALDERNEY. Violet *(on piece)*	80·00
1947	Boxed COMMANDING OFFICER/ 16 MAY 1947 /H.M.S. ALDERNEY. Black.	15·00
1957	Visit of Queen and Duke of Edinburgh, large boxed type. Black	4·00
1962	577 (HAMPSHIRE) FIELD SQN. R.E. (T.A.) (date) Territorial Camp. Violet.	3·00
1962	"Alderney THE Channel Island", publicity cachet States of Alderney. Blue	1·00

Dates of use		Price on cover
1971	Oval REGIMENTAL HEADQUARTERS/ 30th SIGNAL REGT./ 4 SEPT. 1971. Red	3·00
1972	Boxed "Alderney Welcomes/H.R.H. PRINCESS ANNE/May 25th". Blue.	2·50
1972.	"No Sunday Collection. Box cleared Monday".	5·00
1974	Small oval ALDERNEY/CHANNEL ISLANDS. Black	1·00
1975	Small double-circle POSTED IN/ST. ANNES/ALDERNEY. Red or violet.	50
1975	Boxed CHRISTMAS/GREETING/FROM/ALDERNEY and lion. Black or red	50
1975	Double-circle POSTED DURING/ALDERNEY WEEK. Red . . .	50
1975	Boxed STATES OF GUERNSEY/ALDERNEY AIRPORT. Blue .	50

OCCUPATION COVERS

1940–41	Cover from German 83 Infanterie Division	£450
1942–44	Cover from German 319 Infanterie Division	£350
1942–44	German Feldpost cover with code letter "m" or "n".	£750
1943	Re-used cover from German soldier on Alderney to Germany	£750
1942–43	Cover from OT worker with sender's details on reverse	£450
	As above, but with "Insel Frontführer/ALDERNEY/TODT Bei Cherbourg" in red unframed circle on reverse	£550
	Cover from Jewish Concentration Camp with sender's details on reverse.	£450
	As above, but with datestamp added.	£600

SARK

Prior to the establishment of a post office on Sark in 1857, letters were carried between the island and Guernsey by boatmen, who usually charged ½d. per letter. Letters are known dated around 1718 but none of them bears a charge mark of any kind.

(Price from £200)

When Peter Le Pelley was Seigneur of Sark in 1838 he tried to introduce a Post Office and the idea was discussed by the Chief Pleas on several occasions, but it was too revolutionary to be accepted. In those days very few letters were written on the island and most of those were by the Seigneur and the Vicar.

The question was raised again in 1857 and, after long consideration, it was agreed to establish a post office at La Hêche in a thatched cottage and store belonging to a Mr. Queripel, who became the first Sub-Postmaster. Once a day Mr. Queripel carried the mail from La Hêche to the Creux Harbour and returned with the incoming mail. In the first year of the post office 1500 letters were posted in Mr. Queripel's letterbox.

An undated double-arc handstamp (Type **1**) was sent to Guernsey by the G.P.O., London, on 15 July 1857. An example of this mark is known on a letter sent to Gibraltar in 1858 and two other examples, used later, also exist.

The first datestamp issued to Sark was a 29mm rubber single circle (Type **2**) despatched from the G.P.O. in London on 20 June 1885 with the earliest example of use being in violet during 1888. This was replaced by a smaller 21mm steel single circle (Type **3**) with code A believed to have been supplied when Sark became a Money Order and Savings Bank Office from 1 April 1890. It is known used as a backstamp from 18 July 1890, but was not used to cancel stamps until 1902. Later uses of Type **3**, which continued until 1940, sometimes show code B or C. These are scarce.

A rubber stamp of 29mm diameter, shown as Type **3**, was dispatched in 1885. Only one example has been seen used, in 1888, struck in violet.

On 17 March 1960 a single-circle type (**4**) of 24mm diameter was put into use with "SARK·GUERNSEY/CHANNEL ISLANDS" round the circumference and the date in two lines in the centre with an asterisk above.

The Guernsey Post Office Board issued new datestamps to all its sub-offices when it became independent on 1 October 1969 and they were uniform single-circle types. That for Sark reads "Guernsey Post Office/Sark"; it has the date in two lines in the centre with A, B or asterisk above and is 23½mm in diameter (Type **5**). It was replaced by a larger one (26½mm diameter) on 11 November 1970.

A single-circle rubber stamp of 30mm diameter (Type **6**) was issued for use on small packets on 16 June 1970 inscribed "GUERNSEY POST OFFICE/SARK". A replacement, issued 1984, had smaller lettering (Type **7**).

The first double-circle cancellation, Type **8,** was introduced in 1926. An interesting usage is that it may be found on covers prepared during the Occupation when the bisecting of postage stamps was officially permitted. The 2d. Postal Centenary stamp bisected is known on cover or card cancelled with Type **8**. This datestamp was in use throughout the period of the Occupation and can be found with locally made figures for the year date.

In the spring of 1946 this postmark was joined by another showing the same inscription, but with larger bars (Type **9**). This comes with code A, B or asterisk. Both Types **8** and **9** continued in use until 1966 when they were replaced by a new double-circle type (Type **10**). This had "SARK" at the top and "GUERNSEY CHANNEL ISLANDS" at the bottom. It has a thin bar on each side of "SARK" and exists with code A, B or asterisk above the date.

In May 1979 another double circle was issued (Type **11**). This had codes A, B or an asterisk and shows the position of the inscriptions reversed.

Sark uses the new-style parcel post cancellations (Type **12**), rectangular in shape and reading "GUERNSEY POST OFFICE/PARCEL POST/date SARK". The first issued to the island on 20 July 1970 measured 55 × 38mm. Later versions have measured 57 × 34mm (1979), 53 × 36mm (1984) or 48 × 34mm (1990).

Special Cancellations

A small First Day of Issue cancellation was used on 11 November 1970 when the first Christmas stamps were issued in Guernsey the 9d. denomination of which featured St. Peter's Church, Sark.

On 28 May 1975 another special cancellation was used to mark the visit of the Queen Mother.

German Military Mail

During the Occupation German Army mail received an appropriate unit stamp containing the Kenn. number and was then taken to Guernsey for cancelling with the *Feldpost* datestamp. Such mail is scarce as there were very few German troops on the island.

Letters from naval personnel received a handstamp reading "Kriegsmarine/Sark/Hafenuberwachung Stelle" in a 35mm single circle with the eagle and swastika emblem in the centre. There was also a similar handstamp with "Kriegsmarine" removed.

Sark Quatercentenary

The quatercentenary (400th anniversary) of the British settlement of Sark was celebrated in 1965. Letters posted from 1 June received a boxed handstamped cachet reading "ISLE OF SARK/1565 CHARTER 1965/QUATER CENTENARY". The adhesives were cancelled in the normal way.

The Dame of Sark also authorised the issue of pictorial labels inscribed "ISLE DE SERK". Although these carry denominations of 3d., 6d., 9d. and 1s. they performed no postal service.

Local Carriage Labels
Adhesive labels issued by the Commodore Shipping Co. and the Isle of Sark Shipping Co. for carriage of parcels between Guernsey and Sark are outside the scope of this Catalogue.

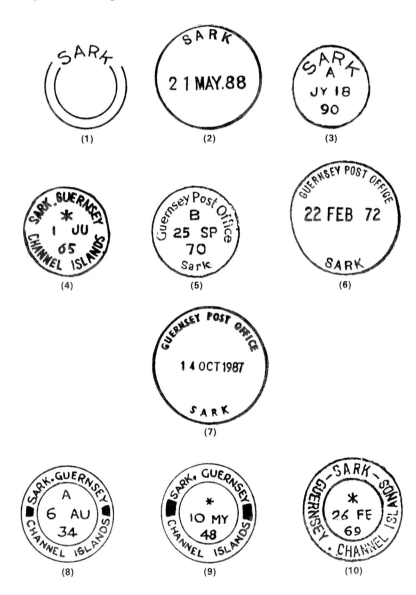

(11)

```
GUERNSEY POST OFFICE
    PARCEL POST

  - 7 DEC 1978


      SARK
```

(12)

```
  ISLE OF SARK
1565 CHARTER 1965
QUATER CENTENARY
```

1965 cachet

Cat. No.	Type No.		Dates of use	Price on cover

Nos. SC1/19: All struck in black (except No. SC2 = violet)

SC1	**1**	SARK double arc	1858	£4000
Single circles				
SC2	**2**	SARK (29mm)	1888	£450
SC3	**3**	SARK (21mm) (code A)	1890–1940	4·00
SC3a		ditto, but code B or C	—	£250
		Adhesive showing large part of cancellation	— .... (*off cover*)	60·00
SC4	**4**	SARK. GUERNSEY/CHANNEL ISLANDS	1960–	10·00
SC5	**5**	Guernsey Post Office / Sark (23½mm) (codes A, B or asterisk	1969	3·00
SC5a		ditto, but 26½mm (same codes)	1970	3·00
SC6	**6**	GUERNSEY POST OFFICE/SARK (30mm)	1970–84	6·00
SC7	**7**	GUERNSEY POST OFFICE/SARK (30mm) (smaller lettering)	1984–	3·00
Double circles				
SC9	**8**	SARK, GUERNSEY / CHANNEL ISLANDS	1926–66	5·00
SC9a		ditto, locally made figures in year	1941–45	15·00
SC9b		ditto on Postal Centenary 2d. bisect	1941	60·00
SC10	**9**	SARK, GUERNSEY CHANNEL ISLANDS (larger bars) (code A, B or asterisk)	1946–66	3·00

Cat. No.	Type No.		Dates of use		Price on cover
SC11	**10**	SARK / GUERNSEY CHANNEL ISLANDS, thin bars (code A, B or asterisk)	1966–69		4·00
SC12	**11**	GUERNSEY POST OFFICE/SARK, thin bars (code A, B or asterisk)	1979–		3·00

Parcel Post cancellations

SC14	**12**	GUERNSEY POST OFFICE/ PARCEL POST / date / SARK (55 × 38mm)	1970–79	(*on piece*)	6·00
SC14a		ditto, but 57 × 34mm	1979–84	(*on piece*)	5·00
SC14b		ditto, but 53 × 36mm	1984–90	(*on piece*)	3·00
SC14c		ditto, but 48 × 34mm	1990–	(*on piece*)	3·00

Special handstamps

SC16	–	First Day of Issue	11.11.70		5·00
SC17	–	Visit of H.M. Queen Elizabeth the Queen Mother	29.5.75		4·00
SC18	–	INTER-ISLAND TRANSPORT	25.8.81		1·00
SC19	–	Royal Visit	24.5.89		1·00

Dates of use		Price on cover

OCCUPATION COVERS

1940–45	Covers sent from Sark to Guernsey	20·00
1940–44	Covers from German forces on Sark	£350
1942–44	Single circle Kriegsmarine/Sark/Hafenuberwachung Stelle (*on piece*)	30·00
1942–44	As above, but without "Kriegsmarine" (*on piece*)	30·00
1944–45	"Fortress cover" from Sark	£750
	See also Section 18. The German Occupation	

CACHETS
Struck in black

1957	Boxed Visit of Queen and Duke of Edinburgh	4·00
1965	Boxed ISLE OF SARK/1565 CHARTER 1965/QUATER CENTENARY	6·00
1972	Boxed "Sark Welcomes/H.R.H. PRINCESS ANNE"	2·50

HERM

A few early letters are known from Herm dated from about 1820, but these were carried privately.

(*Price from* £300)

In the early 1900s several Guernsey vessels ran day excursions to Herm and a postcard is known with an unframed "HERM" struck in black on the picture side and posted on arrival in Guernsey.

When Sir Percival (later Lord) Perry, the Chairman of Ford's, purchased the lease of Herm from Sir Compton Mackenzie in 1925 he took a large staff with him to the island and the Head Postmaster of Guernsey agreed to open a sub-office there. It was in the Mermaid Tavern and was open for only half an hour each day. A special datestamp was provided (Type **1**) which was introduced on 1 May 1925. Special registration labels were also provided. The office was closed down on 30 November 1938 for lack of business.

The island was purchased by the States of Guernsey from the Crown in 1946 and in 1948 it was leased to a Mr. A. G. Jefferies, who tried to get the sub-office reopened, but this was refused on the grounds of insufficient business. Mr. Jefferies therefore instituted a local carriage service, for which special stamps were issued, and this was continued by his successor, Major A. G. Wood, until suppressed by the Guernsey Post Office Board on 1 October 1969. A pigeon-post service to Guernsey was in use until 1950. These local stamps are outside the scope of this Catalogue.

During this period a meter cancel was occasionally used for "official" notices (1d.) or on tourists' postcards (2d.). Examples are known from 1948.

Following Guernsey's postal independence a new sub-office was established on Herm and a 23½mm single-circle datestamp (Type **2**) was issued on 1 October 1969. It was joined by a similar one with diameter 26½mm on 6 January 1971.

A single-circle rubber stamp of 30mm diameter was provided on 16 June 1970 for cancelling small packets (Type **3**).

On 20 July 1970 Herm also received the rectangular-style parcel post cancellation (Type **4**) reading "GUERNSEY POST OFFICE/PARCEL POST/date/HERM ISLAND" measuring 65 × 45mm. A replacement, introduced in 1984, was 47 × 35mm and inscribed "HERM" only at foot.

The first Christmas stamps of Guernsey in 1970 included a 1s. 6d. denomination featuring the St. Tugual Chapel, Herm. A special cancellation reading "Guernsey Post Office/First Day of Issue/11. Nov. 1970//Herm Island" was also produced.

On 1 May 1975 the Guernsey Post Office provided a commemorative cancellation for the 50th anniversary of the opening of the first sub-office in Herm in 1925. This was used in Guernsey (*not* on Herm), and showed an outline map of the island.

(1)

(2)

(3)

```
┌─────────────────────────────┐
│ GUERNSEY POST OFFICE        │
│     PARCEL POST             │
│                             │
│    2 9 AUG 1975             │
│                             │
│  HERM ISLAND                │
└─────────────────────────────┘
```

(4)

Cat. No.	Type No.		Dates of use		Price

Nos. HC1/6: All struck in black

HC1	**1**	HERM GUERNSEY / CHANNEL ISLANDS	1925–38	*cover*	£400
		Adhesive showing large part of cancellation	—	(*off cover*)	50·00
HC2	**2**	Guernsey Post Office/Herm Island, 23½mm	1969–72	*cover*	3·00
HC2a		ditto, but 26½mm	1971–	*cover*	2·00
HC3	**3**	Small-packet rubber stamp	1970–77	*piece*	2·00
HC4	**4**	Parcel Post box type (65 × 45mm) inscr HERM ISLAND	1970–84	*piece*	8·00
HC4a		ditto, but 47 × 35mm and inscr HERM	1984	*piece*	3·00
Special handstamps					
HC5	–	First Day of Issue	11.11.70		2·00
HC6	–	INTER-ISLAND TRANSPORT	25.8.81		1·00
		CACHET			
1903		HERM handstamp. Black	—	*postcard*	£350

JETHOU

The island of Jethou is owned by the Crown and for over 200 years has been leased to private tenants. They have made their own arrangements for dispatch and collection of mail. One or two letters are known dated in the 1820s.

(*Price from* £450)

Excursion trips were made to the island from Guernsey around the turn of the century and picture postcards sold on the vessels sometimes had a rubber cachet applied at the time of sale. A two-line unframed type reading "JETHOU ISLAND/20 MAR.07" is known on a picture postcard of the island with Guernsey datestamp of the same day. Three examples are also recorded of a circular cachet, struck in violet, with the date (day and month only) applied by a second stamp. One is on an unused card, another on one bearing an Edward VII ½d. adhesive, cancelled Guernsey, 6 September 1909, and the third, used in August 1913, shows no date in the cachet.

When Group Captain W. H. Cliff was tenant of Jethou he opened the island to the public and issued local carriage labels in 1960. Two showing the islets of Fauconniere and Crevichon carried their names instead of Jethou. Carriage labels were continued by his successor, Mrs. Susan Faed, until they were suppressed by the Guernsey Post Office Board from 1 October 1969. These issues are outside the scope of this Catalogue.

1909 cachet

CACHETS

1907	Two line JETHOU ISLAND/date. Black	£350
1909–13	Circular JETHOU ISLAND/date/CHAN. ISLES. Violet	£300

BRECQHOU

Brecqhou, a small island off Sark leased to a tenant, is in the Guernsey Bailiwick. No postal markings or identifying cachets exist, except in connection with a set of local carriage labels valid for one day only, 30 September 1969, which were then suppressed by the new independent Guernsey postal authority the following day. The labels are outside the scope of the Catalogue.

LIHOU

Lihou is off St. Saviour's, Guernsey, to which it is joined by a causeway at low tide. No postal markings or identifying cachets exist until 1966. In that year the tenant issued local carriage labels, but these and subsequent items were withdrawn on 30 September 1969 when the independent Guernsey postal authority was set up. The labels are outside the scope of the Catalogue.

14. Sub-offices of Jersey and Guernsey

The sub-office cancellations of Jersey and Guernsey can be divided into twenty-four main types, illustrated below as Types **A** to **X**.

Some of the datestamps vary slightly in detail from the types shown, but such variations in size or lettering are noted where they occur. Details are given, after each entry, of the code letters or other inserts known to exist. Where a measurement is given for a circular mark this refers to its diameter.

The various datestamps are listed according to the date when they were first issued or, where this is not known, the earliest recorded date of use. In most cases the datestamps remained in service for many years and, in some instances, were used for long periods after the issue of a new datestamp. Many of the present sub-office datestamps from both islands have been in continuous use for several years. These items are indicated in the listings by a dagger (†) beside the date of introduction; the prices quoted reflecting their continued availability on registered letters. Some datestamps during the early 1900s are known to have been used at sub-offices in both Jersey and Guernsey on Christmas Day or Boxing Day. These are worth considerably more than the price shown for normal use.

Official registered remittance envelopes, called REM covers, are known used from most Jersey and Guernsey sub-offices in the post-1945 period. These were used by the sub-offices to send surplus cash to the Head Post Office.

(Prices from £35)

For parcel post labels of the sub-offices see Section 23.

Telegraph forms used at the sub-offices of Jersey and Guernsey are known from the 1880s often showing good examples of various datestamps, sometimes with the "P" telegraphic code.

(Prices from £20)

The Type **B** datestamp usually occurs on the early "blank" registration label, Type **RL1**, in use around the turn of the century and is not, generally, found cancelling stamps.

Small circular "seal" handstamps (Type **Q**), diameter 21mm to 30mm, were used in many parts of the British Isles during the early 1900s, primarily on mailbag labels. Some Jersey sub-offices, however, used these in error to cancel stamps. These seals are of "negative" appearance (white letters around a crown on a black background) with the name of the office at the top and the name of the island at the bottom. Seals of a similar type, but 31mm, were issued in the 1950s and 1960s to Alderney, Câtel, Les Baissieres, Roquaine, St. Andrew's and Torteval in Guernsey, but no postal use has been recorded.

Bisected 2d. stamps of King George V and King George VI are known used at the following Guernsey sub-offices during the authorised period (27 December 1940 to 22 February 1941): Braye Road. Cobo, Les Gravées, Market Place, St. Andrew's, St. Martin's, St. Peter-in-the-Wood, St. Sampson's, St. Saviour's, The Vale and Ville au Roi. In addition bisected Jersey and Great Britain stamps are known on covers from certain sub-offices in Jersey during the German Occupation, but these were unauthorised.

Cancellations not seen. Sub-offices recorded as opened, but for which no cancellations have yet been found are: *Jersey*—Pier (1891); *Guernsey*—Câtel Church (1899), La Moye (1891–96).

Rubber handstamps as Type **F** are recorded in the G.P.O. Proof Book records as having been supplied to the following sub-offices, but no examples of their use have yet come to light:

Jersey: St. Martin's, St. Mary's, St. Peter's
Guernsey: Bouet, Câtel Church, Les Gravées, Torteval, Vale.

Registration labels. During the early 1900s Head Post Offices sometimes held stocks of registration labels with a blank space where the datestamp of the office concerned could be struck (Type **RL1**). In addition similar labels, with a blank space where the name or number of the office would normally have been shown, were also used so that the number of a "town" office could be entered in manuscript (Type **RL2**). These two types of label were occasionally issued to offices whose normal stocks had run out and where replacements were not immediately available. Examples are known at a few Jersey sub-offices and are worth more than the usual value of the cover or datestamps used.

Covers used at sub-offices during the German Occupation of the islands between 1940 and 1945 with the registration label of the office concerned are worth considerably more than the price quoted for the datestamp. Registration labels from closed sub-offices were returned to the Head Post Office and were often used there.

Until the recent change to "all-figure" labels in both Jersey and Guernsey, the registration labels showed either the number allocated to each "town" sub-office, or the name of the office in the case of the "country" sub-offices. Registration numbers used by the "town" sub-offices at various times are listed below:

GUERNSEY

Braye Road	Guernsey	9
Cobo (*used in* 1978)	"	15
Collings Road	"	10
Les Gravées	"	1
Market Place (also "country" type in 1930s)	"	2
Quay Branch Office (1948– May 1953)	"	4
St. John's	"	5
St. Sampson's (also "country" type in 1977)	"	6
Vale Road	"	7
Ville au Roi	"	8

In addition No. 3 was used by the Money Order Section and No. 10 (until 1974) by the Posted out of Course duty.

JERSEY

Beresford Street	Jersey	2 or 34
Central Market	"	JE2 or 2
Cheapside	"	JE4 or 4
First Tower	"	6
Five Oaks	"	16
George Town	"	7
Grands Vaux	"	28
Greve D'Azette	"	17 or 34 (1974)
Havre-des-Pas	"	3
Le Squez (1974)	"	34 or 17

Millbrook	''	19
Roseville Street (1962)	''	JE3 or 3
Rouge Bouillon	''	5
Stopford Road	''	JE1 or 1
Town Mills (from 1973)	''	JE1

In addition No. 8 was used by Barclay's Bank, No. 9 by Lloyd's Bank, No. 18 by the Posted out of Course duty and No. 22 either by the same duty (1950s) or by a local firm.

Type **RL1**

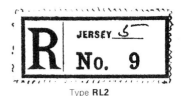

Type **RL2**

"Town" sub-office   "Country" sub-office

POSTMARK TYPES

(A)   (B)   (C)

(D)

(E)

(F)

(G)

(H)

(I)

(J)

(K)

(L)

(M)

(N)

(O)

(P) Skeleton

(Q) Mailbag seal

(R) Parcel Post

(S)

(T)

(U)

(V) Parcel Post

GUERNSEY POST OFFICE
PARCEL POST

1 5 MAY 1970

VILLE AU ROI

(W) Parcel Post

GUERNSEY POST OFFICE PARCEL POST
-7 FEB 1981

VALE ROAD
(X) Parcel Post

JERSEY

Prices are for these sub-office cancellations *on cover*, unless otherwise indicated.

Augrés

Opened 1893, closed 30.9.80

1893	Type **B**, undated, on Type **RL1** registration label		
		on cover	£150
	on Type **RL1** *registration label*.................. *off cover*		10·00
1893	Ditto, but with date (code A or C).................		10·00
1930s	Type **I**, but with CHANNEL ISLANDS in full (asterisk code)...		4·00

Beaumont

Opened 1853

1853	Type **A**, shades of blue, green or black.............	£250
1881	Type **D**, blue or black (21mm) (code C)	80·00
1892	Type **C**, black (code A or without code)	3·00
1920s	Ditto, grey-blue..................................	6·00
1932†	Type **K** (code B until 1960s, then code A)	4·00

Beresford Street

Opened 1909, closed 25.3.72

1909	Type **C** (25mm) (asterisk code)...................	70·00
1909	Type **Q**	£100
1914	Manuscript "2" on Type **RL2** registration label......	15·00
1931	Rectangular parcel post cancellation as Jersey Type **J66**, but inscribed JERSEY St. Heliers)/CHANNEL ISLANDS/BERESFORD STREET....... *on piece*	20·00
1937	Type **H**, inscribed BERESFORD ST. JERSEY/ CHANNEL IS.	5·00

1950s	Ditto, but with code 2 and CHANNEL ISLANDS in full	3·00
1955	Rectangular parcel post cancellation as Jersey Type **J66**, but inscribed JERSEY/CHANNEL ISLANDS/ BERESFORD STREET .... *on piece*	10·00
1961	Type **V**, inscribed JERSEY / (date) / CHANNEL ISLANDS/BERESFORD STREET with PARCEL at left and POST at right................. *on piece*	10·00
1970	Ditto, inscribed BERESFORD STREET / (date) / JERSEY/CHANNEL ISLANDS .... *on piece*	8·00

Carrefour Selous

Opened 1890, closed 30.6.44, reopened 1.1.46, closed 30.9.78

1890	Type **E** (code B, C or without code) ...... *on cover*	8·00
	on Type **RL1** *registration label*	20·00
1935	Type **J** (asterisk code)	6·00
1975	Ditto, but code 9	4·00

Central Market

Opened 1972

1972†	Type **N** (three slightly different types) (code A, B or C)	4·00
1972†	Type **V**. .... *on piece*	4·00

Cheapside

Opened 1888

1888	Type **D** (code C)...............................	70·00
1930s†	Type **H** (two types differing slightly in the size of lettering and asterisk)	4·00

Colomberie

Opened 1905, closed February 1920

1905	Type **C** (asterisk code)..........................	£300

Conway Street

Opened 1903, closed September 1909

1903	Type **D** (23mm) (asterisk code)....................	£250

David Place

Opened 1874, closed July 1914

1874	Type **C** (code A or C)..........................	60·00

Faldouet

Opened 1892, closed 8.12.72

1892	Type **E** (20mm) (code C or without code)	8·00
1930s	Type **L** (asterisk code)	6·00

First Tower

Opened by 1884

1884	Type **E** (19mm) (code C)	6·00
	on Type **RL1** *registration label*	20·00
1914	Type **P**	£400
1914	As Type **E**, but without code	5·00
1930s†	Type **H** (asterisk code)	3·00

Five Oaks

Opened by 1889, closed 1932, reopened 1936, closed 23.7.47, reopened 3.4.50, closed 17.3.83, reopened 25.8.83

1889	Type **D** (22mm) (code C)	8·00
1937†	Type **K** (asterisk code)	3·00
1944	Manuscript "16" on Type **RL2** registration label	15·00

George Town

Opened 1882, closed January 1927, reopened August 1934, closed 20.6.40, reopened 22.8.45

1882	Type **C** (reissued in 1886 showing a slightly different style of lettering)	90·00
1935†	Type **H** (asterisk code)	3·00

Gorey

A receiving house of the Jersey Penny Post was opened in 1830, using the boxed No. 2 handstamp, which carried on into the adhesive period. See Section 3 Jersey Type **J8**.

Opened as a sub-office 1851

1851	Type **A**, blue, blue-green, dirty green or black (a second similar type was introduced in 1857)	£300
1858	Type **D** (20mm) (code A, B, C or P)	50·00
1880	Ditto, in blue (code B)	75·00
1882	Ditto, but 22mm (code A or C)	5·00
1900s	Ditto, (20mm) undated on Type **RL1** registration label	8·00
1906	Type **P** (30mm) (code X)	£350
1906	Type **D** (22mm) (thinner letters) (code A)	3·00

1930st Type **K** (code B or without code) .... 3·00
1960st Type **V**................................ *on piece* 10·00
For instructional marks relating to Gorey, *see* Section 10.

Gorey Village

Opened 1892, closed 20.6.40

1892   Type **D** (22½mm) (mis-spelt COREY).............. 6·00
1930s   Type **H** .... 80·00

Grands Vaux

Opened 5 December 1960, closed 30.6.62, reopened 1.8.62, closed 30.11.82

1960   Type **H** .... 5·00

Great Union Road

Opened by 1903, closed November 1923

1903   Type **D** (asterisk code)........................... £500

Greve D'Azette

Opened 1927, closed 28.6.74

1927   Type **I**, but reading JERSEY, C.I. at foot (asterisk code)   8·00
1927   Type **Q** £100
1940s   Type **H**, but with CH. IS. at foot (asterisk code)..... 5·00

Grouville

Opened 1853, closed 1858, reopened 1890

1853   Type **A** (mis-spelt GRONVILLE) (reissued in 1857
        with slight differences)......................... £450
1890   Type **E** (code A, B or C) .... 8·00
1936   Type **L** (code A or B)............................. 5·00
1973t   Type **H** (code A)................................. 3·00

A postmark as Type **A** with "GROUVILLE" correctly spelt is known, but is not shown in G.P.O. records.

Havre-des-Pas

Opened by 1889, closed September 1962

1889   Type **C** (25mm) (code A or B)..................... 80·00
1930s   Type **H**, but inscribed CHANNEL IS............... 5·00

La Rocque

Opened 1891, closed 15.9.88

1891	Type **C** (code A, B or C)	8·00
1934	Type **J**, but inscribed JERSEY CHANNEL IS. (code A or B)	5·00

Le Squez

Opened 1 July 1974

1974	Temporary c.d.s. reading JERSEY, CHANNEL IS./L/date/9	6·00
1975†	Type **H**	3·00

Maufant

Opened 14 November 1983

1983	Temporary c.d.s. reading JERSEY. CHANNEL IS./L/date/9	6·00
1983†	Type **H**	3·00

Millbrook

Opened by 1851, closed 1.1.44, reopened 10.9.45

1851	Type **A**, blue and shades of black	£250
1873	Type **E** (code A)	£200
1886	Type **C** (code C or without code)	4·00
1913	Ditto, on Type **RL1** registration label..............	20·00
1930	Ditto, but with code U (C on its side)..............	20·00
1930st†	Type **K** (code A, B, asterisk or without code)	3·00

Pier

*An office was opened temporarily in 1891 for six weeks during the potato season. A c.d.s. as Type **C** (23mm) was issued for use on telegrams, but no example has yet come to light.*

Pontac

Opened by 1900, closed 1902

1900	Type **F** (29mm) PONTAC/ST. CLEMENTS. JERSEY .	£450

Quennevais

Opened 18 July 1950

1950†	Type **M** (two slightly different types) (code B or M).	3·00
1971†	Type **N** (asterisk code)............................	3·00

Roseville Street

Opened 1 October 1962

1962†	Type **H**	3·00
1963†	Ditto, but with different arrangement of wording and figure 2 at base	3·00
1967†	Type **V**.................................. *on piece*	3·00
1975†	Type **H**, but with smaller and rounder letters and no space between T and the dot	3·00

Rouge Bouillon

Opened 1889

1889	Type **C** (code B or C)...........................	80·00
1922	Manuscript "5" on Type **RL1** registration label......	15·00
1930st†	Type **H** (asterisk code)...........................	3·00

St. Aubin

A receiving house of the Jersey Penny Post was opened in 1830, using the boxed No. 1 handstamp, which carried on into the adhesive period. See Section 3 Jersey, Type **J7**.

Opened as a sub-office by 1851 (with name "St. Aubins"), name changed to "St. Aubyns" in 1870 and to "St. Aubin" in the early 1900s

1851	Type **A**, ST. AUBINS, blue, bluish green or black....	£250
1865	Type **D**, ST. AUBINS (23mm) (code A or B)	80·00
1870	Type **C**, ST. AUBYNS (code A or P)...............	50·00
1900s	Type **B**, ST. AUBIN, undated on Type **RL1** registration label..	20·00
1900s	Straight-line ST. AUBINS (28 × 4mm) in violet	£200
1903	Type **D**, ST. AUBIN (without code, but showing collection times)	4·00
1925	Type **P**, ST. AUBIN (30mm)......................	£250
1925	Type **C**, ST. AUBIN (code A, B or without code)....	5·00
1932†	Type **K**, ST. AUBIN (code A or B)	3·00
1958	Type **L**, ST. AUBIN. JERSEY. CH. ISLES (1 between long arcs at foot).............................	6·00
1970	Manuscript "ST. AUBIN" on Head Office registration label..	10·00

St. Brelade's Bay

Opened 1890, closed 5.3.77

1890	Type **F**, violet	£130
1900s	Ditto, but smaller letters and "St."	£150
1913	Type **C** (shows dot under T of ST)	25·00
1953	Type **M**, inscribed JERSEY. CH. IS. (asterisk code or without code)	6·00

St. Clements

*A receiving house of the Jersey Penny Post was opened in 1830, probably using the boxed No. 4 handstamp, which carried over into the adhesive period. See Section 3 Jersey, Type **J10**. An undated St. Clements handstamp in Type **A** was sent to this office, but no example has yet been seen.*

St. John's

Opened by 1852, closed 1858, reopened 1879, closed November 1931

1852	Type **A**, black (three types)	£400
1881	Type **D**, (23mm) (code C)	8·00

St. John's Church

Opened 1890, closed 30.6.77, reopened 1.2.78

1890	Type **E** (22mm) (code A, B, D or without code)	8·00
1900s	Ditto, dated or undated, but without code used on Type **RL1** registration label	20·00
1930s	Type **J** (code A, B or without code)	6·00
1976	Temporary Head Office double circle JERSEY/ CHANNEL ISLANDS cancelling registration label on cover	35·00
1976†	Type **I**, ST. JOHN'S CHURCH/JERSEY. CHANNEL ISLANDS	3·00

St. Lawrence

Opened 1854, closed by 1858

1854	Type **A**, black or green (two types)	£450

St. Martin's

Opened 1850, closed 11.11.1983

1850	Type **A**, blue, black or brownish green	£350
1888	Type **C** (25mm) (code A or without code)	3·00
1933	Type **K** (code A, B or asterisk)	6·00
1943	Ditto, on Type **RL1** registration label	25·00

St. Mary's

Opened 1853

1853	Type **A**, blackish green or blue-black	£450
1880s	Type **C** (25mm) (code B or C)....................	8·00
1930st	Type **K**, but solid black circles instead of sectors (code A, B or asterisk)................................	3·00

St. Ouen's

*Opened by 1852 (with name" St. Owens"). The spelling varied during the late 19th century, but settled eventually on the present form in April 1922. Two examples of an unframed St. Owens Type **A** were sent to this office in 1852, but have not been seen used*

1874	Type **E**, ST. OWENS (22mm) (code A, C or P)......	6·00
1882	Type **D**, ST. OUENS (21mm) (code C or P)	£200
1922	Type **C**, ST. OUENS (asterisk code)	10·00
1932t	Type **K**, ST. OUEN'S (code A or B)	3·00

St. Peter's

A receiving house of the Jersey Penny Post was opened in 1830, using the boxed No. 3 handstamp, which carried on into the adhesive period. See Section 3 Jersey, Type **J9**

Opened as a sub-office 1851, closed 20.6.40, reopened 5.9.45

1851	Type **A**, blue or green...........................	£400
1874	Type **D** (21½mm) (code A)......................	5·00
1909	Type **P** (25mm)...............................	£400
1910	Ditto, but 36mm	£350
1910	Type **D** (21mm) (shows dot under T of ST (code A or without code)	5·00
1933	Type **J**, but inscribed JERSEY. CHAN. IS. (code A or B)...	6·00
1968t	Type **I**	3·00

St. Saviour's

A Penny Post is believed to have operated in the 1830s using the boxed No. 5 handstamp, but no example has yet been found. There are no records of a receiving house

Samares

Opened 1887

1887	Type **E** (code A, B, C or without code)	5·00
1912	Ditto, on Type **RL1** registration label..............	15·00
1933t	Type **K** (code B or without code)	3·00

Sion

Opened November 1931, closed 22.4.77

1931	Type **K** (without code)	8·00
1976	Temporary Head Office double circle JERSEY CHANNEL ISLANDS with code N on cover with registratioon label of this office.	35·00
1976	Type **I**, but CHANNEL ISLANDS in full	15·00

Stopford Road

Opened 1914, closed 10.8.73

1914	Type **C** (asterisk code)...........................	£100
1914	Type **Q** (21½mm)	£100
1930s	Type **H**	5·00
1970s	Type **N** (asterisk code).........................	4·00

Town Mills

Opened 1902, closed January 1921, reopened 1973

1902	Type **C** (asterisk code)...........................	£200
1973	Temporary Head Office c.d.s. JERSEY, CHANNEL IS./Z/date/9.	10·00
1974†	Type **H** (code Z or asterisk)	3·00

Trinity

A Penny Post is believed to have operated in the 1830s using the boxed No. 6 handstamp, but no example has been found. There are no records of a receiving house until late 1851

Opened as a sub-office by 1852, closed by 1862, reopened 1890

1852	Type **A** (two types), black, blue-black or dark blue ..	£350
1893	Type **F**, violet...................................	70·00
1893	Ditto, but blue	£100
1924	Ditto, but black	£100
1930s	Type **K** (code A)	3·00

GUERNSEY

Prices are for these sub-offices cancellations *on cover*, unless otherwise indicated.

Arcade

Opened 14 July 1987

1987	Type **U** (code A or B)		3·00
1987†	Type **W** (48 × 35mm).................	*on piece*	3·00

1988†	Type **U** (asterisk code)	3·00
1988†	Type **M**, but GUERNSEY POST OFFICE/ARCADE (code C or D)	3·00

Bouet

Opened 1888, closed 1902

1888	Type **D** (code A)	£400

Braye Road

Opened 1937, closed 9.2.43, reopened 1.5.47, closed 31.3.76

1937	Type **H**	35·00
1969	Type **S**	4·00
1970	Type **W** (53 × 37mm) *on piece*	6·00

Bridge

Opened 2 February 1988

1988†	Type **U** (code A, B, C or D)	3·00
1988†	Type **W** (48 × 33mm)	3·00

Camp du Roi

Opened September 1935, closed 1.7.40

1935	Type **J**, inscribed CHAN. IS. (code A)	£450

An example of this postmark dated 8.10.25 is believed to be a date error.

Câtel

Opened by 1849, closed July 1860, reopened February 1892, closed 19.6.40, reopened 1.5.53, closed 31.12.1986

1849	Type **A**, black or green	£450
1896	Type **E** (22mm) (code A)	8·00
1953	Type **H**	20·00
1969	Type **S**	3·00
1970	Type **W** (53 × 37mm) *on piece*	6·00
1980	Ditto, but 54 × 33mm (also in purple) *on piece*	4·00
1981	Ditto, but 56 × 33mm and accent over A in CATEL *on piece*	3·00

Cobo

Opened November 1887

1887	Type **F**, black	£120
1911	Ditto, but larger lettering and in purple	35·00
1911	Ditto, larger lettering in black or grey	30·00
1918	Type **P** (38mm), black	£400
1918	Type **F** (closer spacing of COBO), black	30·00
1927	Type **G** (30mm), black	60·00
1930	Ditto, but smaller lettering, black	80·00
1933	Type **K** (without code)	6·00
1969	Type **S** (23½mm) (without code)	3·00
1970	Type **W** (53 × 36mm) *on piece*	6·00
1974	Ditto, but smaller lettering in black or purple *on piece*	6·00
1980†	Ditto, but 56 × 34mm *on piece*	3·00
1986	Type **S** (24mm) (without code)	4·00
1988†	Type **U**	3·00

Collings Road

Opened 1.2.1974, closed 31.12.86

1974	Type **P** (30mm)	£200
1974	Type **S** (without code)	3·00
1974	Type **W** (55 × 30mm) *on piece*	6·00
1979	Ditto, but 68 × 40mm *on piece*	6·00
1981	Ditto, but 55 × 34mm *on piece*	4·00
1984	Ditto, but 48 × 34mm *on piece*	4·00

Forest

Opened 1891, closed 1893, reopened June 1899, closed 29.9.78, reopened 1979 but no parcels accepted until March 1989

1899	Type **F**, violet	50·00
1899	Ditto, but in crimson	75·00
1904	Ditto, but larger lettering in violet or black	45·00
1906	Circular (31mm) rubber skeleton FOREST / GUERNSEY, purple	£500
1906	Type **F**, but smaller GUERNSEY, violet	50·00
1917	Ditto, but FOREST larger, purple or black	40·00
1925	Type **G** (two slightly different types)	45·00
1930s	Type **J**, but longer sectors	6·00
1969†	Type **S**	3·00
1970	Type **W** (53 × 36mm) *on piece*	6·00
1972	Ditto, but 57 × 38mm *on piece*	5·00
1989†	Ditto, but 48 × 34mm *on piece*	3·00

L'Islet

Opened 1888, closed 29.6.40, reopened 1.11.45

1891	Type **F**, violet	£250
1900s	Type **C** (with or without collection time above date) .	8·00
1915	Type **D** (normally used for telegrams, rare on mail) . .	50·00
1930s	Type **K** (without code)	8·00
1969†	Type **S** (without code)	3·00
1970	Type **W** (53 × 36mm). . . . . *on piece*	6·00
1977	Ditto, but 58 × 36mm . . . . *on piece*	6·00
1979	Ditto, but 64 × 40mm . . . . *on piece*	6·00
1982†	Ditto, but 48 × 34mm . . . . *on piece*	4·00

Les Baissieres

Opened February 1952, closed 8.7.68

1952	Type **H**, inscribed CHAN. IS.	£100

Les Gravées

Opened November 1886, closed 31.12.1986

1891	Type **C** (code A)	6·00
1949	Type **H**	30·00
1969	Type **S**.	3·00
1970	Type **W** (53 × 36mm). . . . . *on piece*	8·00
1973	Ditto, but name mis-spelt LES GRAVES . . . *on piece*	15·00
1975	Ditto, name corrected and 55 × 38mm . . . *on piece*	4·00
1981	Ditto, but 60 × 33mm . . . . *on piece*	4·00
1984	Ditto, but 48 × 35mm . . . . *on piece*	3·00

Market Place

Opened 1883, closed 21.9.42, reopened 17.12.45, closed 30.6.1987

1883	Type **C** (code A)	80·00
1911	Type **R**, inscribed MARKET PLACE/ GUERNSEY. . . .	
	on piece	£150
1931	Type **V**, inscribed GUERNSEY/CHANNEL ISLANDS/	
	MARKET PLACE with PARCEL POST at right and 1	
	with date at bottom. . . . . *on piece*	20·00
1936	Type **H**, no stop after PLACE (code E or asterisk) . . .	8·00
1958	Type **V**. . . . . *on piece*	15·00
1965	Type **H**, stop after PLACE (code F).	6·00
1969	Type **S** (code E)	3·00
1970	Type **T** (26½mm) (code F)	3·00
1970	Type **W** (55 × 36mm). . . . . *on piece*	6·00
1977	Ditto, but 56 × 34 mm . . . . *on piece*	6·00
1979	Type **X**. . . . . *on piece*	6·00
1981	Type **W** (64 × 39mm). . . . . *on piece*	6·00
1984	Ditto, but 48 × 35mm . . . . *on piece*	4·00
1984	Type **U** (code G).	3·00

Mount Row

Opened 1895, closed August 1896

    1895   Type **F**, violet . . . . *on parcel post label* £500

Pleinmont Road

Opened 1 August 1958, closed 30.11.65

    1958   Type **H** £150

Quay Branch Office

Opened June 1932, closed September 1939, reopened 1.9.48, closed 30.5.53

    1932   Type **O** . . . . 45·00
    1934   Type **H**, inscribed CHANNEL IS. . . . . 45·00

Roquaine

Opened 11 July 1966, closed 31.12.68

    1966   Type **H** . . . . 50·00

St. Andrew's

Opened 1887, closed 26.3.43, reopened November 1945, closed 25.2.1989

    1887   Type **E** (code A or C) £150
    1903   Type **C** (23mm) (without code) . . . . 4·00
    1913   Type **P** (32mm) (asterisk code or without code) £450
    1930s   Type **J** . . . . 8·00
    1969   Type **S** . . . . 3·00
    1970   Type **W** (53 × 37mm) (ST. ANDREW) . . . *on piece* 6·00
    1982   Ditto, but 60 × 34mm . . . . *on piece* 6·00
    1984   Ditto, but 48 × 35mm (ST. ANDREWS) . . *on piece* 3·00

St. John's

Opened January 1934, closed 22.6.40, reopened 8.7.48, closed 31.12.86

    1934   Type **H** . . . . 15·00
    1965   Ditto, but with stop after JOHNS. . . . . 15·00
    1969   Type **S** . . . . 3·00
    1970   Type **W** (53 × 36mm) . . . . *on piece* 6·00
    1975   Ditto, but with larger letters on piece . . . . 6·00
    1980   Ditto, but with small letters for ST. JOHNS
               (59 × 36mm) . . . . *on piece* 4·00

St. Martin's

Opened 1849, closed 1858, reopened 1.5.86

1849	Type **A**, black or dark blue.	£400
1886	Type **C** (24mm) (code A, C or without code)	10·00
1930s	Type **J**	10·00
1961	Type **I** (code A)	10·00
1969†	Type **S**	3·00
1970†	Type **T** (code A or asterisk)	3·00
1970	Type **W**, ST. MARTIN (55 × 37mm), black *on piece*	6·00
1974	Ditto, but 51 × 32mm with smaller lettering, purple *on piece*	6·00
1981	Ditto, ST. MARTINS (60 × 34mm), purple, *on piece*	4·00
1984†	Ditto, ST. MARTIN (48 × 35mm). *on piece*	3·00

St. Peter-in-the-Wood

Opened by 1852 under the name of St. Peters, closed 1857, reopened 1876, name changed to present form in June 1890

1852	Type **A**, ST. PETERS, blue, black, greenish blue or dirty grey	£350
1876	Type **C**, ST. PETERS (code A or C)	60·00
1890	Type **E** (24mm) (code A or without code or date)	6·00
1930s	Type **J**, but solid black circles instead of sectors	6·00
1969†	Type **S**	3·00
1970	Type **W** (53 × 37mm), black *on piece*	6·00
1972	Ditto, but 58 × 39mm *on piece*	6·00
1974	Ditto, but 51 × 32mm with smaller lettering, purple *on piece*	5·00
1981	Ditto, but 60 × 33mm *on piece*	5·00
1982	Ditto, but 54 × 33mm *on piece*	4·00
1983†	Ditto, but 48 × 35mm *on piece*	3·00

St. Sampson's

Opened 1849, closed 31.12.1987

1849	Type **A**, red, blue, greenish grey or green	£300
1865	Type **D** (23mm) (code A, B or C)	80·00
1871	Type **C** (code A)	£100
1886	Type **E**, with dot under T (19mm) (code A, B, C, D or collection time)	6·00
1895	Ditto, but hyphen under T (21mm) (codes A, P or without code)	10·00
1911	Type **R**	£150
1930s	Type **J** (code A, B, C, E, time or without code)	8·00
1948	Type **H** with error GEURNSEY (asterisk code)	£120
1949	Ditto, but spelling corrected (code F or asterisk)	10·00
1954	Parcel post cancellation similar to Guernsey Type **G60**, but inscribed GUERNSEY/CHANNEL ISLANDS/ST. SAMPSON'S. *on piece*	20·00
1957	Type **V** *on piece*	15·00

1963	Type **I**, inscribed GUERNSEY, CH. IS. (code E)	6·00
1969	Type **S** (code F)	2·00
1969	Type **T** (code E or G)	3·00
1970	Type **W** (53 × 36mm)................. *on piece*	6·00
1975	Ditto, but 57 × 32mm with broader lettering *on piece*	4·00
1982	Ditto, but 57 × 35mm with smaller lettering. *on piece*	3·00

St. Saviour's

Opened 1906

1906	Type **F**, violet....................................	35·00
1911	Ditto, but larger lettering with no apostrophe in sub-office name, purple or black	30·00
1917	Ditto, but in crimson...........................	80·00
1922	Type **G**	45·00
1925	Ditto, but GUERNSEY extending to right of ST	45·00
1930s	Type **J**	8·00
1969†	Type **S**, inscribed ST. SAVIOUR.	3·00
1970	Type **W**, inscribed ST. SAVIOUR (53 × 36mm) *on piece*	6·00
1981	Ditto, inscribed ST. SAVIOURS (64 × 40mm) *on piece*	4·00
1984†	Ditto, but 48 × 35mm.................... *on piece*	3·00

Torteval

Opened 1911, closed 21.6.40, reopened 1946

1930s	Type **L** (asterisk code)	10·00
1969†	Type **S**...	3·00
1970	Type **W** (53 × 36mm)................. *on piece*	6·00
1982	Ditto, but 65 × 35mm................. *on piece*	6·00
1983†	Ditto, but 48 × 35mm................. *on piece*	3·00

Vale

Opened as The Vale in 1893, name changed to present form in 1969, closed 31.12.88

1893	Type **E** (20mm) (code A or asterisk)..............	8·00
1918	Type **P** (36mm)...................................	£350
1931	Type **J**, inscribed CHANNEL IS. (without code).....	6·00
1969	Type **S**, inscribed VALE (without code)	3·00
1970	Type **W** (53 × 36mm)................. *on piece*	6·00
1974	Ditto, but VALE in larger lettering (55 × 34mm) *on piece*	6·00
1980	Ditto, inscribed THE VALE (50 × 38mm) . *on piece*	6·00
1982	Ditto, inscribed THE VALE with different size letters (48 × 35mm) .... *on piece*	10·00
1982	Ditto, but THE removed .... *on piece*	3·00

Vale Road

Opened 1895, closed 22.6.40, reopened 1.12.45, closed 31.12.88

1895	Type **D** (22½mm) (asterisk code).................		8·00
1896	Type **F**.......................................		£100
1900s	Type **D** (no code or date) on Type **RL1** registration label.......................................		15·00
1930s	Type **J**.......................................		10·00
1950s	Type **H**, inscribed CHAN. IS. (asterisk code)........		8·00
1969	Type **S**.......................................		3·00
1970	Type **W** (53 × 36mm).................	*on piece*	6·00
1980	Type **X**.............................	*on piece*	8·00
1981	Type **W** (61 × 32mm).................	*on piece*	3·00

Ville au Roi

Opened July 1935, closed 30.6.42, reopened 2.2.48

1935	Type **H**, inscribed CH. IS.		8·00
1969†	Type **S**.......................................		3·00
1970	Type **W** (53 × 36mm).................	*on piece*	6·00
1982†	Ditto, but 60 × 33mm..................	*on piece*	4·00

15. Cachets and Special Markings

The Section is subdivided for Jersey and Guernsey as follows:
(A) Cachets
(B) Slogans
(C) Special Handstamps
(D) Philatelic Exhibition Markings
(E) First Day of Issue Markings

Large numbers of official and private cachets have been used by hoteliers, merchants, the organisers of local fairs and bazaars, railway companies, foreign consulates, etc. Listed below are those cachets and handstamps which indicate a particular method of posting or handling, or which were connected with some philatelic occasion.

JERSEY

(A) Cachets
Cachets are normally collected on complete cover or postcard. The prices below should be *added* to the value of the item to take account of the presence of the cachet clearly struck.

JERSEY CACHETS

1906	Per Train, on postcard. Purple	6·00
1920–21	Via/Mail Boat. Black or red	2·00
1941	Jersey–Guernsey/Mailboat/Channel Islands. Oval. Black or violet	70·00
1973	Posted Jersey Eastern Railway Guard's Van/La Hougue Bie	50
1976	Posted/at/Jersey/Postal Museum/Fort Regent. Boxed. Violet	20

(B1) Individual Slogans
Jersey has frequently replaced the wavy lines of the Universal machine cancellation (Section 9) with slogans, as below. Those slogans which are repeated at intervals are listed separately for convenience.

The prices are for complete covers showing clear strikes of the slogan and its associated datestamp on postage stamps of the letter rate current at the time the slogan was applied. Cut-outs from covers and cards are worth one-quarter of the corresponding item on cover. Where the stamp is already catalogued at a higher figure in used condition, however, the slogan price shown below is to be added when valuing the entire.

JERSEY SLOGANS

Dates of use	Wording	Price on cover
	1931	
	The Best Investment a Telephone	6·00
	1946	
20.5.46 to 15.6.46	Don't Waste Bread Others Need It	1·00
1.7.46 to 31.7.46	Take No Chances Keep Death off the Road	1·00
9.9.46 to 8.10.46	Britain Can Make It Exhibition—1946	1·00
	1947	
23.5.47 to 21.6.47	Volunteer for a Forces Career	1·00
29.9.47 to 27.10.47	Save for the Silver Lining	1·00
20.11.47 to 30.11.47	EP and Wedding Bells	1·00
	1948	
3.5.48 to 27.5.48	A Distinguished Career Nursing	25
	1949	
3.1.49 to 31.1.49	Join the Volunteer Forces	50
1.4.49 to 29.4.49	Mind How You Go On The Road	50
	National Savings Week	50
20.5.49 to 20.6.49	Fly by British Airlines	50
	1950	
1.3.50 to 31.3.50	ROAD USERS PLEASE MIND THE CHILDREN	50
	1953	
3.6.53 to 30.6.53	LONG LIVE THE QUEEN	50
	1955	
7.4.55 to 6.5.55	PLEASE CHECK ADDRESS IF WRONG ADVISE WRITER	20

Dates of use	Wording	Price on cover
	1959	
1.4.59 to 2.5.59	CORRECT ADDRESSING WHAT A BLESSING SAVES US GUESSING	20
5.5.59 to 16.5.59 and 1.11.59 to 12.11.59	CHEAP RATE TRUNK CALLS 6 PM – 6 AM & SUNDAY AFTERNOONS	20
	1960	
1.1.60 to 8.1.60	WORLD REFUGEE YEAR 1959 – 1960	80
7.4.60 to 4.5.60	WORLD REFUGEE YEAR	50
1.11.60 to 26.11.60	CHEAP RATE TRUNK CALLS 6 PM – 6 AM & ALL DAY SUNDAYS	20
	1961	
2.2.61 to 27.2.61 and 17.3.61 to 25.3.61	BUY STAMPS IN BOOKS	20
16.9.61 to 25.10.61	POST OFFICE SAVINGS BANK 1861 1961	50
26.10.61 to 1.11.61	Postal Order Gift Cards MAKE GAY GIFT MESSENGERS	30
2.11.61 to 30.11.61	BBC tv JUBILEE 1936 – 1961	40
	1962	
14.7.62 to 31.7.62	REMEMBER Road accidents can be caused by people like you!	20
1.8.62 to 31.8.62	WORLD HEALTH ORGANISATION FIGHTS MALARIA	30
1.9.62 to 16.9.62	6D RECORDED DELIVERY CHEAP EFFECTIVE 6D	20
17.9.62 to 12.10.62	CIVIL DEFENCE IS COMMON SENSE	20
	1966	
1.10.66 to 31.10.66	CHANNEL ISLANDS 1066 1966 LES ILES NORMANDES	1·00
	1970	
31.7.70 to 4.8.70	JERSEY WELCOMES THE ARCHBISHOP of CANTERBURY 31st JULY – 4th AUGUST	20
	1971	
4.2.71	Opening of Jersey's New Postal H.Q. February, 1971	50
	1972	
18.3.72 to 2.4.72	CHRISTIAN CRUSADE 72 March 18th to April 2nd	50
22.5.72	VISIT OF H.R.H. THE PRINCESS ANNE	1·00
	Used with blue boxed datestamp MAIL OFFICE H.M. YACHT BRITANNIA	6·00
1.10.72 to 31.10.72	ROYAL SILVER WEDDING JERSEY'S STAMP ISSUE 1 NOVEMBER 1972	50
	1973	
2.1.73 to 20.1.73	NEXT STAMP ISSUE 23 JANUARY 1973 LE CENTENAIRE DE LA SOCIETE JERSIAISE	50
30.4.73 to 12.5.73	NEXT STAMP ISSUE 16th MAY 1973 AVIATION HISTORY IN JERSEY	50
15.5.73 to 9.6.73	JERSEY NEW POTATOES ARE AVAILABLE	20
11.6.73 to 18.6.73 and 25.6.73 to 1.7.73	PLANT A TREE IN '73	20
	Struck in red	1·00
19.6.73 to 24.6.73	Cancer Research Campaign CANCER WILL YIELD	25
3.9.73 to 16.10.73	TASTE THE SUNSHINE IN JERSEY TOMATOES	25
9.11.73 to 24.11.73	JERSEY EISTEDDFOD 50th FESTIVAL 26 OCT TO 10 NOV. 1973	25

Dates of use	*Wording*	*Price on cover*

1974

11.3.74 to 31.3.74	SAFETY IS NO ACCIDENT SAFETY AT WORK WEEK MAR. 25-31.	25
14.10.74 to 20.10.74	FIRE SAFETY WEEK 14-20 OCTOBER 1974 JERSEY COUNCIL FOR SAFETY & HEALTH AT WORK	25

1975

5.5.75 to 10.5.75	CHANNEL ISLANDS 1940 – 1945 OCCUPATION OFFICIAL BOOK 8th MAY.	25
23.5.75 to 30.5.75	Jersey Welcomes H.M. Queen Elizabeth The Queen Mother 30th May 1975	40

1976

9.2.76 to 13.2.76	JERSEY LIONS CLUB SWIMARATHON FORT REGENT February 13-15 1976.	20
10.3.76 to 16.3.76	JERSEY TELECOMMUNICATIONS SALUTES WORLD TELEPHONE CENTENARY 1876–1976	20
18.3.76	LAUNCHING OF H.M.S. JERSEY BY H.R.H. THE PRINCESS ANNE.	50
21.3.76 to 27.3.76	MOTHERS UNION CENTENARY 1876 – 1976	20
19.4.76 to 23.4.76	PLEASE SUPPORT THE ARMY BENEVOLENT FUND JERSEY APPEAL	20
24.4.76 to 4.5.76	NEXT STAMP ISSUE "LINKS WITH AMERICA" 29th May WRITE JERSEY BOX 1976.	20
5.5.76 to 11.5.76	7th WEST EUROPEAN AND MEDITERRANEAN CONFERENCE COMMONWEALTH PARLIAMENTARY ASSOCIATION 5TH–11TH MAY.	20
18.5.76 to 31.5.76	1876 1976 OVERSEAS TRADING CORPORATION (1939) LTD. Celebrate 100 Years of Tea Packing in Jersey	20
12.7.76 to 7.8.76	NEXT STAMP ISSUE HIGH VALUE DEFINITIVES 20th AUGUST WRITE JERSEY BOX 1976.	20
24.9.76 to 29.9.76	JERSEY WELCOMES 28TH A.I.P.H. CONGRESS 1976 26–29 SEPTEMBER	20
10.10.76 to 14.10.76	"ALL FOR THE KING" SIR GEORGE CARTERET BIOGRAPHY & MEMORIAL 14TH OCTOBER 1976.	30
18.10.76 to 13.11.76	NEXT STAMP ISSUE LILIAN MARY GRANDIN 25th NOVEMBER WRITE JERSEY BOX 1976	50
19.11.76 to 23.11.76	L'ASSEMBLIEE d'JERRIAIS fondee l' 23 d' Novembre 1951 25e Anniversaire	30
20.12.76 to 2.1.77	NEXT STAMP ISSUE SILVER JUBILEE 7th FEBRUARY WRITE JERSEY BOX 1977.	25

1977

14.2.77 to 21.3.77	JERSEY STAMPS Next Issue 25th March "CURRENCY REFORM" Write box 1977, Jersey	20
29.3.77 to 23.6.77	JERSEY STAMPS Next Issue 24th June "ST. JOHN AMBULANCE CENTENARY" Write box 1977. Jersey. . . .	20
11.4.77 to 23.4.77	DEAF CHILDREN'S WEEK 17th–23rd APRIL 1977.	20
29.6.77 to 28.9.77	JERSEY STAMPS Next issue 29th September "VICTORIA COLLEGE" Write box 1977, Jersey.	20
18.7.77 to 23.7.77	OCCUPATIONAL CENTRE FLAG DAY JERSEY 23rd JULY 1977	20
29.9.77 to 15.11.77	JERSEY STAMPS Next issue 16th November "£2 DEFINITIVE" Write box 1977 Jersey.	20

1978

1.2.78 to 27.2.78	ROYAL JERSEY GOLF CLUB CENTENARY STAMP ISSUE 28 FEB WRITE JERSEY BOX 1978.	20

Dates of use	Wording	Price on cover
1.3.78 to 30.4.78	NEXT STAMP ISSUE EUROPA MONUMENTS 1st MAY WRITE JERSEY BOX 1978	20
1.4.78 to 7.4.78	JERSEY GOOD FOOD FESTIVAL MAY 13th–20th 1978	20
2.5.78 to 8.6.78	NEXT STAMP ISSUE LINKS WITH CANADA OUT JUNE 9th WRITE JERSEY BOX 1978	20
12.6.78 to 25.6.78	NEXT STAMP ISSUE Coronation Anniversary and Royal Visit OUT JUNE 26th WRITE JERSEY BOX 1978.	20
15.7.78 to 21.7.78	OPERATION DRAKE Sea Trials 1978 JERSEY 1980	20
27.7.78 to 4.8.78	HELP The Jersey Life-boat Flag Day 4th August	20
2.10.78 to 14.10.78	nahbo Conference October 13, 14, 15, 1978	20
6.11.78 to 2.12.78	PLANT A TREE NOW NOW NOW	20

1979

2.4.79 to 8.4.79	JERSEY GOOD FOOD FESTIVAL MAY 12TH – 19TH 1979	20
8.4.79 to 21.4.79	JERSEY BADMINTON ASSOCIATION 50th ANNUAL OPEN TOURNAMENT 18 – 21 APRIL	20
4.6.79 to 12.8.79	INTERNATIONAL YEAR OF THE CHILD JERSEY STAMP ISSUE WRITE BOX 60	20
14.8.79	SALVATION ARMY JERSEY CENTENARY 14th AUGUST 1979	20
17.8.79 to 30.9.79 and 8.10.79 to 14.11.79	CONSERVATION JERSEY WILD LIFE TRUST STAMP STAMP ISSUE WRITE BOX 60	20
24.9.79 to 30.9.79	A Gala Performance OPERA HOUSE THEATRE JERSEY Tribute to Tommy Swanson SUNDAY, SEPTEMBER 30th 1979	20
1.10.79 to 9.10.79	10 ANNIVERSARY JERSEY POST OFFICE 1st OCTOBER 1979 UPU DAY 9.10.79	20

1980

1.9.80 to 28.9.80	PLEASE SUPPORT THE ASSOCIATION FOR YOUTH & FRIENDSHIP'S HOSTELS FOR BOYS AND GIRLS	20

1981

16.4.81 to 29.4.81, 3.5.81 to 16.5.81 and 13.7.81 to 26.7.81	YEAR OF THE DISABLED	20
3.5.81 to 16.5.81	GOOD FOOD FESTIVAL 1981	20
1.9.81 to 12.9.81	NORDRING '81 MUSIC FESTIVAL	20

1982

1.3.82 to 7.3.82, 1.6.82 to 7.6.82, 1.7.82 to 7.7.82 and 1.8.82 to 7.8.82	ROYAL BRITISH LEGION IN JERSEY	20
8.3.82 to 28.3.82	BBC LOCAL RADIO	20
18.4.82 to 15.5.82	GOOD FOOD FESTIVAL & SALON CULINAIRE 1982	20
19.7.82 to 25.7.82	JERSEY LIFE-BOAT GUILD	20
11.10.82 to 16.10.82	HELP VARIETY TO HELP A CHILD IN NEED	20

1983

4.1.83 to 17.1.83	JERSEY TELECOMS 10 YEARS TRUNK SERVICE	20
18.4.83 to 8.5.83	JERSEY GOOD FOOD FESTIVAL 1983	20
9.5.83 to 15.5.83	JERSEY WELCOMES THE R.A.F. ASSOC. ANNUAL CONFERENCE 13–15 MAY 83	20
16.5.83 to 22.5.83	ASSOC OF YOUTH & FRIENDSHIP 21ST ANNIV MAY 1983	20

Dates of use	Wording	Price on cover
18.7.83 to 24.7.83	BRITISH MIDLAND. 30 YEARS OF SERVICE TO JERSEY.	20
3.10.83 to 9.10.83	JERSEY & SCHWEPPES SCHWEPPES 1783–1983 BICENTENARY	20

1984

16.4.84 to 24.4.84	JERSEY FRESH.	20
25.4.84 to 5.5.84	"D-U-M-P"	20
6.5.84 to 19.5.84	GOOD FOOD FESTIVAL 1984.	20
25.6.84 to 8.7.84	METHODISM ESTABLISHED IN JERSEY.	20
9.7.84 to 14.7.84	HELP JERSEY HOSPICE CARE.	20
15.7.84 to 21.7.84	JERSEY ROTARY DIAMOND JUBILEE.	20

1985

1.4.85 to 7.4.85	JERSEY HOCKEY EASTER FESTIVAL	20
5.5.85 to 18.5.85	GOOD FOOD FESTIVAL 1985.	20
8.9.85 to 14.9.85	RAF ASSOCIATION (JERSEY BRANCH) DIAMOND JUBILEE.	20

1986

10.3.86 to 16.3.86	DON'T DELAY, STOP SMOKING TODAY FOR LIFE	20
16.6.86 to 22.6.86	SUPPORT THE ROUND JERSEY RELAY	20
22.9.86 to 28.9.86	BRITISH PHARMACEUTICAL CONFERENCE	20
9.11.86 to 15.11.86	CENTENARY OF THE JERSEY BLIND SOCIETY.	20

1987

3.5.87 to 16.5.87	NATIONAL DEAF CHILDREN'S WEEK	20
22.5.87 to 28.6.87	CENTENARY OF ST JOHN AMBULANCE BRIGADE.	20
8.6.87 to 14.6.87	MEN OF THE TREES GOLDEN JUBILEE	20
20.7.87 to 2.8.87	PARISH RATE DRAFT REGISTER OF ELECTORS	20
3.8.87 to 27.9.87	CTV 25. CHANNEL TELEVISION 25 YEARS OF BROADCASTING	20
5.10.87 to 11.10.87	INTERNATIONAL YEAR OF SHELTER FOR THE HOMELESS	20

1988

15.5.88 to 27.5.88	TELETHON 88.	20

1989

27.3.89 to 23.4.89	MISSION JERSEY	20

1990

19.3.90 to 24.3.90	NATIONAL PHYSIOTHERAPY WEEK.	20
13.5.90 to 26.5.90	TELETHON 90.	20
24.6.90 to 7.7.90	JERSEY EVENING POST CENTENARY	20
25.6.90 to 30.6.90	HELP BIRTHRIGHT RESEARCH.	20
22.10.90 to 28.10.90	SOROPTIMIST INTERNATIONAL.	20

1991

2.1.91 to 15.1.91	100 YEARS OF SAVING LIVES	20
1.4.91 to 7.4.91	CHANNEL ISLANDS AIR SEARCH	20
8.4.91 to 21.4.91	CRIME PREVENTION WEEK	20
20.5.91 to 26.5.91 and 19.8.91 to 25.8.91	PLEASE SUPPORT HAMPTONNE	20
30.9.91 to 27.10.91	THE SAMARITANS – 30 YEARS IN JERSEY	20

(B2) Annual or Periodic Slogans
The wording of the slogan is followed by the dates of use; exact dates are given where known, otherwise the years only.

THE TELEPHONE MAKES LIFE EASIER .... 2·00
    1932
    1933
POST EARLY for CHRISTMAS (holly leaves) 20
    1946
    1947
    1948
    1949
    1.12.50 to 20.12.50
    1.12.51 to 20.12.51
    1.12.52 to 20.12.52
    2.12.53 to 21.12.53
    6.12.54 to 20.12.54
    9.12.55 to 21.12.55
    1.12.56 to 19.12.56
    9.12.57 to 18.12.57
    5.12.58 to 19.12.58
    5.12.59 to 20.12.59
BLOOD DONORS ARE STILL URGENTLY NEEDED 20
    1947
    1948
    1949
    1950
    1.2.51 to 28.2.51
    1952
    1.9.53 to 3.10.53
    1954
    16.5.55 to 10.6.55
CIVIL DEFENCE JOIN NOW
    1.11.51 to 30.11.51
    1952
    1953
    4.10.54 to 27.10.54
    12.9.55 to 7.10.55
    2.10.56 to 17.10.56
POSTAGE ON LETTERS for EUROPE 4D 20
    1.9.52 to 1.10.52
    1.6.54 to 30.6.54
HAVE YOU TAKEN OUT YOUR LICENCE FOR RADIO – TV? 20
    3.1.57 to 30.1.57
    12.3.58 to 16.5.58
    4.3.59 to 24.3.59
    5.5.60 to 20.6.60
    16.4.61 to 14.5.61
    2.4.62 to 30.4.62
    1.4.63 to 29.4.63
EXPRESS GOOD WISHES BY GREETINGS TELEGRAMS. . . 20
    1.2.58 to 12.3.58
    4.7.59 to 5.8.59
    2.9.60 to 12.9.60
    18.10.60 to 26.10.60
    30.7.61 to 20.8.61
KING GEORGE'S JUBILEE TRUST........................ 20
    4.6.60 to 28.6.60
    1.3.61 to 10.3.61

POST EARLY FOR CHRISTMAS (candle)................   20
   7.12.60 to 21.12.60
   9.12.61 to 19.12.61
   9.12.62 to 20.12.62
   10.12.63 to 21.12.63
   15.12.64 to 20.12.64
   9.12.65 to 20.12.65
   1.12.66 to 21.12.66
   12.12.67 to 19.12.67
   8.12.68 to 20.12.68
JERSEY FOR A HAPPY SPRINGTIME HOLIDAY   20
   1964
   1965
   1966
   1967
   1968
   1969
   1.1.70 to 31.3.70
   1.1.71 to 3.2.71 and 5.2.71 to 31.3.71
   3.4.72 to 30.4.72
   2.4.73 to 29.4.73
   1.4.74 to 28.4.74
JERSEY FOR SUNNY AUTUMN HOLIDAYS   20
   1964
   1965
   1966
   1967
   1968
   1.7.69 to 12.10.69
   1.7.70 to 30.7.70 and 5.8.70 to 18.10.70
   1.7.71 to 16.10.71
   1.7.72 to 31.8.72
   2.7.73 to 2.9.73
   1.7.74 to 1.9.74
JERSEY FOR SUNSHINE IN THE WINTER................   20
   1964
   1965
   1966
   1967
   1968
JERSEY for CHRISTMAS HOLIDAYS   20
   1965
   1966
   1967
   1968
   13.10.69 to 31.12.69
   19.10.70 to 31.12.70
JERSEY FOR SUNNY SUMMER HOLIDAYS   20
   1.4.70 to 30.6.70
   1.4.71 to 30.6.71
PLEASE REMEMBER THE JOINT CHRISTMAS APPEAL ...   20
   3.12.73 to 30.12.73
   29.11.74 to 26.12.74
   23.11.75 to 20.12.75
   20.12.76 to 24.12.76
   5.12.77 to 16.12.77
DESPAIRING? SUICIDAL? 25555 SAMARITANS JERSEY..   20
   1.11.76 to 31.10.77 (when machines not fitted with other
      slogans)
   30.10.78 to 5.11.78
   23.4.80 to 29.4.80
POST YOUR CHRISTMAS GREETINGS EARLY   20
   1.12.76 to 19.12.76

```
     21.11.77 to 4.12.77
     3.12.78 to 16.12.78
JERSEY LIONS CLUB SWIMARATHON FORT REGENT. . . .      20
     12.2.77 to 18.2.77
     6.2.78 to 11.2.78
     19.2.79 to 24.2.79
     18.2.80 to 23.2.80
     15.2.81 to 21.2.81
     21.2.82 to 27.2.82
     20.2.84 to 26.2.84
     18.2.85 to 24.2.85
     17.2.86 to 23.2.86
     9.2.87 to 15.2.87
     8.2.88 to 14.2.88
     6.2.89 to 12.2.89
     19.2.90 to 25.2.90
     11.2.91 to 17.2.91
POPPY APPEAL PLEASE GIVE GENEROUSLY . . . . . . . . . . . .      20
     1.11.77 to 12.11.77
     29.10.79 to 4.11.79
     25.10.81 to 7.11.81
     31.10.82 to 13.11.82
     31.10.83 to 13.11.83
     29.10.84 to 11.11.84
     4.11.85 to 9.11.85
     27.10.86 to 8.11.86
     26.10.87 to 7.11.87
     30.10.88 to 12.11.88
     30.10.89 to 11.11.89
support The Jersey Society for Mentally Handicapped Children
     Inc. For all information 'phone 54622 . . . . . . . . . . . . . . . . . .      20
     11.6.78 to 1.7.78
     1.3.79 to 7.4.79
     22.4.79 to 30.4.79
     3.6.79 to 30.6.79
     21.6.82 to 27.6.82
Jersey STAMPS WORTH COLLECTING BOX 1978 . . . . . . . .      20
     From 28.6.78 when no other slogan in use
Support SCHIZOPHRENIA RESEARCH CAMPAIGN FOR
     INFORMATION PHONE 51244 . . . . . . . . . . . . . . . . . . . . . .      20
     19.5.79 to 2.6.79
     24.6.85 to 30.6.85
NATIONAL SCHIZOPHRENIA FELLOWSHIP . . . . . . . . . . . . .      20
     14.4.80 to 22.4.80
     17.5.81 to 23.5.81
     6.9.81 to 12.9.81
     16.4.82 to 22.4.82
     27.6.83 to 3.7.83
     1.6.84 to 7.6.84
     12.8.84 to 18.8.84
     10.12.84 to 16.12.84
     25.3.85 to 31.3.85
     23.9.85 to 29.9.85
     16.12.85 to 22.12.85
     17.3.86 to 23.3.86
CHOOSE GENUINE JERSEY ROYAL NEW POTATOES. . . . .      20
     2.6.80 to 22.6.80
     8.6.81 to 28.6.81
KEEP JERSEY TIDY . . . . . . . . . . . . . . . . . . . . . . . . . . . . . . . . .      20
     6.4.81 to 12.4.81
     6.6.83 to 12.6.83
SHOPLIFTERS COST YOU £'s £'s £'s . . . . . . . . . . . . . . . . . . . . .      20
     15.6.81 to 21.6.81
```

13.7.81 to 19.7.81
17.8.81 to 23.8.81
20.6.83 to 26.6.83
18.7.83 to 24.7.83
22.8.83 to 28.8.83

DON'T DRINK AND DRIVE 20
7.12.83 to 20.12.83
21.5.84 to 27.5.84
20.8.84 to 26.8.84
12.11.84 to 25.11.84
17.12.84 to 23.12.84
2.12.85 to 15.12.85
23.12.85 to 29.12.85

JERSEY POLICE. FOR SAFETY'S SAKE. BELT UP 20
4.3.85 to 10.3.85
15.4.85 to 4.5.85
19.5.85 to 2.6.85
17.6.85 to 23.6.85
1.7.85 to 7.7.85
22.7.85 to 4.8.85

SARK TO JERSEY ROWING RACE 20
8.7.85 to 13.7.85
29.6.86 to 4.7.86
5.7.87 to 11.7.87

INDUSTRY YEAR 20
From 23.6.86 when no other slogan in use

JERSEY SCHIZOPHRENIA FELLOWSHIP 20
7.7.86 to 13.7.86
15.9.86 to 21.9.86
1.12.86 to 7.12.86
25.5.87 to 31.5.87
28.9.87 to 4.10.87
13.3.89 to 19.3.89
26.6.89 to 2.7.89
9.10.89 to 15.10.89
4.12.89 to 10.12.89
16.9.91 to 22.9.91

POLIO PLUS CAMPAIGN. 20
12.10.87 to 25.10.87
24.4.88 to 7.5.88

JERSEY DEAF CHILDREN'S WEEK 20
8.5.88 to 14.5.88
7.5.89 to 13.5.89
29.4.90 to 12.5.90
22.4.91 to 5.5.91

JERSEY ROAD SAFETY PANEL "DRIVE DRY" 20
16.12.88 to 31.12.88
12.6.89 to 25.6.89
11.12.89 to 24.12.89
10.12.90 to 31.12.90

FOR RELIEF OF GLAUCOMA 20
3.7.89 to 9.7.89
13.11.89 to 18.11.89
3.12.90 to 9.12.90

JERSEY POST. 20
From 1.6.89 when no other slogan in use

PLEASE USE YOUR POSTCODE 20
From 2.4.90 when no other slogan in use

WEAR YOUR POPPY WITH PRIDE 20
29.10.90 to 11.11.90
28.10.91 to 9.11.91

(C) Special Handstamps

Numerous special handstamps have been used by the independent postal administration in Jersey. Prices are for covers, each franked with postage stamps of the letter rate current at the time. Where the postage stamp is already catalogued at a higher figure in used condition, this should be *added* to the price given below. Markings for philatelic exhibitions overseas are listed separately for convenience.

JERSEY SPECIAL HANDSTAMPS

Dates of use	Event	Price on cover
5.5.70 and 28.9.70	Visit of M.V. *Kungsholm* to Jersey	75
20.5.70	Trustee Savings Bank Conference	1·00
19.6.70	Dunkirk Veterans Association	60
14.8.70	Visit of M.V. *Gripsholm* to Jersey	75
18.8.70	Interlink Development Ltd.	1·00
26.10.70	Railway Centenary Exhibition	60
15.2.71	Normacol Golden Jubilee (in violet)	2·00
1.4.71	30th Anniversary of Jersey's first 1d. stamp	30
6.5.71, 15.8.71 and 1.10.71	Posted on board M.V. *Kungsholm*	60
6.5.71	Imperial Life of Canada Convention	40
15.5.71	Re-enactment of Siege of Gorey Castle	50
12.6.71	Visit of Cardinal Heenan	20
7.8.71	Posted on board M.V. *Gripsholm*	60
1.9.71 and 18.9.71	Exhibition of Postal History Société Jersiaise	50
2.10.71	Postal History Society Conference	60
16.10.71	Commonwealth Postal Conference Visit to Jersey	60
2.11.71	21st Birthday of Channel Islands Specialists' Society	50
1972	Last day of £.s.d. stamps	30
1.4.72	BEA Channel Islands 1947–1972 25 Years	50
7.4.72	50th Anniversary of Formation of 2 Sqn RAF Regt BFPS 1282	50
7.5.72, 13.8.72 and 29.9.72	Posted on board M.V. *Kungsholm*	60
28.5.72	Re enactment of Battle of Port de la Mare	30
7.8.72	Posted on board M.V. *Gripsholm*	60
26.9.72	Exposition Grande Bretagne au Printemps 26 Sep – 17 Oct Paris	3·00
16.5.73	50th Anniversary Aero Philatelic Club	40
29.5.73	Engagement of Princess Anne	1·50
5.8.73	Posted on board M.V. *Kungsholm*	60
13.8.73	Posted on board M.V. *Gripsholm*	60
15.9.73	33rd Anniversary of Battle of Britain	30
26.9.73	Lions Club	30
1.10.73	Opening of new Post Office in Broad Street, St. Helier	40
1.11.73	65 Years of Scouting in Jersey	30
1973	Opening of Jersey Philatelic Bureau, Broad Street	20
5.3.74	Royal Artillery Association Jubilee	30
20.4.74	French Rotary Conference	30
24.4.74	La Corbière Lighthouse Centenary	30
27.4.74	21st National Assembly of Skal Clubs	30
20.7.74	Opening of St. Ouen's Manor	30
31.7.74	Sir Winston Churchill Centenary	40
31.7.74	150th Anniversary of R.N.L.I.	50
12.9.74	50th Anniversary of La Hougue Bie Tomb	30
14.9.74	Battle of Britain	50

Dates of use	Event	Price on cover
30.9.74	Greetings from A. W. Pope Travel Bureau	30
30.11.74	Centenary of Birth of Churchill.	40
16.1.75	Swearing-in of new Bailiff.	30
15.3.75	25th Anniversary of Channel Islands Specialists' Society . . .	50
9.5.75	30th Anniversary of Liberation	30
2.8.75	Siege of Gorey Castle.	30
4.8.75	75th Birthday of Queen Mother	75
8.9.75	European Architectural Heritage Year	30
29.9.75	Hans Christian Andersen Exhibition.	30
30.10.75	10th Anniversary of the Red Arrows	40
21.12.75	56 Squadron R.A.F.	40
1975	Launching of Lifeboat	40
26.2.76	230 Squadron R.A.F.	40
5.3.76	40th Anniversary of first flight of Spitfire	30
10.3.76	Opening Maison Variety Tent 52	40
15.4.76	35 Jarig Bestaan 320 (Dutch) Squadron	40
29.5.76	Visit of Lord Mayor of London	30
8.6.76	56 Squadron R.A.F.	40
31.10.76	Houdini 50th Anniversary	30
1.3.77 to 4.3.77	Reunion of Association des Parlementaires de Langue Française.	30
27.3.77	Official Welcome of H.M.S. Jersey . . . . in black	1·00
	in red	1·25
28.4.77	Introduction of Hawk into R.A.F.	40
2.6.77	60 Squadron R.A.F.	40
7.6.77	Jersey Silver Jubilations	30
16.2.78	Jersey Scottish Society Jubilee	25
14.4.78	Multi District 105 Lions Convention	25
18.4.78	Inauguration of Sea Rangers Group	25
13.5.78 and 19.5.78	Good Food Festival.	25
15.5.78	Sub-Postmasters' Federation Conference	25
10.6.79	Edgar Percival Aircraft Designer and Test Pilot	25
25.7.79	70th Anniversary of First Crossing by Air of the Channel . . .	25
27.7.79	30th Anniversary of the First Flight of the Comet	25
28.7.79	Army Air Day	25
2.8.79	150th Anniversary of Bethlehem Methodist Church St. Mary	25
9.10.79	Jersey Post Office 10th Anniversary U.P.U. Day	25
1.12.79	40th Anniversary Formation of Air Transport Auxiliary.	25
14.12.79	5th Anniversary of Channel Islands Collectors Club Inc. (U.S.A.).	40
23.12.79	60th Anniversary of No. 1 Flying Training School	25
23.2.80	Rotary International 1905–1980.	25
11.5.80	40th Anniversary of R.A.F. Innsworth	25
24.6.80	Tercentenary of the De la Salle Brothers.	25
4.8.80	80th Birthday of HM Queen Elizabeth The Queen Mother . .	25
10.8.80	Lifeboat Open Day (in blue)	25
15.9.80	40th Anniversary Battle of Britain	25
20.9.80	Centenary Jersey College for Girls 1880–1980	25
28.10.80	75th Anniversary Jersey Football Association	25
1.11.80	30th Anniversary of Channel Islands Specialists' Society . . .	40
4.11.80	5th Anniversary of FGCI (German Channel Islands Collectors Society).	50
29.11.80	Operation Drake Welcome Home Eye of the Wind	25
31.12.80	Last Day of European Nature Conservation Decade	25
1-3.10.81	Rotary District III Conference	25
19.11.81	Bomber Command Museum Appeal	25
31.12.81	Disbandment of No. 617 Squadron R.A.F.	25
1.2.82	65th Anniversary Formation of No. 100 Squadron R.A.F. . . .	25

Dates of use	Event	Price on cover
28.2.82	Disbandment of No. 35 Squadron R.A.F.	25
22.3.82	Introduction of the Washington to the Royal Air Force	25
1.4.82	64th Anniversary of Formation of the Royal Air Force	25
12.4.82	70th Anniversary of First Use of the Aeroplane in War	25
13.4.82	70th Anniversary of Formation of the Royal Flying Corps	25
26.4.82	First Award of the Victoria Cross to an Airman	25
1.6.82	Reformation of No. 9 Squadron R.A.F.	25
13.6.82	Jersey Ladies Lifeboat Guild 50th Anniversary (in blue)	25
15.6.82	25th Anniversary of Operation Grapple	25
10.7.82	First Woman to Fly the Atlantic Solo.	25
20.7.82	41st Anniversary of the Guinea Pig Club	25
23.7.82	Army Air 82 Middle Wallop.	25
12.8.82	First Victoria Cross Awarded to Bomber Command	25
15.8.82	40th Anniversary of Formation of Pathfinder Force	25
16.9.82	Commemorating 40th Anniversary of First Deportations to Germany	25
15.10.82	60th Anniversary of the First Air Control Operation	25
15.12.82	Introduction of Liberator Mk.3 to the Royal Air Force	25
24.12.82	30th Anniversary of the First Flight of the Victor.	25
21.4.83	New £1 Coin Issue St. Helier	25
3.5.83	40th Anniversary Award of Victoria Cross to Sqn Ldr Trent .	25
14.5.83	Biggin Hill International Air Fair.	25
17.5.83	40 Years Operational Use of Mitchell by R.A.F.	25
11.6.83	40th Anniversary Empire Test Pilots School.	25
18.6.83	Royal Air Force Brize Norton Air Day	25
21.6.83	First Flight of Production Version of Handley Page Heyford.	25
9.7.83	Hendon Pageant	25
15.8.83	First Successful Ascent of Manaslu North-East Nepal	25
3.9.83	44th Anniversary First Bomber Command Operation over Germany	25
7.9.83	40th Anniversary of the Last Stirling Operational Sortie	25
4.10.83	Boys Brigade Centenary Founded 4th Oct 1883 Glasgow	25
25.10.83	44th Anniversary of the First Flight of the Halifax.	25
21.11.83	200th Anniversary of Manned Flight.	25
24.11.83	61st Anniversary of the First Flight of the Virginia	25
19.12.83	30th Anniversary Breaking London-Cape Town & Return Canberra Record	25
22.12.83	19th Anniversary of Maiden Flight of the Lockheed SR71 .	25
15.8.83	First Successful Ascent of Manaslu North-East Nepal	25
3.9.83	44th Anniversary of the First Bomber Command Operation over Germany.	25
7.9.83	40th Anniversary of the last Stirling Operational Sortie	25
4.10.83	The Boys Brigade Centenary.	25
25.10.83	44th Anniversary of the 1st flight of the Halifax RA	25
21.11.83	200th Anniversary of Manned Flight.	25
24.11.83	61st Anniversary of the 1st Flight of the Virginia	25
19.12.83	30th Anniversary of the Breaking of London – Cape Town & Return Record by the Canberra	25
22.12.83	19th Anniversary of the Maiden Flight of the Lockheed SR-71	25
31.3.84	31st Anniversary of the last flight of the Wellington.	25
10.4.84	Commemorating the 1st Award of the Air Force Cross to an Airman.	25
13.4.84	50th Anniversary of the Start of the B17 Fortress Project	25
1.5.84	50th Anniversary of the Introduction of the Overstrand to RAF Service	25
19.5.84	Biggin Hill International Air Fair.	25
1.6.84	Presentation of New Standard to 208 Squadron.	25

Dates of use	Event	Price on cover
9.6.84	Mildenhall Air Fete	25
9.6.84	Commonwealth Postal Conference	25
12.6.84	Distinguished Flying Cross	25
7.7.84	Hendon Open Day	25
18.7.84	Chivenor Open Day	25
19.7.84	66th Anniversary of the 1st Seaborne Landplane Bombing Operation	25
15.8.84	Commemorating the 1st Award of the Victoria Cross to an Airman	25
1.9.84	Reformation of 27 Squadron	25
8.9.84	Farnborough International '84	25
27.9.84	Chartered Insurance Institute National Conference	25
12.10.84	Commemorating the 1st Appointment of an Airman to the Distinguished Service Order	25
1.11.84	Reformation of 216 Squadron	25
15.11.84	Cheshire Home Jersey	25
1.1.85	70th Anniversary of No 10 Squadron	25
1.2.85	70th Anniversary of the Formation of No 17F Squadron	25
14.2.85	70th Anniversary of No 11 Squadron	25
12.4.85	50th Anniversary of the 1st Flight of Britain First	25
8.5.85	40th Anniversary of V.E. Day	25
9.5.85	Liberation Anniversary 1945 – 1985	25
15.5.85	60th Anniversary of No 502 Squadron Royal Auxiliary Air Force	25
21.5.85	40th Anniversary of Delivery of Lincoln to Bomber Command	25
31.5.85	75th Anniversary of the Girl Guide Association	25
1.6.85	The Award of the Distinguished Service Cross to Airmen	25
15.6.85	Inaugural Lufthansa Flight Jersey to Frankfurt	25
23.6.85	Digital Schneider Trophy Race	25
1.8.85	Appointment to the Most Honourable Order of the Bath	25
15.8.85	40th Anniversary of V.J. Day	25
1.10.85	The Award of the Military Medal to Airmen	25
23.10.85	Rank Theatres Jersey Conference	25
4.11.85	Forschungs Gemeinschaft CI (Club of C.I. Collectors)	25
1.12.85	Appointment to the Most Excellent Order of the British Empire	25
4.1.86	Assermertation du Bailli – Swearing in of the Bailiff of Jersey	25
4.3.86	Halley's Comet Society	25
4.3.86	Domesday Book 900th Anniversary	25
10.3.86	50th Anniversary of the 1st Flight of the Battle	25
1.4.86	70th Anniversary of No 38 Squadron	25
15.4.86	70th Anniversary of No 49 Squadron	25
15.4.86	Conspicuous Gallantry Medal	25
22.4.86	70th Anniversary of the Formation of 70 Sqn	25
10.5.86	Shoreham Philatelic Society	25
14.5.86	Centenary of the Royal Liver Delegation	25
17.5.86	Jersey New Potato Fair	25
1.6.86	Aircrew Europe	25
30.6.86	Disbandment of No 57 Squadron	25
5.9.86	Jersey Travel Mart 12–14 Oct '86	25
22.9.86	Small Countries Conference of the Commonwealth Parliamentary Association	25
30.9.86	50th Anniversary of the Closure of Jersey Railway	25
1.10.86	Air Efficiency Award	25
1.12.86	Distinguished Flying Medal	25
1.5.87	RAF mentioned in Despatches	25
2.5.87	Royal Visit	25
10.5.87	Inaugural Lufthansa Flight to Dusseldorf	25

Dates of use	Event	Price on cover
17.5.87	U.C.W. 68th Annual Conference	25
1.7.87	George Medal RAF	25
1.9.87	Air Force Medal	25
25.5.89	Royal Visit	25
28.4.90	40th Anniversary of the Channel Islands Specialists' Society	25
9.5.90	Naming of the New Lifeboat St Helier Jersey	25
1.7.90	50th Anniversary of the Occupation of Jersey	25
4.8.90	90th Birthday of Her Majesty Queen Elizabeth the Queen Mother	25
4.9.90	50th Anniversary Battle of Britain	25

(D) Philatelic Exhibition Markings

At many of the world's philatelic exhibitions since 1971 the Jersey stand has provided special markings for covers (franked with Jersey stamps) presented for postmarking.

In the list below, (H) signifies a handstamp used for cancelling the stamps; the others are cachets, i.e. commemorative markings for the envelope.

Date of use	Event	Price on cover
12.3.71	Interpex, New York (H)	6·00
4.6.71 to 14.6.71	Basle Philatelic Exhibition	2·00
24.4.71 to 9.5.71	Foire de Paris	2·00
25.9.71 to 26.9.71	Assindia, Essen	2·00
17.3.72 to 19.3.72	Interpex, New York (H)	3·00
24.6.72 to 9.7.72	Belgica, Brussels	2·00
1.11.72	BPE, London	50
2.3.73 to 4.3.73	Expo 73, Anaheim	3·00
9.3.73 to 11.3.73	Interpex, New York	3·00
11.5.73 to 20.5.73	Ibra, Munich	2·00
25.5.73 to 27.5.73	Compex 73, Chicago	2·00
31.10.73 to 3.11.73	BPE, London	1·00
26.2.73 to 3.3.73	Stampex, London	1·00
7.6.74 to 16.6.74	Internaba Exhibition	2·00
29.7.74 to 31.7.74	Philatex, Bournemouth	1·00
21.9.74 to 29.9.74	Stockholmia	2·00
30.10.74 to 2.11.74	BPE, London	1·00
22.11.74 to 24.11.74	ASDA, New York	1·00
29.11.74 to 1.12.74	Stamp Expo North, San Francisco	1·00
4.4.75	Espana 75, Madrid (H)	2·00
6.6.75	Arphila 75, Paris (H)	2·00
21.11.75 to 23.11.75	ASDA, New York (H)	50
13.12.75	Themabelga, Brussels (H)	2·00
29.5.76	Interphil, New York (H)	50
20.8.76	Hafnia 76 (H)	50
14.10.76	Italia 76, Milan (H)	50
29.10.76	Rhein-Ruhr Posta 76, Essen (H)	50

Dates of use	Event	Price on cover
19.11.76 to 21.11.76	ASDA, New York	50
28.8.77 to 4.9.77	San Marino 77	30
16.11.77 to 20.11.77	ANPSS, New York	50
20.5.78 to 25.5.78	Naposta 78	50
9.6.78 to 18.6.78	Capex, Toronto	50
26.8.78 to 28.8.78	Riccione	30
1.11.78 to 5.11.78	Essen Stamp Fair	30
15.11.78 to 19.11.78	ANPSS, New York	40
10.3.79	Rhein-Ruhr Posta 79, Essen	40
13.6.80 to 22.6.80	Norwex 80, Oslo (H)	40
3.10.80 to 12.10.80	Espamer 80, Madrid (H)	40
22.5.86 to 1.6 86	Ameripex, Chicago	30
9.6.86 to 20.6.86	Stamplink (M.V. *Earl Granville*)	30
13.6.87 to 21.6.87	Capex	30
16.10.87 to 25.10.87	Hafnia, Copenhagen	30
1.6.88 to 12.6.88	Finlandia	30
7.7.89 to 17.7.89	Philexfrance, Paris	30
17.11.89 to 3.12.89	World Stamp Expo, Washington	30
3.5.90 to 13.5.90	Stamp World, London	30
2.6.90 to 10.6.90	Belgica, Brussels	30
24.8.90 to 2.9.90	New Zealand, Auckland	30
16.11.91 to 24.11.91	Philanippon, Tokyo	30

(E) "First Day of Issue" Markings

With the 2½d. Regional stamps of 8 June 1964 (S.G. 9) Jersey began using the machine cancellation introduced generally in the British Isles, namely the words "FIRST DAY OF ISSUE" shown on an envelope and printed as a slogan alongside a circular datestamp (Type **A**). The datestamp is 21mm in diameter and as used on the 8 June 1964 included the time of posting. It was originally inscribed "JERSEY" at the top and an arc below but a later version has the arc replaced by "CHANNEL ISLANDS". Later use was without the time of posting.

Normally the datestamp is to the left and the slogan to the right, but the positions have been transposed (examples noted in 1969). The independent Jersey postal administration have continued using this envelope-type slogan from time to time, primarily to cancel single adhesives on covers posted on the first day of issue.

From 13 September 1965 (Battle of Britain issue) a 38mm diameter cancel (Type **B**) reading "JERSEY. CHANNEL ISLANDS/FIRST DATE OF ISSUE/date" was used for all G.B. special issues until 20 February 1967 (E.F.T.A. issue), with the exception of the Battle of Hastings Anniversary issue of 14 October 1966 for which a special 21mm diameter First Day of Issue handstamp was applied. A 26mm handstamp (Type **C**) came into use with the Wild Flowers issue of 24 April 1967. This was made of rubber and inscribed "FIRST DAY OF ISSUE" at the top, "CHANNEL ISLANDS" at the bottom with the date and "JERSEY" in two lines across the centre.

With the Liberation issue of 9 May 1970 a single-circle handstamp, diameter 24mm and inscribed "FIRST DAY OF ISSUE/JERSEY CHANNEL ISLANDS", was put into use. In three lines across the centre are:

(Type **D**) "date/PHILATELIC/BUREAU" or
(Type **E**) "date/PHILATELIC/SERVICE".

The centre details have been modified at times to give the date in four lines, but from 1974 it was always in two lines with the diameter reduced to 22mm (Type **F**).

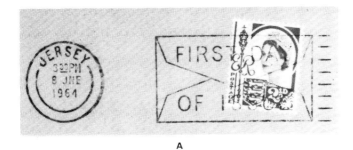

A

A

B

C

D

E

F

Jersey first-day cancellations

Pictorial Handstamps. For the Inauguration issue of the independent postal administration a handstamp in the form of a shield was applied on the first day, 1 October 1969. Since then many issues have had special first day cancellations of a pictorial character related to the dsigns of the stamps. They are normally applied to covers bearing full sets only, the prices for which are given in *Collect Channel Islands and Isle of Man Stamps*.

GUERNSEY

(A) Cachets

Cachets are normally collected on complete cover or postcard. The prices below should be *added* to the value of the item to take account of the presence of the cachet clearly struck.

GUERNSEY CACHET

1970   Director of Postal Services. Boxed. Violet.   50

(B1) Individual Slogans

The wavy lines of the Universal machine cancellation (Section 9) have from time to time been replaced by slogans, as below. Those slogans which are repeated at intervals are listed separately for convenience.

The prices are for complete covers showing clear strikes of the slogan and its associated datestamp on postage stamps of the letter rate current at the time the slogan was applied. Cut-outs from covers and cards are worth one-quarter of the corresponding item on cover. Where the stamp is already catalogued at a higher figure in used condition, however, the slogan price shown below is to be added when valuing the entire.

GUERNSEY SLOGANS

Dates of use	Wording	Price on cover
	1947	
20.11.47 to 30.11.47	EP and Wedding Bells	50
1.3.50 to 31.3.50	ROAD USERS PLEASE MIND THE CHILDREN	50
	1953	
3.5.53 to 30.6.53	LONG LIVE THE QUEEN	1·00
	1954	
1.9.54 to 28.9.54	SAVE TIME BUY 2½d. STAMPS IN BOOKS 3'9D. A BOOK	50
	1960	
1.1.60 to 9.1.60	WORLD REFUGEE YEAR 1959 – 1960	1·00
7.4.60 to 4.5.60	WORLD REFUGEE YEAR	1·00
	With "324" in triangle instead of c.d.s. (bulk postings)	2·00
1.11.60 to 26.11.60	CHEAP RATE TRUNK CALLS 6 PM – 6 AM & ALL DAY SUNDAYS	50
	1961	
2.2.61 to 27.2.61 and		
17.3.61 to 25.3.61	BUY STAMPS IN BOOKS	50
16.9.61 to 25.10.61	POST OFFICE SAVINGS BANK 1861 1961	50
2.11.61 to 30.11.61	BBC tv JUBILEE 1936 – 1961	50
	1962	
14.7.62 to 31.7.62	REMEMBER Road accidents can be caused by people like you!	50
1.8.62 to 31.8.62	WORLD HEALTH ORGANISATION FIGHTS MALARIA	50
	1966	
27.1.66 to 3.2.66	HELP SAVE YOUR DOCTOR'S TIME	1·00
7.3.66 to 30.4.66	DR. BARNARDO'S HOMES 1866 – 1966 100 YEARS OF CHILD CARE	50
1.10.66 to 31.10.66	CHANNEL ISLANDS 1066 1966 LES ILES NORMANDES	1·00
	1970	
26.5.70 to 25.1.71	OBESITY SHORTENS LIFE TREAT IT SERIOUSLY (used on Medical Mailing International bulk postings only)	3·00
	1971	
1.2.71 to 17.2.72	STAMP OUT OVERWEIGHT (mainly used on Medical Mailing International bulk postings)	2·00

Dates of use	Wording	Price on cover
12.5.71 to 18.5.71	ROYAL LIVER FRIENDLY SOCIETY ANNUAL CONFERENCE COMMENCING 12 MAY 1971 GUERNSEY	50
11.9.71	GUERNSEY SCOUT ASSOCIATION DIAMOND JUBILEE 1911 1971	1·00

1972

10.4.72 to 15.4.72	GUERNSEY TSB 150 Years of Service SAVINGS WEEK 10–15 April, 1972	40

1975

5.5.75 to 10.5.75	OCCUPATION 1939–45 CHANNEL ISLANDS OFFICIAL HISTORY 8 MAY	25

1976

11.12.76 to 24.12.76	Beau Sejour LEISURE CENTRE OFFICIAL OPENING	25

1979

1.10.79 to 30.9.80	1969–1979 TEN SUCCESSFUL YEARS COLLECT GUERNSEY STAMPS NOW	25

1982

25.1.82 to 30.4.82	BBC RADIO GUERNSEY 1116kHz/269m .... on the Air from March 16th	25
12.5.82	ROYAL LIVER FRIENDLY SOCIETY ANNUAL CONFERENCE COMMENCING 12 MAY 1982 GUERNSEY	1·00
1.10.82 to 30.10.82	La Societe Guernesiaise Centenary Exhibition 7th–31st October 1982	50

1984

25.6.84 to 5.7.84	METHODISM ESTABLISHED IN GUERNSEY – 1784	50
6.7.84 to 21.7.84	N.S.P.C.C. CENTENARY YEAR 1984	50

1985

12.5.85 to 18.5.85	SMILE WEEK	50
27.8.85 to 7.9.85	The friendliest friendly society ANCIENT ORDER OF FORESTERS National Conference GUERNSEY 31st Aug – 7th Sept 1985	50

1987

1.7.87 to 31.7.87	GUERNSEY FESTIVAL SEPT. 6–20 1987	25
23.8.87 to 5.9.87	CHANNEL TELEVISION 25 YEARS OF BROADCASTING.	25
15.11.87 to 21.11.87	GUERNSEY DEAF AWARENESS WEEK	25

1988

4.4.88 to 14.4.88	"JESUS IS ALIVE!"	1·00
16.5.88	the samaritans 25th ANNIVERSARY 1983 – 1988 IN GUERNSEY (shows wrong year date)	1·00
17.5.88 to 29.5.88	the samaritans 25th ANNIVERSARY 1963 – 1988 IN GUERNSEY	50
26.6.88 to 2.7.88	Citizens Advice Bureau 1978 1988	50
8.8.88 to 21.8.88	WEST SHOW 17th–18th August 1988 75th ANNIVERSARY	50
14.9.88 to 17.9.88	GUERNSEY AUTOCROSS CLUB 1968 1988 20th ANNIVERSARY	50
28.9.88 to 4.10.88	1967 VENTURE SCOUTING 1988 21ST BIRTHDAY	50

Dates of use	Wording	Price on cover
13.11.88 to 19.11.88	Guille-Alles LIBRARY 1888 – 1988 EXTENSION CENTENARY	50
	1989	
15.1.89 to 19.1.89	WI 40 YEARS OF FUN AND FRIENDSHIP	50
21.3.89 to 28.3.89	PRIAULX LIBRARY 1889 1989 CENTENARY	50
2.5.89	GUERNSEY ENVIRONMENT 2000	25
	1990	
22.5.90	Telethon'90 CHANNEL TELEVISION	25
	1991	
5.5.91 to 11.5.91	THUMBS UP TO HEALTHIER LIVING	25

GUERNSEY SLOGANS FROM "PAID" DIE

The following three slogans were struck in red.

5.10.73 to 19.10.73	GUERNSEY issues Stained Glass Windows 24 Oct 1973 . .	10·00
23.11.73 to 11.1.74	GUERNSEY issues RNLI commemoratives 15 Jan 1974 . . .	10·00
30.1.74 to 16.2.74	GUERNSEY issues second series Low Value Definitives 2 APRIL 1974	10·00

(B2) Annual or Periodic Slogans
The wording of the slogan is followed by the dates of use.

POST EARLY for CHRISTMAS (holly leaves)	25
1.12.50 to 20.12.50	
1.12.51 to 20.12.51	
1.12.52 to 20.12.52	
2.12.53 to 21.12.53	
6.12.54 to 20.12.54	
9.12.55 to 21.12.55	
1.12.56 to 19.12.56	
9.12.57 to 18.12.57	
5.12.58 to 19.12.58	
5.12.59 to 20.12.59	
ARE YOU ON THE NEW VOTERS LISTS? –CHECK NOW . . .	25
17.1.51 to 24.1.51	
16.1.52 to 23.1.52	
16.1.53 to 24.1.53	
19.1.54 to 24.1.54	
30.11.54 to 5.12.54	
28.11.55 to 5.12.55	
2.12.59 to 4.12.59	
27.11.60 to 6.12.60	
1.12.61 to 7.12.61	
29.11.62 to 8.12.62	
BLOOD DONORS ARE STILL URGENTLY NEEDED	25
1.2.51 to 28.2.51	
1.9.53 to 3.10.53	
16.5.55 to 10.6.55	

CIVIL DEFENCE JOIN NOW 25
    1.11.51 to 30.11.51
    4.10.54 to 27.10.54
    12.9.55 to 7.10.55
    2.10.56 to 17.10.56
    26.9.57 to 18.10.57
POSTAGE ON LETTERS for EUROPE 4D 25
    1.9.52 to 1.10.52
    15.7.53 to 13.8.53
    1.6.54 to 30.6.54
PLEASE CHECK ADDRESS IF WRONG ADVISE WRITER .. 25
    3.11.53 to 29.11.53
    8.4.55 to 6.5.55
HAVE YOU TAKEN OUT YOUR LICENCE FOR RADIO – TV? 25
    3.1.57 to 30.1.57
    12.3.58 to 16.5.58
    4.3.59 to 24.3.59
    5.5.60 to 20.6.60
    16.4.61 to 14.5.61
    2.4.62 to 30.4.62
    1.4.63 to 29.4.63
    7.4.64 to 30.4.64
EXPRESS GOOD WISHES BY GREETINGS TELEGRAMS... 25
    1.2.58 to 12.3.58
    4.7.59 to 5.8.59
    2.9.60 to 12.9.60
    18.10.60 to 26.10.60
    30.7.61 to 20.8.61
CIVIL DEFENCE IS COMMON SENSE.................... 25
    1.10.58 to 31.10.58
    22.9.60 to 17.10.60
    17.9.62 to 12.10.62
CHEAP RATE TRUNK CALLS 6 PM – 6 AM & SUNDAY
AFTERNOONS.. 25
    17.11.58 to 24.11.58
    5.5.59 to 16.5.59
    1.11.59 to 12.11.59
PLEASE PUT YOUR CORRECT ADDRESS ON YOUR OWN
NOTEPAPER 25
    4.4.59 to 30.4.59
    1.2.60 to 29.2.60
KING GEORGE'S JUBILEE TRUST....................... 25
    4.6.60 to 28.6.60
    1.3.61 to 10.3.61
POST EARLY FOR CHRISTMAS (candle)................. 25
    7.12.60 to 21.12.60
    9.12.61 to 19.12.61
    9.12.62 to 20.12.62
    10.12.63 to 21.12.63
    15.12.64 to 20.12.64
    9.12.65 to 20.12.65
    1.12.66 to 21.12.66
    12.12.67 to 19.12.67
    8.12.68 to 20.12.68
Postal Order Gift Cards MAKE GAY GIFT MESSENGERS ... 25
    25.10.61 to 31.10.61
    1.11.62 to 29.11.62
6D RECORDED DELIVERY CHEAP EFFECTIVE 6D 25
    1.2.62 to 28.2.62
    1.9.62 to 16.9.62
    13.10.62 to 31.10.62
    6.9.63 to 28.9.63
    2.5.64 to 31.5.64

14.9.64 to 3.12.64
GUERNSEY THE BRITISH HOLIDAY ABROAD............ 25
    23.6.66 to 30.9.66
    1.11.66 to 30.11.66
    26.12.66 to 30.11.67
    26.12.67 to 30.11.68
    26.12.68 to 30.9.69
    2.10.69 to 12.12.69
FIRST CLASS MAIL (used to indicate that Guernsey $2\frac{1}{2}$p.
franked mail was entitled to First Class treatment in the
British postal system) .... 1·00
    21.5.71 to 2.7.71
    3.9.84 to 17.12.85
COLLECT GUERNSEY STAMPS For details write to 25
    1.10.80 to 30.1.82
    11.5.82 to 30.9.82
    1.11.82 to 23.6.84
    4.8.84 to 11.5.85
    19.9.85 to 28.2.86
COLLECT GUERNSEY STAMPS AND COINS (no rules).... 25
    1.3.86 to 20.6.87
    1.8.87 to 8.11.87
COLLECT GUERNSEY STAMPS AND COINS (rules top and
bottom)... 25
Since 9.11.87 when no individual slogan was in use
ST. PETER PORT (view) 25
    2.1.91 onwards

(C) Special Handstamps

The first special handstamp was introduced in 1967 for a philatelic occasion, the 23rd Annual Conference of the Postal History Society. It was rectangular and reproduced the Guernsey scroll (Type **G2**). Since then numerous other markings, circular or rectangular, have been used. Prices for covers are given below, each franked with postage stamps of the letter rate current at the time. Where the postage stamp is already catalogued at a higher figure in used condition, this should be *added* to the given price.

Markings for philatelic exhibitions overseas are listed separately for convenience.

GUERNSEY SPECIAL HANDSTAMPS

Dates of use	Event	Price on cover
21.10.67	POSTAL HISTORY SOCIETY 23rd ANNUAL CONFERENCE	1·50
9.2.70	Union Street/ Oldest Pillar box in British Isles..............	40
18.2.71	THE 30TH. ANNIVERSARY OF GUERNSEY'S FIRST POSTAGE STAMP	30
7.4.71	THE 30TH. ANNIVERSARY OF GUERNSEY'S FIRST HALFPENNY STAMP..................................	30
4.9.71	CLASS IV POWERBOAT CHAMPIONSHIPS NATIONAL FINALS	75
2.11.71	CHANNEL ISLANDS SPECIALISTS' SOC. 21st YEAR	50
25.1.72	SAVINGS BANK FOUNDER'S DAY 1822 1972	25

Dates of use	Event	Price on cover
22.5.72	SECOND WORLD CONFERENCE OF GUERNSEY BREEDERS	1·50
26.9.72 to 17.10.72	EXPOSITION GRANDE BRETAGNE – PARIS	25
21.1.73	No. 201 SQUADRON ROYAL AIR FORCE	25
15.5.73	GUERNSEY VARIETY CLUB CHARTER DAY	30
4.7.73	GUERNSEY–AMSTERDAM BY CHANNEL ISLANDS AIRWAYS	25
25.9.73	50th Anniversary Guernsey Air Service	25
1.5.74	COMMONWEALTH PARLIAMENTARY REGIONAL CONFERENCE	25
16.10.74	SIXTIETH ANNIVERSARY 201 SQUADRON ROYAL AIR FORCE 1914 – 1974	25
15.3.75	324 CHANNEL ISLANDS SPECIALISTS' SOCIETY 1950 1975	30
1.5.75	50th ANNIVERSARY HERM SUB POST OFFICE	70
9.5.75	30th ANNIVERSARY of the LIBERATION	30
28.5.75	visit of H.M. Queen Elizabeth The Queen Mother	75
1.9.75	GUERNSEY AIR RIFLE ASSOCIATION 75 ANNIVERSARY	30
8.9.75	EUROPEAN ARCHITECTURAL HERITAGE YEAR 1975	30
7.6.77	Royal Silver Jubilee	25
26.6.77	Police Open Day	25
28.10.77	Commissioning of H.M.S. GUERNSEY	25
15.9.78	60th ANNIVERSARY RAF 1918–1978	25
23.4.79	Rcn Congress & Exhibition Guernsey 23–27 April 1979	25
3.5.79 to 8.5.79	The Booksellers Association Of Great Britain & Ireland	25
22.9.79	79 Ambex Guernsey September 22–25	25
9.10.79	UNIVERSAL POSTAL UNION 100 Anniversary UPU Day	25
14.12.79	CCIC 5th ANNIVERSARY	25
22.4.80	SWEARING-IN OF NEW LIEUTENANT GOVERNOR	25
9.5.80	A Symposium on Channel Islands' Archaeology 9th–11th May	25
4.8.80	80th Birthday of Her Majesty Queen Elizabeth the Queen Mother	25
7.10.80	NEW BELFRY NOTRE DAME DU ROSAIRE	25
1.11.80	30th Anniversary Meeting Channel Islands Specialists' Society	25
4.11.80	FORSCHUNGSGEMEINSCHAFT CHANNEL ISLANDS FCGI–GOCI–5th ANNIVERSARY	25
3.12.80	The Institute of Bankers 1930–1980 Golden Jubilee	25
5.8.81	THE SALVATION ARMY CENTENARY	25
25.8.81	INTER-ISLAND TRANSPORT	25
2.10.81 to 4.10.81	British Philatelic Federation Sixty-Third Congress	25
3.10.81	GUERNSEY AERO CLUB Tenth International Air Rally	25
16.10.81	WORLD FOOD DAY	25
7.11.81	G.S.S.P.H.	25
15.4.82	NEW COIN ISSUE 20p	25
21.11.82	COMMEMORATING GUERNSEY'S OWN No. 201 SQN	25
5.3.83	Lions International District 105D 1983 CONVENTION	25
7.4.83	NEW £1 COIN ISSUE	25
19.9.83	AERODROME OWNERS ASSOCIATION 1983 Conference 19–22 Sept	25
15.11.83	TRADES FAIR 83 BEAU SEJOUR	25
15.11.83	GUERNSEY CHAMBER OF COMMERCE 175 years 1808–1983	25
3.5.84	SARNIA ARTS & CRAFTS CLUB 1924 – 1984 RETROSPECTIVE Guernsey Museum & Art Gallery	25
6.8.84	ANCIENT ORDER OF FORESTERS FRIENDLY SOCIETY 1834 – 1984	25

Dates of use	Event	Price on cover
18.9.84	THE MUSEUMS ASSOCIATION CONFERENCE 18–22 SEPTEMBER	25
16.10.84	70th Anniversary 201 Squadron R.A.F. 1914 – 1984	25
23.11.84	BBC CHILDREN IN NEED	25
22.1.85	GUERNSEY SEA ANGLERS' CLUB	25
22.5.85	Victor Hugo (signature) 1802 – 1885	25
1.7.85	National Trust of Guernsey 1960 – 1985	25
13.7.85	THE GLOBAL JUKE BOX LIVE AID	25
4.11.85	FORSCHUNGS-GEMEINSCHAFT CHANNEL ISLANDS 10 YEARS FGCI	25
2.6.86	CHRIST – OUR PEACE THE SALVATION ARMY	25
23.8.86	THE GUERNSEY SWIMMING CLUB	25
12.9.86	GUERNSEY PHILATELIC SOCIETY 1936 – 1986	25
10.9.87	ISLANDS GAMES GUERNSEY	25
5.5.89	1939 – 1989 GUERNSEY'S OWN NO. 201 SQN	25
5.9.89	GWR STEAMSHIP CENTENARY	25
5.12.89	THE UNIVERSAL FOURPENNY POST 150th ANNIVERSARY	25
28.5.90	CTV CHANNEL TELEVISION ITV TELETHON 90	25
4.8.90	HER MAJESTY QUEEN ELIZABETH THE QUEEN MOTHER 90TH BIRTHDAY	25
2.7.91	ROLEX SWAN REGATTA	25

(D) Philatelic Exhibition Markings

Guernsey participates in many philatelic exhibitions around the world and special markings are applied to covers (franked with Guernsey stamps) presented for postmarking. (H) signifies a handstamp, the remainder are cachets.

Dates of use	Event	Price on cover
9.3.73 to 11.3.73	Interpex, New York	1·25
4.7.73	Apex, Manchester (H)	1·00
7.6.74 to 16.6.74	Internaba, Basel	60
4.4.75	Espana 75, Madrid (H)	60
6.6.75	Arphila, Paris (H)	75
1976	Interphil 76	75
20.8.76	Hafnia 76, Copenhagen (H)	60
29.10.76 to 1.11.76	Briefmarken-Messe, Essen	4·00
1976	Italia	75
28.8.77 to 4.9.77	San Marino	50
7.10.77 to 13.10.77	Espamer, Barcelona	50
20.5.78 to 25.5.78	Naposta	40
9.6.78	Capex, Toronto (H)	40
26.8.78 to 28.8.78	Riccione	40
8.9.78 to 10.9.78	Torino	40
20.9.78 to 24.9.78	Eurphila, Rome	40
1.11.78 to 5.11.78	Essen	50
10.3.79 to 12.3.79	Recklinghausen	30
16.3.79 to 18.3.79	Stamphilex, New York (H)	40
24.10.79 to 25.10.79	Mannheim	30

Dates of use	Event	Price on cover
24.2.81 to 28.2.81	Stampex, London	30
28.4.81 to 3.5.81	NAPOSTA, Frankfurt	30
22.5.81 to 31.5.81	WIPA, Vienna	30
29.9.81 to 2.10.81	BPE, London	30
19.11.81 to 22.11.81	ASDA, New York	30
23.2.82 to 28.2.82	Stampex, London	30
28.4.82 to 2.5.82	Essen	30
11.6.82 to 21.6.82	Philexfrance, Paris	30
6.10.82 to 9.10.82	BPE, London	30
18.11.82 to 21.11.82	ASDA, New York	30
15.2.83 to 20.2.83	Stampex, London	30
21.5.83 to 29.5.83	Tembol, Basle	30
27.10.83 to 30.10.83	BPE, London	30
17.11.83 to 20.11.83	National Postage Stamp Show, New York	30
6.3.84 to 11.3.84	Stampex, London	30
27.4.84 to 6.5.84	Espana, Madrid	30
26.5.84 to 31.5.84	Essen	30
16.10.84 to 20.10.84	BPE/Stampex, London	30
26.2.85 to 3.3.85	Super Stampex, London	30
10.4.85 to 13.4.85	Essen	30
28.8.85 to 7.9.85	Stockholmia	30
4.3.86 to 9.3.86	Super Stampex, London	30
22.5.86 to 1.6.86	Ameripex, Chicago	30
9.6.86 to 20.6.86	Stamplink (M.V. *Earl Granville*)	30
6.10.86 to 25.10.86	Hafnia, Copenhagen	30
14.10.86 to 19.10.86	BPE, London	30
30.10.86 to 2.11.86	ASDA	30
3.3.87 to 8.3.87	Super Stampex, London	30
6.3.87 to 8.3.87	Interpex, New York	30
13.6.87 to 21.6.87	Capex	30
22.9.87 to 27.9.87	Autumn Stampex, London	30
16.10.87 to 25.10.87	Hafnia, Copenhagen	30
22.10.87 to 25.10.87	ASDA, New York	30
30.10.87 to 1.11.87	Stamp Expo, New York	30
6.11.87 to 8.11.87	Stamp Expo, Anaheim	30
6.1.88 to 17.1.88	Boat Show, London	30
1.3.88 to 6.3.88	Super Stampex, London	30
14.4.88 to 17.4.88	Essen	30
1.6.88 to 12.6.88	Finlandia	30
27.9.88 to 2.10.88	Autumn Stampex, London	30
18.10.88 to 23.10.88	Filacept, The Hague	30
20.10.88 to 23.10.88	ASDA	30
28.10.88 to 30.10.88	Anaheim	30
28.2.89 to 5.3.89	Spring Stampex, London	30
7.7.89 to 17.7.89	Philexfrance, Paris	30
17.10.89 to 22.10.89	Autumn Stampex, London	30
8.11.89 to 11.11.89	ASDA	30
17.11.89 to 3.12.89	World Stamp Expo, Washington	30
12.1.90 to 14.1.90	Orcoexpo, Los Angeles	30
27.2.90 to 4.3.90	Spring Stampex, London	30
19.4.90 to 22.4.90	Essen	30
3.5.90 to 13.5.90	Stamp World, London	30
2.6.90 to 10.6.90	Belgica, Brussels	30
24.8.90 to 2.9.90	New Zealand, Auckland	30
16.10.90 to 21.10.90	Autumn Stampex, London	30
1.11.90 to 4.11.90	ASDA, New York	30
26.2.91 to 3.3.91	Spring Stampex, London	30

(E) "First Day of Issue" Markings

A 2½d. Regional stamp (S.G.6) issued in Guernsey on 8 June 1964 saw the introduction of the general machine cancellation of Great Britain. This is Type **A**, having the words "FIRST DAY OF ISSUE" on an envelope and printed as a slogan to the right of a circular datestamp inscribed "GUERNSEY" and containing an arc. After postal independence Type **A** saw further use, though the datestamp now read "GUERNSEY POST OFFICE", with the Brock issue on 1 December 1969. On 12 August 1970 (Agriculture issue) and later the envelope slogan was transposed to the left. A 38mm diameter handstamp (Type **B**), similar to that issued for Jersey, was used between 13 September 1965 and 20 February 1967, except for the Battle of Hastings issue in 1966 when a 21mm diameter mark with "CHANNEL ISLANDS" above the date was used (Type **C**). Type **D**, a 26mm rubber handstamp was introduced on 24 April 1967. It reads "FIRST DAY OF ISSUE" around the top and "CHANNEL ISLANDS" around the bottom with the date and "GUERNSEY" across the centre in two lines. Two different sizes of lettering have been seen on examples used for the Regional definitives on 4 September 1978.

With postal independence on 1 October 1969 Guernsey introduced a new circular datestamp, Type **E**. This was 23½mm in diameter inscribed in upper and lowercase with "Guernsey Post Office" around the top and "First Day of Issue" around the foot. The date appears in one line in the centre, with "Philatelic/Bureau" in small letters below. There were a number of different settings of this type which remained in use until 1989.

A similar mark, but with all inscriptions in capitals, was used between 2 August 1977 and 13 February 1979 (Type **F**). An unusual First Day of Issue mark appeared for the Europa series of 22 May 1981. This was without the line around the circumference and did not show "Philatelic Bureau" in the centre (Type **G**).

A

B

C

Guernsey first-day cancellations

Pictorial Handstamps. Specially designed cancellations, often pictorial, have been used on first day covers for many later issues beginning with the 1971 Decimal definitives.

For prices of first day covers bearing complete sets see *Collect Channel Islands and Isle of Man Stamps.*

16. Airmails and Hovercraft Mail

Early Airmail Flights (to 1969)

Ballons Montés from Paris are known addressed to Guernsey and Jersey, as are covers flown from London to Windsor on the 1911 Coronation Aerial Post, but the first airmail from the Channel Islands was flown from the French Navy's seaplane base in St. Peter Port, Guernsey in 1917. The various experimental and official airmail services between 1917 and 1969 are described below, and are listed and priced at the end of this section.

French Seaplane Base in Guernsey, 1917–18. A French seaplane base was established in Guernsey at the southern end of St. Peter Port harbour in July 1917. Huts were erected by the Royal Navy and a Bessonau shed was sent from France.

The base was under the command of Lieutenant de Vaisseau Le Cour Grandmaison. There were three pilots (Lambert, Bourgault and Sylvestre) of whom one was an officer, and three observers (Rolin, Parmentier and Boissand). It was intended to have twelve seaplanes at the base but only two were sent in July. In September it was decided that the strength of the base be raised to sixteen patrol aircraft.

Bad weather in the winter caused real difficulties. On 19 December 1917 the motor launch was lost. The commander of the Normandy squadrons was unable to supply the torpedo boat that the base needed. The position was bad for take-off and landing and, because of the winds, the roofs of the portable hangars were in a very bad state. In view of this the Commandant recommended that the base be transferred to Cherbourg.

In January 1918 the strength of the base was eleven Telliers and ten F.B.A.s. In February and March activity was much reduced because of damage to the crane.

Enseigne de Vaisseau Flandrin replaced Lieutenant Le Cour de Grandmaison as commanding officer of the base.

The seaplane base remained in Guernsey until December 1918, when the aircraft were flown to Cherbourg and the 150 men attached to the base left the island.

Four cachets were used on mail sent from the base, which was carried to Cherbourg by seaplanes of the squadron and posted there.

The first cachet was of the general French naval type inscribed "MARINE FRANCAISE SERVICE A LA MER" around an anchor. This is quite common used elsewhere, but is rare from Guernsey where an example is known dated as early as 22 July 1917.

Before moving to Guernsey the squadron had been based at Venice. When transferred the unit made use of their existing cachet (similar to Type **2**), but with the previous location, possibly "VENICE", removed. Examples are known on two cards sent in September 1917 by Quartermaster Engineer G. Sauvée from "Centre Aviation Maritime Guernesey" to Cherbourg.

The third cachet (Type **1**) is unframed and reads, in three lines, "CENTRE d'AVIATION/MARITIME/de GUERNESEY". An example is known struck in violet on a card dated 1 December 1917 bearing Christmas greetings. The fourth cachet has an anchor in the centre and "ESCADRILLE D'AVIATION MARITIME DE GUERNSEY" in a double circle (Type **2**). This is known struck in blue on several cards from members of the squadron and on a cover addressed to Croydon bearing a British stamp. One example, dating from 1919, is known used at Cherbourg after the unit had returned to France.

U.S. army engineers served at the base from August 1918. Covers sent by them are often franked with British stamps and cancelled by the American APO at Cherbourg.

Such mail may also carry the Type **2** cachet. It is believed that the American unit may not have left the island until March 1919.

CENTRE d'AVIATION
MARITIME
DE GUERNESEY.

(1)   (2)

Southampton—Guernsey Flight, 1919. The earliest recorded flight from England to the Channel Islands was on 5 October 1919, during the Railway Strike period, when an unsuccessful attempt was made to carry *Lloyds Weekly News* from Southampton to Guernsey, the pilot of the machine being compelled to alight on the sea near Alderney. Papers were imprinted "By Seaplane, Special Edition", and after the accident were overprinted with a message from the pilot apologising for his failure.

Early Air Mail Covers. Covers with "By Air Mail" stickers posted from Jersey (and possibly Guernsey) in 1929 or in the early 1930s are very occasionally seen. These are usually addressed to India, being carried by sea to England and then onwards from Croydon Airport. The first flight to Karachi was on 30 March 1929. Such covers are scarce (*from* £60).

Experimental Flight, 1935. In an effort to demonstrate to the postal authorities how great a saving of time could be effected by carrying mail by air to the Channel Islands, Whoopee Sports Ltd. had a small quantity of covers (less than 100) addressed to Roborough Aerodrome, Plymouth, and posted locally at 5 p.m. on Friday, 27 June 1935. These were flown to Jersey at noon on 28 June and arrived at 1.15 p.m., landing on the beach. The letters were then re-stamped and re-addressed with a grey label covering the old address and were re-posted in Jersey, receiving the 4.15 p.m. cancellation on the same day. The service, however, proved unsuitable for mail-carrying purposes, due to the non-existence of an aerodrome and the fact that the time-table varied with the tides.

Official Flight, 1937. An aerodrome was constructed in Jersey in 1937 and a contract for the transport of first-class mail was awarded to Jersey Airways, the first flights taking place on 1 June. The plane from Jersey left at 6.25 a.m. and arrived at Southampton at 7.37 a.m. with 335lb of mail. That from Southampton left at 7.50 a.m., arriving at Jersey at 8.50 a.m. with 229lb of mail.

An angular cachet (Type **3**) reading "JERSEY AIRWAYS LTD/FIRST/AIR/MAIL/ FLIGHT/1ST JUNE/1937" was applied to covers handled at the Company's offices in London, Jersey or Southampton. Each office used a distinctive coloured ink as follows: London—green, Jersey—blue, Southampton—violet. A similar cachet struck in red was used by a well-known dealer, A. Phillips, on letters from Newport, Monmouthshire. The Jersey and Southampton covers were also endorsed "FROM JERSEY" or "FROM SOUTHAMPTON" in the same coloured ink as the cachet.

Covers with meter stamps of Jersey Airways are scarcer than those with adhesives. The slogan attached to the Jersey Airways meter stamp reads "JERSEY (emblem) AIRWAYS/VICTORIA RLY STATION PHONE VICTORIA 5692/5/1½ HRS – – LONDON – FARE £5/OR FROM/EXETER – SOUTHAMPTON – BRIGHTON". After "£5" the letters "RTN" are inserted vertically in tiny type.

(3)

(*Illustrations reduced*)

(4)

(5)

Covers addressed to the town office of Jersey Airways Ltd. received on arrival a straight-line cachet reading "for Jersey Airways Limited/1 JUN 1937" in blue. Covers addressed to the London office of the airline received on arrival a circular cachet in black reading LONDON/1 JUN 1937/OFFICE.

Guernsey Flights, 1939. The Southampton–Guernsey service by Guernsey Airways Ltd. commenced on 8 May 1939, a plane leaving Southampton at 8 a.m. and arriving at Guernsey at 8.59 a.m. Flown covers usually bear the 11.45 p.m. postmark of Southampton dated 7 May 1939, but twenty covers dispatched from London bear the 12.45 a.m. postmark of London dated 8 May 1939. Some covers received the cachets shown as Types **4** and **5**, the rectangular cachet usually being struck in purple and the circular in green. The aircraft was RMA G-ACZP and the pilot B. Walker.

The first flight from Guernsey took place on 22 May 1939. The plane left Guernsey at 6.28 a.m. and arrived at Southampton at 7.25 a.m. The pilot was J. B. W. Pugh. The usual postmark seen on flown covers is St. Peter Port, Guernsey, 5 a.m. 22 May 1939. Covers have been seen bearing both cachets (Types **4** and **5**) with the dates altered, struck very faintly in black. Privately printed souvenir covers of several kinds exist.

Jersey–Guernsey Flight, 1939. Also on 22 May, mail was flown for the first time from Jersey to Guernsey, the plane leaving Jersey at 6 a.m. and arriving at Guernsey 15 minutes later. No special cachets were applied and genuine flown covers are rare. They normally bear the 5 a.m. Jersey postmark of 22 May 1939. The aircraft was RMA G-ADVK and the pilot J. B. W. Pugh.

The return flight from Guernsey to Jersey did not take place until 10 July 1939. Details of time of departure, etc., are not known. Very little mail was carried owing to inadequate notice being given of the institution of the service. The usual postmark is that of Guernsey timed 5 a.m. on 10 July 1939. Regular services continued until war was declared on 3 September 1939, when all air services between Southampton and the Islands ceased.

Shoreham–Channel Islands Service, 1939. A service between Shoreham and the Islands was resumed on 8 November 1939, running to Jersey and Guernsey on Mondays, Wednesdays and Fridays, and from the Islands on Tuesdays, Thursdays and Saturdays. Daily services operated from 11 December, until the German Occupation on 1 July 1940, when all services were suspended.

Resumption of Air Services, 1945. On 10 September 1945 air services between Southampton and Jersey and Guernsey were resumed in both directions, and also the inter-island services. Special souvenir covers were prepared and were flown from Southampton at 6.30 a.m., Jersey at 9.20 a.m., and Guernsey at 10.05 a.m. Some covers received a circular cachet (Type **6**) in purple applied in Jersey on mail to and from the island, or a rectangular one (Type **7**) in blue applied to mail entering Guernsey. Some covers sent from Guernsey to Jersey also received the rare "GUERNSEY CH. IS. PARCEL DEPOT" cancellation (Type **G34**) dated "10 SP 45".

(6) (7)

Guernsey–Alderney Service, 1946. The first flight from Guernsey to Alderney took place on 18 June 1946 and the return flight was made on the same day. No special markings were applied to letters flown, of which there were eleven from Guernsey to Alderney and forty from Alderney to Guernsey, but they were initialled by the Sub-Postmaster and backstamped with the Alderney datestamp.

B.E.A. Take-over, 1947. When the airlines were nationalised in 1947 the Channel Islands services were taken over by British European Airways and the rectangular datestamps of the Jersey, Guernsey and Southampton offices were applied to letters carried on some flights under the new regime from 1 April. The Jersey stamp was in violet and was lettered A at the bottom; the Guernsey stamp was in violet and was lettered T at the bottom; and the Southampton one was in red and was lettered A at the bottom. Last-day covers under the old service on 31 March have a circular cachet of Channel Islands Airways. This was the parent company of both Jersey and Guernsey Airways and was formed in 1934.

First Alderney–Southampton Direct Mail, 1947. On 20 May 1947 a direct flight was made from Alderney to Southampton and twelve letters were carried by arrangement with the pilot and the Sub-Postmaster of Alderney. They were autographed by the pilot and posted on arrival at Southampton.

Scottish Airlines Flight, 1952. Scottish Airlines inaugurated a regular passenger service between Prestwick and Jersey in the summer of 1952, and on the first flight on 14 June 1952 the pilot, Captain J. C. Grant, carried seven letters which were posted on arrival in Jersey. The covers were stamped in four lines in violet "SCOTTISH AIRLINES/PRESTWICK–JERSEY/FIRST FLIGHT/14 JUN 1952" and were signed by the pilot. Covers on the return flight bear a three-line cachet in black "SCOTTISH AIRWAYS/JERSEY–PRESTWICK/14 JUN 1952".

B.E.A. Airway Letter Services, 1953. On 20 October 1953 British European Airways extended their Airways Letter Service to the Channel Islands, using the then current B.E.A. stamps for prepayment of their charges. The rates charged were 7d. for letters up to 2oz, 1s. from 2oz to 4oz, and 1s. 6d. from 4oz to 1lb, in addition to the ordinary inland postage. Letters had to be properly stamped and handed into the B.E.A. office or airport endorsed "To be called for" or "To be posted on arrival". The letters were then flown to the destination and those marked "To be posted on arrival" were dropped into the nearest pillar box and the postage stamps were cancelled by the Post Office. A letter from London to Jersey would have the B.E.A. stamp cancelled in London and the postage stamp would be cancelled in Jersey by B.E.A., either with the rectangular datestamp of the local office, with a rubber stamp reading "CANCELLED", or by pen. The flights were made between Jersey and London, Guernsey and London, Jersey and Guernsey, and Guernsey and Alderney.

On 25 November 1953 the B.E.A. rates were raised to 8d., 1s. 2d., and 1s. 9d. and new stamps were issued. The rates were raised to 9d., 1s. 3d. and 1s. 11d. on 1 September 1954, using stamps of the same design with the values printed in black instead of in the colour of the stamps.

On 27 June 1956 the rates were increased to 10d., 1s. 5d., and 2s. 2d. and new stamps of smaller format were issued. When the rates were raised again on 1 July 1957, to 11d., 1s. 6d., and 2s. 4d., stamps of the same design were used.

The reason for the almost annual increases in rates was the increased railway freight charges. The charge for airway letters must be the same as that for railway letters and when British Rail put their charges up the Postmaster General insisted that British European Airways did the same.

Only during the 1953 and 1954 rate increases were first day covers flown between London and Guernsey and London and Jersey, although, of course, genuine commercial covers can be found flown on later dates.

Because of difficulties with H.M. Customs at London Airport, British European Airways were forced to suspend their Airway Letter Service to London from Jersey and Guernsey from 24 July to 2 September 1956, and then discontinue it altogether. There was no embargo on the carriage of letters to the Islands from Britain. Some covers handed in at Guernsey on 24 July were marked "Received before embargo" and were carried in the normal way.

The rate was increased from 11d. to 1s. on 4 October 1961 and 100 covers were flown from London to Jersey. They bear the datestamps of the Air Mail Branch, London, and Jersey Airport.

A new series of Airway Letter stamps was issued in 1964 and covers bearing the 1s. stamp were flown from London to Jersey on 27 May.

A further series was issued in 1970 and letters bearing the 3s. 7d. stamp were flown from London to Guernsey and Jersey on 1 May. On 15 February 1971 covers with decimal 18p, 21p and 26p stamps were flown to Guernsey and Jersey.

Throughout its existence B.E.A. used several four-lined boxed or unboxed datestamps to cancel the Airway Letter Service stamps, either at the Guernsey and Jersey airports or at the town offices. Although each datestamp differed slightly they were all of a similar design which read "B.E.A./date/GUERNSEY (or JERSEY)/AIRPORT" and "B.E.A./date/JERSEY (or GUERNSEY)/TOWN". Violet was the normal colour of ink, but black and red are also recorded. Another one read similarly for Alderney.

Cambrian Airways Flight, 1964. On 2 December 1964 Cambrian Airways carried letters from Bristol to Guernsey and from Cardiff to Jersey. Special 1s. Cambrian Airways Air Letter stamps were used.

Helicopter Flight, 1965. On 1 November 1965 B.E.A. carried 100 covers from Jersey to Guernsey and 100 covers from Guernsey to Jersey by helicopter. They carried 1s. B.E.A. Airway Letter stamps cancelled at the airports. The covers from Jersey had a black rectangular cachet featuring a helicopter and inscribed FIRST SCHEDULED HELICOPTER FLIGHT/JERSEY – GUERNSEY. The covers from Guernsey had a similar cachet in green inscribed GUERNSEY – JERSEY.

At this time, Jersey airport was closed to aeroplanes for four months for the extension of runways so a helicopter service was established by B.E.A. and B.U.A. using a 25-seater Sikorsky S-61NG-ASNM of B.E.A. Helicopters Ltd. This made three round trips daily between Jersey and Guernsey, connecting with scheduled services at Guernsey Airport.

British United Airways Flight, 1966. On 5 August 1966 British United Airways carried a dozen covers from Paris to Jersey. They were franked by French 60c. stamps and carried a red boxed cachet reading "BRITISH UNITED/PARIS JERSEY/5 Aout 1966". On arrival in Jersey they received the British United datestamp of Jersey Airport.

Anniversary of First Airmail, 1969. To commemorate the thirtieth anniversary of the first airmail from Guernsey to England, special covers were flown on 22 May by L. E. Batchelor in a Cessna 172. The aircraft first called at Jersey to carry mail from Jersey to Guernsey and there picked up mail for England. The flight terminated at Thruxton. There were 150 matched pairs of covers signed by the pilot and a further 350 unsigned covers. A few of the original 1939 covers were also reflown.

Inauguration of New Postal Administrations, 1969. To commemorate the inauguration of the new Jersey and Guernsey Postal Administrations, British European Airways carried 1000 covers from each island to Heathrow. Both covers carry the B.E.A. insignia and the inscription "1st October 1969 British European Airways Commemorate the Inauguration of the States of Jersey Postal Administration (States of Guernsey Post Office)".

The Jersey covers bear the Jersey 2s. 6d. stamp featuring the airport and were cancelled with the special Jersey first-day postmark. They also have the boxed B.E.A. Jersey Airport datestamp of 1 October 1969. The Guernsey covers have the Guernsey $\frac{1}{2}$d., 1d., 1$\frac{1}{2}$d. and 5d. stamps cancelled with the special Day of Issue postmark.

Modern Flights (from 1971 onwards)

The flights from 1971 onwards are too numerous to describe in detail and, with certain exceptions, are less important. They are not included in the priced list at the end of this Section.

Hovermail Flights

Channel Islands hovermail first started in 1969. The Hovermail Collectors' Club organised the majority of these first flights and, with one exception, less than 100 covers were carried on each flight. The one exception was the visit to the Islands by VT1.001 of Vosper Thorneycroft Ltd. in 1971. This craft carried out six special flights and several thousands of dealers' covers were on board although the craft also carried a very limited number of private covers and official mail of Hovertravel Ltd.

From 1976, hovermail posted in the waters around the Channel Islands has been dealt with in the same manner as paquebot mail, the first usage of mail posted at sea on board hovercraft. Apart from this paquebot mail which has been handled in accordance with U.P.U. regulations, no official mail has been carried either to or from the Channel Islands by hovercraft. There have been no organized flights with special cachets since 1978.

JERSEY AIRMAIL COVERS

*Inter-island flight. For convenience of reference the cover is listed under *both* islands and marked with an asterisk.

1870

Ballons Montés from Paris, addressed to Jersey . . . .   *from* £350

1911

9/15.9.11   Coronation Aerial Post, London to Windsor, addressed to Jersey *from* 80·00

1935

28.6.35   Whoopee Sports Ltd. experimental flight £100

1937

1.6.37	Jersey Airways Ltd. (Type **3**). Blue	15·00
1.6.37	As above, but violet (Southampton)	15·00
1.6.37	As above, but green (London)	20·00
1.6.37	As above, but red (Newport, Mon., applied by A. Phillips)	10·00
1.6.37	Jersey Airways London. Meter stamp on first flight cover	15·00
1.6.37	"For Jersey Airways Limited/1 June 1937" straight-line cachet	18·00
1.6.37	LONDON/1 JUN 1937/OFFICE circular cachet. Black	12·00

1938

9.7.38   First Flight Paris–Dinard–Jersey by Air France. No cachet . . . .   30·00

1939

22.5.39*	Jersey to Guernsey inter-island, no cachets	35·00
22.5.39*	As above, but signed by pilot (J. B. W. Pugh)	40·00
10.6.39*	Guernsey to Jersey inter-island, no cachets	40·00

1945

10.9.45	Resumption of air services souvenir cover, no cachets	15·00
10.9.45	Circular cachet JERSEY/AIRWAYS (Type **6**). Purple	20·00

1946

First Flight of Bristol Wayfarer, Filton–Jersey. Signed by pilot, J. Pegg   40·00

1947   10·00

1.4.47   B.E.A./JERSEY/A rectangular datestamp. Violet. In use from this date

1948

10.5.48   B.E.A. Advertising letter sent in f.d.c. of Channel Islands Liberation
Issue. Envelope imprinted BRITISH EUROPEAN AIRWAYS . . . . .   12·00

1952

14.6.52	SCOTTISH AIRLINES/PRESTWICK–JERSEY. Violet	45·00
14.6.52	SCOTTISH AIRWAYS/JERSEY–PRESTWICK, unframed. Black	35·00

1953

B.E.A./JERSEY/AIRPORT, boxed datestamp. Black, red or violet . . .   8·00

1954

1.9.54   National Institute of Oceanography card dropped in the Atlantic by
R.A.F. washed ashore on Jersey . . . .   40·00

1964

17.7.64	Large double-circle FREEDOM/GROUP datestamp, on cover to Jersey	40·00
2.12.64	First Flight by Cambrian Airways from Cardiff to Jersey. With special 1s. Airway Letter stamp cancelled with boxed Cambrian Airways Ltd. cachet	25·00

1965

1.11.65	FIRST SCHEDULED HELICOPTER FLIGHT/JERSEY–GUERNSEY and helicopter. Black	35·00

1966

5.8.66	BRITISH UNITED/PARIS JERSEY boxed datestamp. Red	40·00

1968

28.5.68	B.E.A./JERSEY/AIRPORT boxed datestamp. Blue. BRITISH EUROPEAN AIRWAYS/FRET/ORLY circular cachet. Violet	30·00

1969

22.5.69*	Jersey–Guernsey–England Airmail 30th Anniversary Flight	10·00
31.5.69	Re-introduction of Jersey to Portsmouth service. CHANNEL AIRWAYS/PORTSMOUTH AIRPORT, HANTS boxed cachet	12·00
31.5.69	Re-introduction of Portsmouth to Jersey Service. CHANNEL AIRWAYS/PORTSMOUTH AIRPORT, HANTS boxed cachet	12·00
13.7.69	Jersey–Caen Flight. BRITISH UNITED/ISLAND AIRWAYS/JERSEY AIRPORT datestamp in black and FIRST FLIGHT/JERSEY CAEN unframed cachet	6·00
13.7.69	As above, but with unframed cachet PREMIER VOL/CAEN JERSEY and date. Black	6·00
1.10.69	B.E.A. commemoration of new postal administration. Boxed B.E.A./JERSEY/AIRPORT datestamp in violet on f.d.c. to London	5·00
2.12.69	50th Anniversary England–Australia Flight, with Inauguration stamp and special circular cancellation	*from* 15·00

1970

24.2.70	Jersey–Derby Flight. British Midland Airways/JERSEY unframed datestamp	5·00
28.3.70	Plymouth–Jersey Flight WESTWARD/AIRWAYS LTD unframed cachet. Black	5·00
29.3.70	Jersey–Plymouth Flight WESTWARD/AIRWAYS LTD unframed cachet. Black	5·00
1.5.70	New B.E.A. Airway Letter stamps (3s. 7d., 4s. 3d., 5s. 2d.) on flown cover Heathrow–Jersey	2·50
2.5.70	Jersey–Manchester Flight BRITISH UNITED/JERSEY/AIRPORT boxed datestamp in blue with "409" in triangle (Type **J78b**)	6·00
7.5.70	R.A.F. Flight. Red oval datestamp H.Q. OPERATIONS WING/R.A.F. WADDINGTON and "409" in triangle (Type **J78b**)	12·00
8/9.5.70	Plymouth–Guernsey–Jersey Flight by Aurigny Air Services, with Aurigny Airport cachets in blue. Signed by pilots	11·00
9.5.70	25th Anniversary of Liberation of Channel Islands f.d.c. flown by B.E.A.	8·00
5.6.70	Jersey–Quimper Flight. Four-line unframed cachet in black	10·00
20.6.70	25th Anniversary of re-opening of civil airways in Jersey. B.E.A./JERSEY/AIRPORT	1·50
13.9.70	Jersey–Lessay Flight. Boxed BRITISH/ISLAND AIRWAYS/JERSEY AIRPORT datestamp in black	10·00

GUERNSEY AIRMAIL COVERS

*Inter-island flight. For convenience of reference the cover is listed under *both* islands and marked with an asterisk.

1870

Ballons Montés from Paris, addressed to Guernsey .... *from* £1500

1911

9/15.9.11   Coronation Aerial Post London to Windsor, addressed to Guernsey
from 80·00

16.9.11   Coronation Aerial Post Windsor to London addressed to Guernsey
from £120

1917

Circular ESCADRILLE D'AVIATION MARITIME DE. Violet £400
Circular MARINE FRANCAISE/SERVICE A LA MER £350
CENTRE d'AVION/MARITIME/de GUERNESEY three line. Violet
(Type **1**) £400

1918

Circular ESCADRILLE D'AVIATION MARITIME DE GUERNESEY
(Type **2**). Blue and violet.................................. £300
U.S. Army Post Office MPES 768 .... £200

1919

5.10.19   Newspaper with BY/SEAPLANE/SPECIAL/EDITION .... 50·00

1939

8.5.39   Southampton–Guernsey GUERNSEY AIRWAYS (Type **4**). Purple or
black .... 15·00
8.5.39   Southampton–Guernsey GUERNSEY AIRWAYS (Type **5**). Green or
black .... 15·00
8.5.39   Southampton–Guernsey. Without cachet, but signed by pilot
(B. Walker) .... 18·00
22.5.39   Guernsey–Southampton. Souvenir cover .... 12·00
22.5.39   As above but with Type **4** and Type **5** cachets .... 20·00
22.5.39   As above, without cachets, but signed by pilot (J. B. W. Pugh) .... 20·00
22.5.39*   Jersey to Guernsey inter-island, no cachets..................... 25·00
22.5.39*   As above, but signed by pilot (J. B. W. Pugh) .... 35·00
10.6.39*   Guernsey to Jersey inter-island, no cachets..................... 35·00

1945

10.9.45   Resumption of Air services Souvenir cover, no cachets............ 12·00
10.9.45   JERSEY AIRWAYS (Type **7**). Blue or violet .... 15·00

1946

18.6.46*   Guernsey to Alderney, no cachets £100
18.6.46*   Alderney to Guernsey, no cachets .... 80·00

1947

31.3.47   Large double-circle CHANNEL ISLANDS/AIRWAYS/GUERNSEY
OFFICE. Black .... 12·00
1.4.47   B.E.A. GUERNSEY T rectangular datestamp. Violet. In use from this
date .... 8·00
1.4.47   B.E.A. SOUTHAMPTON A rectangular datestamp. Red. In use from
this date .... 8·00

1953

B.E.A./GUERNSEY/AIRPORT boxed datestamp. Violet or black.... 7·00
B.E.A./GUERNSEY/TOWN boxed datestamp. Violet or black ...... 7·00

1954

7.8.54	Herm Island B.E.A. Feeder Service.	35·00
7.8.54	As above, but with manuscript "Delayed by Storm"	40·00
1.9.54	National Institute of Oceanography card dropped in Atlantic by R.A.F. washed ashore on Guernsey	50·00
1.9.65	As above, but washed ashore on Sark.	£100

1964

	B.E.A./GUERNSEY/AIRPORT datestamp, unframed. Black	5·00
2.12.64	First Flight by Cambrian Airways from Bristol to Guernsey. With 1s. Airway Letter stamp cancelled with boxed CAMBRIAN AIRWAYS LTD. datestamp	15·00
2.12.64	Cambrian Airways Flight from Guernsey to Jersey. With 1s. Airway Letter stamp cancelled with B.E.A. GUERNSEY AIRPORT unframed datestamp	15·00

1965

1.11.65	FIRST SCHEDULED HELICOPTER FLIGHT/GUERNSEY–JERSEY and helicopter. Green	15·00

1969

31.3.69	B.E.A./GUERNSEY/AIRPORT, large boxed datestamp in violet and B.E.A./LAST FLIGHT/JERSEY–GUERNSEY, unframed cachet in black. On last inter-island flight by B.E.A.	12·00
22.5.69*	Guernsey-England Airmail 30th Anniversary Flight to Thruxton.	12·00
1.10.69	B.E.A. commemoration of new postal administration on f.d.c. to London. Circular first day postmark	5·00

1970

1.5.70	New B.E.A. Airway Letter stamps (3s. 7d., 4s. 3d., 5s. 2d.) on flown cover Heathrow–Guernsey.	2·50
9.5.70	25th Anniversary of Liberation of Channel Islands f.d.c. flown by B.E.A.	8·00
10.11.70	Manston–Guernsey flight by Invicta Air Cargo. With single-line INVICTA AIR CARGO (1969) LIMITED. Black.	9·00

ALDERNEY AIRMAIL COVERS

*Inter-island flight. For convenience of reference the cover is listed under *both* islands and marked with an asterisk.

1946

| 18.6.46* | Guernsey to Alderney, no cachets .... | £100 |
| 18.6.46* | Alderney to Guernsey, no cachets .... | 80·00 |

1947

| 20.5.47 | First Flight Alderney–Southampton .... | 45·00 |

1953

| 20.10.53 | B.E.A./ALDERNEY/TOWN boxed datestamp. Violet .... | 10·00 |

1954

| 1.9.54 | National Institute of Oceanography card dropped in Atlantic by R.A.F. washed ashore on Alderney................................. | £100 |

1970

| 16.11.70 | Inaugural Flight by Aurigny Air Services, Alderney–Cherbourg and return. With unframed cachet AURIGNY/date/ALDERNEY/ AIRPORT or AURIGNY/date/AEROGARE/CHERBOURG .... | 5·00 |
| 2.12.70 | Return of the Islanders to Alderney. AURIGNY/ALDERNEY/ AIRPORT unframed datestamp in black .... | 5·00 |

CHANNEL ISLANDS HOVERMAIL COVERS

1969

4.5.69   Gorey–Carteret by 14 amateur-built hovercraft . . . .   30·00

1970

21.1.70   Carteret–Gorey by SR.N6 024 of Hoverwork Ltd. . . . .   15·00
27.1.70   Gorey–Carteret by SR.N6 024 of Hoverwork Ltd. . . . .   15·00
3.2.70   Jersey-Ryde I.O.W. by SR.N6 024 of Hoverwork Ltd. . . . .   18·00
20.4.70   Browndown (Gosport)–Alderney by SR.N6 XV614 of 200 Hovercraft
          Trials Squadron RCT. . . . .   18·00
24.4.70   Alderney–Browndown by SR.N6 XV616 of 200 Hovercraft Trials
          Squadron RCT . . . .   18·00

1971

4.1.71   Gosport–Jersey by VT1.001 of Vosper Thorneycroft Ltd. Dealer's
         cover . . . .   2·50
4.1.71   As above. Signed by Captain . . . .   3·50
4.1.71   As above, but Hovertravel official cover with Hovertravel Ltd. cachet
         in   red . . . .   5·00
6.1.71   Jersey–Guernsey by VT1.001 of Vosper Thorneycroft Ltd. Dealer's
         cover . . . .   2·00
6.1.71   As above, but private cover signed by Commander . . . .   5·00
6.1.71   Guernsey–Jersey by VT1.001 of Vosper Thorneycroft Ltd. Dealer's
         cover . . . .   2·00
6.1.71   As above, but private cover signed by Commander . . . .   5·00
7.1.71   Jersey–Dinard by VT1.001 of Vosper Thorneycroft Ltd. Dealer's cover   2·50
7.1.71   As above, but Hovertravel official cover with Hovertravel Ltd. circular
         cachet in red. . . . .   5·00
7.1.71   Dinard–Jersey by VT1.001 of Vosper Thorneycroft Ltd. Dealer's cover   2·50
7.1.71   As above, but Hovertravel official cover with Hovertravel Ltd. circular
         cachet in blue. . . . .   5·00
4.2.71   Jersey–Gosport by VT1.001 of Vosper Thorneycroft Ltd. Dealer's
         cover with special Postal Strike Hovercraft stamp. . . . .   2·50
4.2.71   As above, but Hovertravel official cover with Hovertravel Ltd. cachet
         in green . . . .   6·00
4.7.71   Jersey–Alderney by SR.N5 XT492 of Interservice Hovercraft Unit. . .   8·00
5.7.71   Alderney–Lee-on-Solent by SR.N5 XT492 of Interservice Hovercraft
         Unit . . . .   13·00

1972

26.4.72   Browndown–Herm by SR.N6 XV614 of 200 Hovercraft Trials
          Squadron, Royal Corps of Transport . . . .   10·00
26.4.72   Herm–Samsonport by SR.N6 XV614 of 200 Hovercraft Trials Sqn.
          RCT . . . .   10·00
27.4.72   Samsonport–Alderney by SR.N6 XV614 of 200 Hovercraft Trials Sqn.
          RCT . . . .   10·00
27.4.72   Herm–Sark by SR.N6 XV614 of 200 Hovercraft Trials Sqn. RCT . . . .   10·00
27.4.72   Sark–Jersey by SR.N6 XV617 of 200 Hovercraft Trials Sqn. RCT . . .   10·00
28.4.72   Herm–Browndown by SR.N6 XV617 of 200 Hovercraft Trials Sqn.
          RCT . . . .   10·00

1974

27.2.74   Browndown–Alderney by SR.N6 MK5 XT657 of 200 Hovercraft Trials
          Sqn. RCT . . . .   7·50
1.3.74   Alderney–Browndown by SR.N6 MK5 XT657 of 200 Hovercraft Trials
         Sqn. RCT . . . .   7·50
17.6.74   Lee-on-Solent–Guernsey by SR.N6 XV859 of Interservice Hovercraft
          Unit . . . .   7·50
19.6.74   Guernsey–Lee-on-Solent by SR.N6 XV859 of Interservice Hovercraft
          Unit . . . .   7·50

1975

25.6.75	Southampton–Jersey by HM2 303 of International Hoverservices Ltd. Posted at sea, receiving Jersey Paquebot on G.B.	7·50
26.6.75	Jersey–Carteret by HM2 303 of International Hoverservices Ltd. on charter to Hovercross Ltd.	3·00
26.6.75	Carteret–Jersey by HM2 303 of International Hoverservices Ltd. on charter to Hovercross Ltd.	3·00
1.7.75	Carteret–Jersey by HM2 303 of International Hoverservices Ltd. on charter to Hovercross Ltd. (first passenger operations)	3·00
18.7.75	Carteret–Sark by HM2 303 of International Hoverservices Ltd. on charter to Hovercross Ltd.	3·00

1976

12.7.76	Southampton–Jersey by HM2 GH-2018 of International Hoverservices Ltd. Posted at sea, receiving Jersey Paquebot on G.B.	6·00
14.7.76	Carteret–Jersey by HM2 GH-2018 of International Hoverservices Ltd. on charter to Hovercross Ltd. Posted at sea in French waters, receiving Jersey Paquebot on France	9·00
4.8.76	Jersey–Sark by HM2 GH-2018 of International Hoverservices Ltd. on charter to Hovercross Ltd. Posted at sea in international waters, receiving Sark postmark and Guernsey Paquebot on G.B.	9·00
4.8.76	As above, but posted in Jersey waters, receiving Sark postmark and Guernsey Paquebot on Jersey	9·00
4.8.76	Sark–Jersey as above, but posted in Sark waters, receiving Jersey postmark and Paquebot on Guernsey	9·00
13.9.76	Jersey–Cherbourg by HM2 GH-2018 of International Hoverservices Ltd. Posted at sea in Jersey waters, receiving Cherbourg Paquebot on Jersey	10·00
15.9.76	Jersey–Le Havre by HM2 GH-2018 of International Hoverservices Ltd. Posted at sea in Jersey waters, receiving Le Havre Paquebot on Jersey	10·00
18.9.76	Jersey–Southampton by HM2 GH-2018 of International Hoverservices Ltd. Posted at sea in Jersey waters, receiving Southampton Paquebot on Jersey	6·00

1977

23.5.77	Jersey–Carteret by HM2 GH-2018 of International Hoverservices Ltd. on charter to Hovercross Ltd. Posted at sea in Jersey waters, receiving Carteret Paquebot (Type **27c**) on Jersey	6·00
8.8.77	Sark–Carteret by HM2 GH-2018 of International Hoverservices Ltd. on charter to Hovercross Ltd. Posted at sea in Sark waters, receiving Carteret Paquebot (Type **27c**) on Guernsey	6·00
8.8.77	Carteret–Sark by HM2 GH-2018 of International Hoverservices Ltd. on charter to Hovercross Ltd. Posted at sea in French waters, receiving Sark postmark and Guernsey Paquebot on France	6·00
12.8.77	Guernsey–Carteret by HM2 GH-2018 of International Hoverservices Ltd. on charter to Hovercross Ltd. Posted at sea in Guernsey waters and Carteret Paquebot (Type **27c**) on Guernsey	6·00

1978

28.6.78	Poole–Alderney by HM2 GH-2023 of International Hoverservices Ltd. Posted at sea in international waters, receiving Alderney postmark and Guernsey Paquebot on G.B.	6·00
28.6.78	Alderney–Poole by HM2 GH-2023 of International Hoverservices Ltd. Posted at sea in Alderney waters, receiving Bournemouth and Poole Paquebot on Guernsey	6·00
29.6.78	Poole–Alderney by HM2 GH-2024 of International Hoverservices Ltd. Posted at sea in English waters, receiving Guernsey Paquebot on G.B.	6·00
6.7.78	Alderney–Poole by HM2 GH-2024 of International Hoverservices Ltd. Posted at sea in Guernsey waters, receiving Bournemouth and Poole Paquebot on Guernsey	6·00

17. Mails between the Channel Islands and France

Prior to 1843 letters were carried privately between the Channel Islands and France and were handed to agents on either side of the Channel for onward transmission. The agent would hand them to the captain of a ship who, in turn, would hand them to another agent at the port of arrival. For this service a fee of 3d. (or 3 decimes in France) was charged, 1d. going to each agent and 1d. to the captain of the ship.

The Foreign Post Offices

By Ordinance of the Royal Court of Guernsey dated 23 August 1823 a Foreign Post Office was set up in Guernsey for the purpose of dealing with letters to and from Alderney and the neighbouring coast of France. Two Guernseymen, Georges S. Syvret and Matthieu Barbet, held the monopoly of this service, making a charge of 2d. per letter, payable by the addressee, 1d. of which went to the Master of the ship bringing it. The Ordinance was twice strengthened, first on 13 December 1823 and again in March 1833, and was not repealed until January 1841.

According to a report made by George Louis, a Post Surveyor, who visited Jersey in 1829, a similar office (known as the French Post Office) was functioning there. It was run by Theodore Fontaine, and was concerned with the collection and dispatch of mails between St. Helier, Granville and St. Malo.

Louis believed this office to be sanctioned in some way by the French Government and a letter exists which seems to confirm that this office was an official agency of the French Post Office.

The letter was written by Theodore Fontaine on 4 May 1842 to the Director-General of Posts, Paris, and requested "that as he (Fontaine) had to dispatch express packets every day to the Postmasters of St. Malo and Granville which called for the use of large quantities of wrapping paper, could he be supplied with some for the use of his office, also some wax".

On the front of the letter is the address and the word Service, also the red "OUTRE-MER ST. MALO" datestamp of 4 Mai 1842 (Type **16**); inside is yet another datestamp, this time in blue and reading Cabinet Particulier (Postes) 6 Mai 1842.

Both Foreign Post Offices were officially suppressed on 1 June 1843 in consequence of a new Anglo-French Postal Convention which came into force on that date. Under this Convention all mail to or from France was to be delivered to the British Post Office, and the French Postal Authorities agreed that it should not be sent through any other channels. Neither of the Foreign Post Offices used any postal markings.

French Ports of Entry and Departure

The huge field of markings for French maritime mail has implications for the Channel Islands. Postal history is rich in two centuries of cancellations and markings used to record ports of entry for foreign mail and ports of departure for letters leaving France on the high seas. Paquebot mail, involving ports of call for letters posted on board ship, is dealt with in Section 12.

The first marking known to have been used on mail from the Channel Islands is "D'JARSEY", unframed and measuring 21 × 3mm, applied at St. Malo in 1683 (Type **1**). It appears to have been little used, as only two examples are known. A type (**2**) reading "DE S'MALO" was used in 1698 and 1699.

Another marking found is "D'ANGLETERRE" struck in black from 1699 to 1720 and used on letters from England as well as from the Channel Islands (Type **3**). This was followed in 1720 by a larger "ANGLETERRE" which can be found struck in red, blue or black until 1802 (Type **4**).

From 1823 letters routed via England are found marked "ANGLETERRE PAR BOULOGNE" (or "CALAIS" or "ROUEN") in two lines (Type **5**). Letters going direct from the Islands to the adjacent French ports have "GRANDE BRETAGNE/PAR GRANVILLE" (or "CHERBOURG" or "ST. MALO") in two lines (Type **6**). This latter mark was used on letters from the Channel Islands only. The St. Malo mark exists with damage (a misshapen "G" to "GRANDE") after about 1830. An 1823 letter from Jersey is known with "Angleterre par" in manuscript above the handstamped "ST MALO".

Other markings are found on letters from Jersey and Guernsey, but are not, of course, restricted to mail from those islands; they may be described as follows.

Type **7** is "SMALO" in black measuring 27 × 4mm and recorded on letters from Guernsey dated 1776 and 1777. A similar version (with full stop) reads "S. MALO" and is known used between 1755 and 1783.

Type **8** is "ST. MALO" in black measuring 28 × 3½mm and is known on a letter from Guernsey dated 1790. In the same type is "GRANVILLE" in black and this measures 36 × 4mm (the "G" is slightly larger, 6mm high). It is recorded on a letter from Jersey of 1781. "MORLAIX" in Type **8** is known on a letter of 1816.

Type **9** is a two-line marking. A letter from Guernsey of 1793 is known struck with "34/ST. MALO" in black (dimensions 5 × 3½mm and 28 × 3½mm). Another Guernsey letter, dated 1817, bears "34/ST. SERVAN" in this type (8 × 5mm and 38 × 5mm). Recorded during 1823–29 is "48/CHERBOURG".

The "34/ST. SERVAN" in Type **9** exists on a letter from Sark of 1819 with the words "Colonies par" written in manuscript above it.

The figures "34" and "48" are French Departmental numbers, which occur in further markings. Type **10** reads "DEB 48/CHERBOURG" (known 1815) and there is also "DEB 34/ST. MALO" (known 1828–30). "DEB" probably means "Debourse" (expended, disbursed). Type **11** is "P21P/ST. BRIEUC" (known 1820) and, similarly, "P34P/ST. MALO" (known 1828–31).

In 1788 the French had begun designating ports of entry for mail arriving by sea with the words "COLONIES PAR" and the name of the port. In relation to Channel Islands mail St. Malo, Cherbourg and Granville are recorded in Type **12**.

These are unframed. One of the scarcest French pre-adhesive marks is Type **13**, used in 1818, a boxed "COL. PAR CHERBOURG".

The postal designation "COLONIES" was dropped in 1828 in favour of "PAYS D'OUTREMER" and name of port (e.g. "PAYS D'OUTREMER/PAR NANTES"). Such boxed markings were in use till 1831 though none is so far recorded on Channel Islands mail.

In August of 1831 the name of the port was deleted and the framed "PAYS D'OUTREMER" (Type **14**) in black or red was used in conjunction with a large circular datestamp. One version of this has fleurons at each side and the French Departmental number at the foot (Type **15**); the other type is without fleurons (**15a**). This c.d.s. is known used in 1830 with the "GRANDE BRETAGNE PAR CHERBOURG" mark and in 1833 with "GRANDE BRETAGNE PAR ST. MALO".

Small circular datestamps, 20mm in diameter, struck in black or red were brought into use in March 1839 (Type **16**). These read "OUTRE-MER" at the top and "ST. MALO" (or "GRANVILLE" or "CHERBOURG" or "PORT-BAIL") at the bottom with the date in three lines across the centre. They are found on letters from the Channel Islands as well as from many other places abroad.

The Postal Conventions

The Postal Convention of 1843 provided for official exchange of mail between various British and French ports and for Packets between the Channel Islands and St. Malo. It also provided for mails to be carried by private steamers between Jersey and Guernsey and Cherbourg, Granville and St. Malo. The service between Jersey and Cherbourg was suppressed in 1845, but a cover dating from 1849 is known. Rates of postage were 6d. per $\frac{1}{2}$oz from England and 3d. per $\frac{1}{2}$oz from the Channel Islands. This was the rate to the French port of arrival and an additional 5 decimes per $\frac{1}{4}$oz was added for the French inland rate.

The Convention also provided for *boîtes mobiles* (movable boxes) in which letters could be posted and cancelled at the port of arrival. At a number of English ports special handstamps bearing the framed letters "M.B." were applied to letters, but although it seems likely that similar ones were issued to the Channel Islands none has so far been recorded. On the French side, however, letters from the Channel Islands were marked with a small circular datestamp reading "ILES-C" at the top and bearing the name of the port, Cherbourg (very rare), Granville or St. Malo at the bottom (Type **17**). The "C" stands for "CANAL", a French version of Channel. Such marks were also used on ordinary letters to France not posted in the movable box. The marks were usually struck in red, although an example from St. Malo is known in black, and were in use until about 1889. A second version of the St. Malo mark had the inscriptions in larger type.

A mark made specially for use on letters from Jersey and Guernsey was a flat-topped "3" (Type **18**). It was introduced in the 1830s to indicate the 3 decimes ship charge due (raised from 2 decimes in 1830) and continued in use after 1843, presumably indicating the 3d. per $\frac{1}{2}$oz rate. Another mark which was also retained was the underlined "6" (Type **12a**) which is known used on double letters from about 1830, and in later years showed the postage due on unstamped and unpaid mail. Raymond Salles in his "Encyclopédie de la Poste Maritime Francaise", Volume VIII, indicates that this underlined "6" came into use after the 1843 Convention and states that it was struck on all Island letters which, on arriving in France, received one of the "ILES-C" marks. He considered that the mark referred to the 6d. per 1 oz rate then operating from the Channel Islands. As, however, it is known stamped on pre-adhesive mail of 1830, etc. his assumption cannot be correct. A similar mark, an underlined "9", is known on covers from Hamburg passing through Le Havre during the 1830s.

Two covers are known from this first *boîte mobile* service. One is from Jersey to France and has a single G.B. 1855 4d. on blue paper cancelled with the "3176" small-figures lozenge of St. Malo and the "ILES-C ST. MALO" c.d.s. of 8 January 1856. The other cover is addressed from Jersey to St. Malo. It bears a pair of the G.B. 1855 4d. on blue paper cancelled with the "1441" small-figures lozenge of Granville and the "ISLE-C GRANVILLE" c.d.s. of 10 May 1856.

Handstruck 6, 7 and 8 decimes marks (equivalent to 6d., 7d. and 8d.) can be found on letters fom the Islands (Type **19**). They are usually struck in black and denote the amount of postage due, calculated at double rates, to be collected in France. When used on covers from the *Boîte Mobile* service they are extremely rare, the entires being usually prepaid. From 1849, when France first issued stamps, the postage due on unpaid letters was fixed at 7 decimes per $\frac{1}{4}$oz, being raised to 8 decimes in 1855–56. The 1856 Convention set the postage rate (from 1 January 1857) at 4d. per $\frac{1}{4}$oz for both G.B. and C.I. letters. An additional conference in 1869 reduced this to 3d. per 10g or $\frac{1}{3}$oz, but the entry of both France and Britain into the U.P.U. in 1875 fixed the foreign rate at 2$\frac{1}{2}$d. per 30g (1oz) for the next 45 years.

The 1856 Anglo-French Convention also provided for another *Boîte Mobile* service of which full details are given later in this section. This service came into existence on 1 January 1857 when the current rates of postage were as follows:

1.1.1857–30.6.1870	4d. per $\frac{1}{4}$oz (7.5g)
1.7.1870–31.12.1875	3d. per $\frac{1}{3}$oz (10g)
1.1.1876–11.6.1921	2$\frac{1}{2}$d. per 1 oz (30g)
12.6.1921–1939	3d. per 1oz

It is interesting to note that the 1856 Convention reduced the rate from England to France from 6d. to 4d., but abolished the reduced Channel Islands rate of 3d. The use of adhesive stamps on letters from the U.K. to France was not made compulsory until the 1856 Convention. Postage could be prepaid in cash instead, but if posted unpaid stampless covers were charged to the recipient at twice the correct postage rate.

The 1843 Convention was divided into a series of Articles, each of which was concerned with some service, place or detailed rate of postage. Article 57 laid down that any letter originating in Great Britain, or passing through Great Britain on route to France, on which the postage had not been prepaid had to be stamped with a mark indicating the particular Article to which reference should be made. These cachets were rectangular and those referring to G.B. and the Channel Islands were Articles 9 and 10 respectively. In April 1844 boxed marks reading "ART-9" were sent to the office of the Secretary of the G.P.O. for dispatch to Guernsey and Jersey, but no example of their use has yet come to light. They were probably not sent as Article 9 referred to the fixing of the rate from the U.K. to France at 1s. per oz, and it was Article 10 which covered the C.I. rate of 6d. per oz although this mark has not been seen either.

The Boîte Mobile Service

Under Article II of the Postal Convention between Great Britain and France dated 24 September 1856, in addition to the regular mail service, letters were to be exchanged between several British and French ports, such mails being carried by private vessels of either country, a gratuity of 1d. being paid on each letter. This means of communication became so constant that all the vessels carried a *boîte mobile* (movable box) on board for collecting such letters, and postmarks were brought into use for letters so posted.

The steamers of the London & South Western Railway ran from St. Helier to St. Malo and Granville on alternate weekdays, carrying the regular mails between the Islands and France. They also carried a movable letterbox in which letters, which had not been passed through the Post Office, could be posted up to the time of sailing, and afterwards by passengers on board. On arrival at the destination these boxes were taken to the Post Office, where the letters were removed for cancelling.

There appears to have been no Guernsey movable box on this service. Letters were carried direct to St. Malo from Guernsey for many years by the *Fawn*, a 47-ton cutter. The captain was given letters by the Post Office and also received them from private persons. There is no evidence that the cutter *Fawn*, or the steamer of the same name, had a movable box on board.

The *Boîte Mobile* service ceased at the outbreak of war in 1939.

Letters from the Channel Islands. Letters from Jersey and Guernsey had the British stamps cancelled with the normal French numeral obliterator (lozenge of dots). In addition the covers received a date postmark, at first octagonal (Type **20**) and later circular (Type **21**). These read "ANGL. B.M." at the top and name of the port below.

For Type **20** the ports recorded are: St. Malo, Cherbourg and Granville. For Type **21** they are: St. Malo, Granville, Plérin and Port-Bail. A variant of the Plérin Type **21** has "ANGLETERRE" in place of "ANGL. B.M.". A variation of Type **21** for St. Malo is known inscribed "ANG. B.M./ST. MALO" only. This is known in red or black used on widely scattered dates between 1867 and 1904. These "B.M." marks were applied to mail from private vessels which was handed in at the Bureau Ambulant. Mail from the Government packet via St. Malo was handled by the Bureau Sédentaire and cancelled with a double circle "ANGL./ST. MALO" known from 1870. A similar mark is recorded from Port-Bail in the following year.

The lozenge of dots obliterators contained different figures identifying the ports. Small figures (Type **22**) were used at first, but when the French post offices were renumbered on 1 January 1863 larger figures were introduced (Type **23**). The numbers for the major ports were:

	Small Figures	Large Figures
Cherbourg	842	1002
Granville	1441	1706
St. Malo	3176	3734

In the large-figure series Binic was numbered 480 and Port-Bail 2984. The 3734 obliterator occurs in small figures, transferred to St. Malo and used as a supplementary cancellation to the large-figure 3734, above.

Mails to Cherbourg probably went by French ships from Guernsey. There was also a service from Southampton to Le Havre which had no connection to the Channel Islands. As yet, no covers from the Channel Islands have been recorded with an entry mark of Le Havre and there is no mention of the town in either of the Postal Conventions as one of the ports through which mail to and from the Islands might pass. Cards from France to the Channel Islands do exist sent by this route and these carry the "SOUTHAMPTON–FRANCE M.B." mark.

The lozenge obliterations were withdrawn in April 1876 and ordinary town datestamps were then used. Few examples of Types **20** and **21** exist after this date although scattered instances of use, especially at Granville, continue to 1911. Prices are quoted for complete covers cancelled with such datestamps and bearing British stamps.

About 1906 St. Malo brought into use a single-circle datestamp "ANG. B.M./SAINT-MALO" (Type **24**) in place of the ordinary town cancellation and this remained the case until the Second World War.

Letters from the French Ports. On arrival at St. Helier, letters from France had the stamps cancelled with the Jersey "409" obliterator and Type **25** worded "JERSEY/FRANCE/MB" was applied to the cover clear of the stamps. The letters "MB" refer, of course, to "movable box" and, because of its shape the cancellation is called a "milestone". It was dispatched from the G.P.O. on 24 November 1856 and the earliest recorded date of use is 26 April 1858.

On 25 July 1873 a similar datestamp (Type **26**) was sent to Jersey. The lettering is larger and the wider-spaced "M.B." now has a stop between "M" and "B". The cancellation originally had straight sides, but it became distorted in use through its long life, the last recorded date being 24 August 1939. Before 1914 the month preceded the day in the date-line; thereafter their positions were transposed, as illustrated (Type **26a**). This change was made in all cancels throughout the U.K. The cancellation, normally in black, is known used in red in 1938 on a single stamp, but this was probably accidental.

The Proof Book in the Post Office records shows an M.B. datestamp as having been dispatched to Guernsey at the same time (1856) as the one to Jersey. So far no stamps or covers are known bearing this marking, however. Instead the French stamps were cancelled with a Guernsey barred-oval obliterator ("324") in a single or duplex or an ordinary datestamp.

For Jersey French stamps up to the "Peace and Commerce" types, first issued 1876, are found cancelled by the barred oval "409" in single or duplex with the "milestone" (Type **25**) struck on the cover. Later issues are found cancelled with the "milestone" alone. The Bordeaux issues of France (1870–71) are particularly desirable items on *boîte mobile* covers. A single French *Ballon Monté* is also known with the M.B. milestone mark.

In general, French stamps with Jersey and Guernsey cancellations are much scarcer than British stamps cancelled in France. From about 1904 French stamps can be found cancelled with the current datestamps of the Islands.

Boîte Mobile from Smaller Ports.
Several ports cancelled mail from movable boxes, though there was no reference to them in the 1856 Convention which had covered only St. Malo, Cherbourg, Granville and Le Havre (from Southampton only). For this reason details of them are given here.

Port-Bail. Port-Bail is on the west coast of the Cotentin peninsula and from about 1868 to 1885 letters were sent there from Gorey in Jersey. Little is known of the mail service: the sailings are believed to have been irregular and concentrated on summer excursion steamers which ceased when the port became silted-up in 1885. Port-Bail possesed a circular datestamp Type **21**, since it is known on a letter from Jersey dated 14 April 1869 which arrived in France the following day. This was struck in red, but another in black is known from 1871. Few covers or loose stamps with Port-Bail markings are known, although one example of the "OUTREMER" (Type **16**) is known in 1871 and there is also a 1874 cover from Jersey with the Port-Bail town c.d.s.

Plérin. Plérin, in the Bay of St. Brieuc, is another port at which mail from the Channel Islands was occasionally landed. It also had a circular datestamp Type **21** and this is known on covers from Guernsey dated 1872–1880. The double-circle town datestamp was also used on some covers from Jersey in 1885–86.

Binic. Another small port in the Bay of St. Brieuc near Plérin, Binic also received mail from the Islands. Sailings were made from Guernsey by the cutter *Reindeer* and later by the *Echo*. Early this century the *Fawn*, belonging to the St. Malo and Binic Steamship Co. Ltd., based on Guernsey, also made regular sailings to the port. A part cover from Guernsey to Binic dated 1872 is known bearing a pair of the 1858 1d. red cancelled with Type **23**, the "480" large-figures lozenge of Binic. A number of postcards from Guernsey to Binic exist bearing Edward VII stamps cancelled with the Binic/Cotes-du-Nord datestamp of 1905–08. An oval "B.M." stamp was applied to each card (Type **27**), a marking of a land *boite mobile* occasionally used on mail arriving from the Islands. One such cover is endorsed "paquebot" in manuscript. A similar oval "B.M." mark is known from St. Malo.

Carteret. The little port of Carteret is situated on the west coast of the Cotentin peninsula, near to Port-Bail. From about 1894 letters were carried from Gorey by the vessels of the Compagnie Rouennaise de Navigation, the paddle-steamers *Cygne* and *Jersey*. In recent years letters have been carried by the *Torbay Belle* and *Les Deux Léopards*, belonging to the Compagnie Navigation Carteret, but only if they bear French stamps.

Two types of cancellation (of equal value) are known on British stamps used on postcards routed via Carteret. The first consists of three concentric circles, the outer one being made up of dots, with the word "CARTERET" at the top, "MANCHE" at the bottom and the date in three lines in the centre. Examples are known from 1898 to 1908. The second type consists of a single circle 26½mm in diameter, with "CARTERET" at the top, "MANCHE" at the bottom and the date in three lines in the centre. Examples are known used from 1908 to 1914. The existence of a card addressed to Chester suggests that this route was occasionally used for mail to the British mainland. The first type was intended as a transit or dispatch mark and the second as an arrival cancel.

Some cards from France to Jersey, sent through Carteret uncancelled, received the "JERSEY–FRANCE MB" mark at St. Helier.

Two types of "PAQUEBOT" mark are known used on these cards. The first (Type

27a) measured 29 × 4½mm and was used from 1901 to 1911. The second (Type **27b**) measured 27 × 4mm and was used from 1911 to 1914. For some time ordinary bags of mail were also carried between Jersey and Carteret and letters to and from France are known with the Carteret transit mark. In the early 1970s, Hovermail covers posted at sea in Island waters may be found with a later type of Carteret "PAQUEBOT" mark (Type **27c**). *For details of such covers see Section 16.*

St. Brieuc. For a number of years in the late nineteenth and early twentieth centuries there were regular shipping services between the Channel Islands and St. Brieuc in the Côtes-du-Nord. It seems likely that mail was carried on these services and British stamps with the "3533" large-figures lozenge or with later St. Brieuc datestamps may possibly exist.

Other ports with which there was an occasional link were Tréguier, Portriex, Le Légué and Regnéville.

The "P-F" and "P-D" Handstamps

As a result of the 1843 Convention "P-F" and "P-D" handstamps were issued to the Guernsey and Jersey Post Offices. Letters going beyond France could only be prepaid for the English and French postage—hence "P-F" (Paid to Frontier). The marking "P-D" indicated Paid to Destination.

Only one example, on a cover of 1849 to Oporto, is known of the Jersey "P-F" mark.

The oval "P-D" stamp (Type **28**) was used from 1843 to 1862 and is known struck in red, black, blue and a dirty green. A single "P." in an oval (Type **28a**) has been seen in red on an 1847 cover from Jersey to Rome via St. Malo and a 13mm double-ring circle inscribed "PD" (Type **28b**) is known used in 1862. The circular "PD" stamp (Type **29**) was used from 1863 to 1875, generally in black, but occasionally in red. In 1875 a small oval Type **30** was struck in black or red. It had sloping letters and, like Type **29**, did not have a hyphen between the letters. A replacement for this was sent from the G.P.O. on 16 July 1879.

Guernsey had an oval "P-F" stamp (Type **31**) in use in 1843–44, struck in dull red. An oval "P-D" stamp (Type **32**) was in use from 1843 to 1872, struck in red at first and then in the colour of the datestamp. A version without the hyphen is known in black on a cover from Guernsey to St. Malo dated 12 August 1872, with damage to the top. The circular "P-D" stamp (Type **33**) was used from 1856 to 1875 and was struck in the colour of the datestamp, blue or black. A 13mm diameter type with thinner letters can be found on covers of 1866–1873 (Type **34**).

Letters to France from Jersey and Guernsey via Calais and Boulogne in 1856–57 are known with a larger circular "P D" stamp with thicker letters and in 1866 with a smaller type in red or black. These were almost certainly applied in London. Some of these covers have a large handstruck "PAR LONDRES". This was privately applied by P. Beghin of Jersey. Small square or rectangular "P D" marks on letters *to* the Islands were sometimes applied on dispatch and so are French markings.

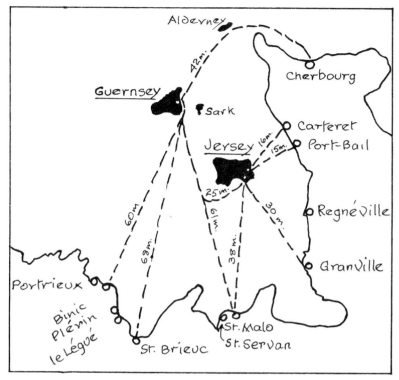

C.I.–France Shipping Routes

D'JARSEY
(1)

**GRANDE BRETAGNE
PAR GRANVILLE**
(6)

SMALO
(7)

S⸳T MALO
(8)

**34
S⸳T SERVAN**
(9)

**COLONIES PAR
S⸳T MALO**
(12)

(12a)

COL. PAR CHERBOURG

(13)

PAYS D'OUTREMER

(14)

(15)

(16)

(17)

3

(18)

(19a)

(19b)

Cat. No.	Type No.		Dates of use	Colour	Price on cover
CF1	**1**	D'JARSEY	1683	Black	£2000
CF2	**2**	DE S'MALO	1698–99	Black	£250
CF3	**3**	D'ANGLETERRE	1699–1720	Black	80·00
CF4	**4**	ANGLETERRE	1720–1802	Red, blue or black.	40·00
CF5	**5**	ANGLETERRE PAR BOULOGNE	1823–30	Black	50·00
CF6		ANGLETERRE PAR CALAIS	1823–30	Black	60·00
CF7		ANGLETERRE PAR ROUEN	1823–30	Black	£100
CF8	**6**	GRANDE BRETAGNE/PAR GRANVILLE	1823–33	Black	£180

Cat. No.	Type No.		Dates of use	Colour	Price on cover
CF9	**6**	GRANDE BRETAGNE/PAR			
		CHERBOURG	1823–32	Black	£350
CF9a		ditto	1823	Red-brown	£250
CF10		ditto with Type **15** (Cherbourg			
		c.d.s.)	1830	Black	£300
CF11		GRANDE BRETAGNE/PAR			
		ST. MALO	1823–34	Black or red	£150
CF12	**7**	SMALO	1776–77	Black	£100
CF13		S. MALO	1755–83	Black	80·00
CF14	**8**	ST. MALO	1790	Black	60·00
CF14a		ditto with manuscript			
		"Angleterre par"	1823	Black	£120
CF15		GRANVILLE	1781	Black	50·00
CF16		MORLAIX	1816	Black	80·00
CF17	**9**	34/ST. MALO	1793	Black	60·00
CF18		34/ST. SERVAN	1817	Black	40·00
CF19		ditto, with manuscript "Colonies			
		par"	1819	Black	£300
CF20		48/CHERBOURG	1823–29	Black	60·00
CF21	**10**	DEB 48/CHERBOURG	1815	Black	60·00
CF22		DEB 34/ST. MALO	1828–30	Black	40·00
CF23	**11**	P21P/ST. BRIEUC	1820	Black	60·00
CF24		P34P/ST. MALO	1828–31	Black	50·00
CF25	**12**	COLONIES PAR/ST. MALO	1803–26	Black	80·00
CF26		COLONIES PAR/CHERBOURG	1818–27	Black	£250
CF27		COLONIES PAR/GRANVILLE	1815–23	Red or black	£150
CF28	**12a**	Underlined 6	1830–46	Black or red	30·00
CF29	**13**	Boxed COL. PAR CHERBOURG	1818	Black	£350
CF30	**14**	PAYS D'OUTREMER with			
	15/15a	ST. MALO (34) c.d.s.	1831–38	Black	60·00
CF31	**14**	PAYS D'OUTREMER with			
	15/15a	GRANVILLE (48) c.d.s.	1834–39	Black	60·00
CF32	**16**	OUTRE-MER/ST. MALO c.d.s.	1839	Black	£220
CF33		ditto	1839–43	Red	£120
CF34		OUTRE-MER/GRANVILLE			
		c.d.s.	1839–42	Red or black	£180
CF35		OUTRE-MER/CHERBOURG			
		c.d.s.	1841	Red	£250
CF35a		OUTRE-MER/PORT BAIL c.d.s.	1871	Black	£300
CF36	**17**	ILES-C/CHERBOURG c.d.s.	1845–49	Red	£400
CF37		ILES-C/GRANVILLE c.d.s.	1843–79	Red	£120
CF37a		ditto	1873	Black	£150
CF38		ILES-C/ST. MALO c.d.s.	1843–56	Red	60·00
CF39		ditto	1856–89	Red	60·00
CF40		ditto, ILES-C larger	1871	Red	60·00
CF41		ILES-C/ST. MALO	1848	Black	£100
CF42	**18**	Flat-topped 3	1839–46	Red	40·00
CF43	**19**	Handstruck 6	1850s	Black	80·00
CF44	**19a**	Handstruck 7	1849–50s	Black	80·00
CF45	**19b**	Handstruck 8	1850s	Black	80·00
CF46		ditto with manuscript "timbre			
		insuffisante"	1854	Black	£280

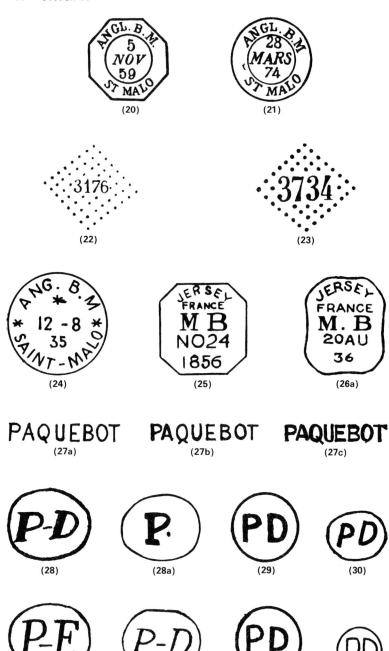

(20)

(21)

(22)

(23)

(24)

(25)

(26a)

PAQUEBOT
(27a)

PAQUEBOT
(27b)

PAQUEBOT
(27c)

(28)

(28a)

(29)

(30)

(31)

(32)

(33)

(34)

Cat. No.	Type No.		Dates of use	Colour	Price on cover

Octagonal datestamps

CF47	**20**	St. Malo	1857–67	Red	£150
CF48		Cherbourg	1857	Red	£250
CF49		Granville	1857–92	Red	£200
CF50		ditto	1890–1911	Black	50·00

Circular datestamps

CF51	**21**	St. Malo (ANGL. B.M.)	1867–76	Red	£130
CF51a		ditto	1893–1904	Black	80·00
CF51b		St. Malo (ANG. B.M.)	1887–1900	Red	£200
CF51c		ditto	1867–1904	Black	£150
CF51d		St. Malo (ANGL.)	1870	Black	£120
CF52		Granville (ANGL. B.M.)	1870–71	Red	£200
CF53		Plérin (ANGL. B.M.)	1872–80	Red	£400
CF53a		Plérin (ANGLETERRE)	1881	Black	£300
CF54		Port-Bail (ANGL. B.M.)	1869	Red	£300
CF54a		Port-Bail (ANGL.)	1871	Black	£300

Lozenge, small figures

CF57	**22**	842 Cherbourg	1857	Black	—
CF58		1441 Granville	1856–62	Black	£400
CF60		3176 St. Malo	1856–62	Black	£350
CF61		3734 St. Malo	1863	Black	£480

Lozenge, large figures

CF62	**23**	480 Binic	1872	Black	£600
CF63		1002 Cherbourg	1863–76	Black	£500
CF64		1706 Granville	1863–76	Black	£350
CF65		2984 Port-Bail	1866–70	Black	£350
CF66		3734 St. Malo	1863–76	Black	£250

Ordinary French datestamps with British stamps

CF67	—	Binic c.d.s.	1905–08	Black	£150
CF67a	—	ditto with manuscript "paquebot"	1907–08	Black	£250
CF67b	—	ditto used as transit mark	1900	Black	40·00
CF68	—	Port-Bail c.d.s.	1869–79	Red or black	£350
CF69	—	Carteret c.d.s.	1898–1914	Black	60·00
CF70	—	ditto, with French Paquebot (Types **27a/b**)	1901–14	Black	85·00
CF70a		ditto, but on cover to G.B.	1906	Black	£100
CF71	—	Granville c.d.s.	1876–1939	Black	50·00
CF72	—	ditto, with French Paquebot	1912	Black	£150
CF73	—	Plérin c.d.s.	1885–98	Black	£400
CF73a	—	ditto, used as transit mark	1900	Black	45·00
CF73b	—	ditto, with manuscript "paquebot"	1912	Black	£120
CF74	—	St. Malo c.d.s.	1876–1906	Black	30·00
CF74a	—	Le Havre (transit mark)	1910–23	Black	35·00

St. Malo datestamp

| CF75 | **24** | ANG.B.M/SAINT-MALO | 1906–39 | Black . . . . | 80·00 |

MB datestamps

CF76	**25**	"Milestone" datestamp	1856–73	Black	£600
CF77	**26**	Larger lettering	1873–1900	Black	£130
CF78		ditto	1900–26	Black	£100
CF79	**26a**	Day-month-year	1914–39	Black	£100

Cat. No.	Type No.		Dates of use	Colour	Price on cover
Barred ovals on French stamps					
CF80	—	Guernsey "324"	1853–61	Black	£1000
CF81	—	ditto	1862–71	Black	£800
		On 1870–71 Bordeaux issue	—	Black	£1400
CF82	—	Jersey "409"	1853–61	Black	£450
CF83	—	ditto	1862–79	Black	£500
		On 1870–71 Bordeaux issue	—	Black	£800
B.M. in oval					
CF84	**27**	Stamps cancelled St. Malo	—	Black	45·00
CF85		Stamps cancelled Binic	1905–08	Black	45·00
P-F and P-D handstamps					
CF86	**28**	Jersey oval P-D	1843–62	Red, black, yellow, orange, grey, blue or green . .	50·00
CF86a		Jersey P-F	1849	Red	£200
CF87	**28a**	Jersey oval P.	1847	Red	£130
CF88	**28b**	Jersey circular double-rim P-D	1862	Black	60·00
CF89	**29**	Jersey circular PD	1863–75	Black or red	40·00
CF90	**30**	Jersey small oval PD	1875–79	Black or red	30·00
CF91	**31**	Guernsey P-F	1843–44	Red	50·00
CF92	**32**	Guernsey oval P-D	1843–72	Red, black, blue or green	40·00
CF93		Guernsey oval PD (no hyphen)	1903	Black	80·00
CF94	**33**	Guernsey circular PD (17mm)	1856–75	Blue or black	25·00
CF95	**34**	Guernsey circular PD (13mm)	1866–73	Black or red	40·00
Jersey and Guernsey datestamps on French stamps					
CF96	—	Single or double circles	early 1900s onwards	Black	*from* £125
CF97	—	ditto on reply paid postcards	1960s–70s	Black	*from* 10·00

Notes. In the case of lozenge obliterations (Types **22** and **23**), prices are for those on the 3d. and 4d. adhesives, which were the most commonly used values. Covers bearing other values are worth considerably more.

Types **20** and **21** were normally used in conjunction with Types **22** and **23**.

The value of Types **28** to **34** depends on the adhesives and the other postal markings on the cover.

Prices for markings on mail between the U.K./Channel Islands and France are for letters originating in or dispatched to the Islands. Those to or from the mainland are often worth less.

18. The German Occupation

German forces were in occupation of the Channel Islands between 30 June 1940 and 9 May 1945.

The Course of Events

The War Cabinet in London had decided to demilitarise the Islands. All British regular forces were withdrawn by 21 June 1940 and many civilians were evacuated to Britain by 23 June.

With the military evacuation the Lieutenant-Governors of Jersey and Guernsey departed and civil administration had to be reorganised. Emergency bodies were accordingly set up to which many powers of the normal local government (the States) were transferred. In Guernsey the States of Deliberation set up a controlling Committee with the Procureur (Major A. J. Sherwill) as President on 21 June. In Jersey the Assembly of the States formed a Superior Council under the Presidency of the Bailiff (A. M. Coutanche) and this first met on 24 June.

The first German troops flew into Guernsey on the evening of 30 June 1940 and the main force arrived during the following day. On 1 July Jersey was occupied and on 2 July the island of Alderney. A detachment crossed from Guernsey to Sark on 4 July to complete the operation. Because of the demilitarisation the invasion proceeded without military opposition, although loss of life and casualties occurred during air-raids.

German military government became effective in August 1940 with the Channel Islands considered as part of France (*Département de la Manche*). *Feldkommandantur 515* (Field Command 515), responsible for all the Islands, was located in Jersey. It had a *Nebenstelle* (branch) on Guernsey and lesser organisations elsewhere. The *Kommandantur* itself had separate divisions for military and civil affairs; the *Wehrmacht* (armed forces) were, of course, a body separate from this military government organisation.

Since Jersey and Guernsey continued in allegiance to the British Crown the local civil administration remained. To recognise the reality of the Occupation new laws were henceforward approved by the German *Kommandant* and the Bailiff.

Currency

German currency was principally in circulation during the Occupation alongside British. When, some time after the invasion, the Germans eventually took control of the banks an official rate of exchange was fixed at 9.36 *Reichsmarks* to the pound, so that 1 RM was worth about 2s. 1½d. Because of souvenir hunting and hoarding small change became scarce and the Islands printed notes of low denomination expressed in sterling.

Early Communications

The immediate result of the arrival of the Germans was that communications with the mainland of Britain abruptly ceased. Attempts were made by the islanders to make contact, but very few messages can have arrived; there are only three known at present that did.

The method adopted was to send such letters in a cover addressed to the British Vice-Consul in Lisbon for forwarding. One Guernseyman who had a friend interned in France wrote to him by the same means hoping that he might be able to pass on the news to England via the Red Cross (which was not yet functioning in Guernsey). This cover, which was handed in at the German *Feldpost* on the island, bore a strip of three 1d. stamps. These were not cancelled and one has been removed. As the internee died in camp it is not known if he ever received the letter, but the cover bears the censor stamp of *Front–Stalag 131* at St. Lô, France, which suggests it did reach its destination.

Another cover bears a 3d. Postal Centenary stamp (S.G. 484) that has been left uncancelled. These Vice-Consul, Lisbon, covers were outer wrappers and contained letters to be forwarded. This second example has the name and address of the sender, a Guernsey woman, on the back. It also bears the *Front–Stalag 131* censor stamp. It also reached the Vice-Consul and the message arrived safely in Wales.

Another method was to try to send news to families in Britain via the British Vice-Consul in Washington (also neutral territory at that time), but none of these letters ever left the Islands as the Postal Authorities were unable to forward them to the U.S.A. They, also, are very scarce.

A method allowed to refugees in Britain wishing to communicate with their relatives in the Channel Islands was via P.O. Box 506, Lisbon, the address of Thomas Cook & Son, the official forwarding agents for mail within, to and from enemy-occupied countries and Great Britain. They could write letters with severely limited contents and place them in stamped envelopes and send them under cover to Thomas Cook & Son, London, together with a 2s. postal order. The writers could not give any address, but were to instruct their correspondents to write back c/o Post Box 506, Lisbon. Several covers sent by this service are in existence (*see* illustration) but bear a handstamp "Detained in France during German Occupation".

Mail via Lisbon with "detained" handstamp

From October 1940 communication with the Islands via the Red Cross organisation was established, but at first only the name and address of the enquirer could be transmitted. By the end of the year a message of not more than twenty-five words was allowed. No replies or messages from the Islands could be sent until

13 January 1941. On that date a Red Cross Bureau was opened in Guernsey. A Jersey Bureau was opened in March 1941. The Red Cross Message Service is dealt with in Section 19 of this Catalogue.

The Feldpost

The initial occupation of the Channel Islands by German forces was by elements of the 216th Infantry Division, which was part of the Army in France. The division's *Feldpostamt* (Field Post Office) was at Montmartin-sur-Mer, which had the Kenn. (code) No. 205. These codes appeared to the left of the date (see Type **1**), on registered mail only and were also written on the registration label. For ordinary *Feldpost* covers these numbers were replaced by hyphens. Mail from the forces in the Islands was collected and transported back to Montmartin-sur-Mer for cancelling.

There appears to have been a stationary military post office established in Jersey shortly after the initial occupation as a branch of *Feldpostamt 372* (which was at Cherbourg and used the Kenn. No. 447). It is reported to have had the Kenn. No. 405, which was also used at St. Lô, and at present we know of only one registered cover from Jersey of this period using that number. The office was in Falle's shop as 12–14 Beresford Street.

The 319th Infantry Division moved into the Channel Islands on 19 April 1941 and replaced the elements of the 216th. The Kenn. number for the Jersey office was then changed to 712 (Type **1**) and a Guernsey office was established at Le Jardinet, St. Martin's. This was given the number 937, but since it was for all practical purposes a sub-office of the main *Feldpost* office in northern France, the suffix "a" was added whenever the number was inserted in manuscript on registration labels. Where the number 937 appears in label *without* the suffix this indicates that the letter concerned was taken direct to France and was then registered at the main office. In such cases (which are very unusual) the handstruck *Feldpost* datestamp would include the code letter "a" above the date. Other code letters would indicate the island from which an item of mail originated. The cancellers in Jersey were either "f", "g" or "h", and those in Guernsey "b", "d" or "e". The letter "c" is unrecorded. Bundles of letters all addressed to a particular *Feldpost* office often showed the requisite code written on the top item of the stack.

In addition to the datestamp (Type **1**) most covers also carry a *Feldpost* cachet, of similar design but without a date, which shows the five-figure code number assigned to each unit. These were usually in black, but can be found in red from, it is believed, officers' correspondence. Such numbers for the *Luftwaffe* had an "L" prefix and those for the Navy "M".

Local records in the islands report the opening of both offices as 6 January 1941 and philatelic covers are known from this date.

Mail carried by the *Feldpost* was subject to German censorship at one of fifteen Primary Censor offices, each of which was assigned a different code letter. Most Channel Islands mail was dealt with by the Frankfurt office where handstamps showed the code "e" or by Paris which used "x". Letters in transit through these offices, but not censored there, were marked by handstamps showing a capital "A" followed by the office code, both within a circle.

At first, correspondence was restricted to Germany, Italy, Belgium and Occupied France, but in spite of this one letter arrived in Jersey from Ireland (a neutral country) on 17 April 1941. Several others are known which were turned back after reaching Germany, even though they had already been censored three times; they usually bear a censor mark of Frankfurt. At the end of May some other countries were added to the list of those with which correspondence could be carried out.

All civilian mail from both Islanders or Germans, to any part of Occupied Europe had to go through the *Feldpost* at a charge of 25pf. for letters and 15pf. for postcards. German forces, of course, received free postage and quite a lot of official correspondence, much of it registered, went back to Germany. All military mail had a handwritten (or sometimes handstamped) five-digit *Feldpostnummer* to identify it.

From 1942 onwards, mail for abroad had to be handed in at the *Feldpost* unstamped but with the necessary cash. Stamps were affixed and then cancelled. Many Jersey, and a few Guernsey, covers are also known bearing one of the locally-produced stamps cancelled at a British post office in the islands to establish proof of origin. Although philatelic, these covers are quite acceptable if they bear the correct rate of postage in German definitive stamps (commemorative stamps were not available at the Field Post Offices, but were sometimes supplied by German stamp dealers to soldiers returning from home leave). Items with either commemorative stamps or the wrong foreign rate are worth much less. Various covers are known with mixed German, French and British stamps or German and Channel Islands stamps. They are also known with airmail labels or with a red boxed handstamp "MIT SCHNELLBOOT/BEFÖRDERT". These are all philatelic items and, although of some interest if they have the correct German postal rates and censor marks, are worth much less than genuine private correspondence.

One or two covers with Jersey and Guernsey stamps cancelled by a small oval handstamp inscribed "JERSEY-GUERNSEY/MAIL BOAT/CHANNEL ISLANDS" are reported to have been carried on the States of Jersey vessels S.S. *Normand* or M.V. *Spinel* to Granville and put into the post there.

A small batch of philatelic registered covers accepted by favour from a Jerseyman (which was strictly against regulations) had the stamp cancelled with Type **1** dated 1 August 1944 and marked "ZURUCK" (returned) in red. They were returned on 26 September. *See* No. GO11 in the Catalogue listing.

"Fortress" Covers

After the Allied landings in Normandy in June 1944, the German *Feldpost* system in the area, including Channel Islands traffic, closed for several weeks. The Granville *Feldpost* office (which handled Channel Islands mail) was reduced to the status of a sub-office and its business was transferred to St. Malo, but when that town fell to the advancing Allies on 18 August 1944 the last link between the Channel Islands and the rest of Occupied Europe was broken. Like Lorient and St. Nazaire, the Channel Islands became besieged "fortresses". The nine months from that point until the Liberation is known as the "siege" or "fortress" period.

Commencing on the night of 24 September 1944 a series of twenty-three supply flights took place between Germany and Guernsey. The aircraft employed were Heinkel He 111s or Junkers Ju 188s of *Transportgeschwader 30*. They normally took off from either Frankfurt or Strasbourg, landed in Guernsey, discharged their cargo, refuelled and returned to Germany immediately. Most, but not all, of the aircraft carried mail, both in and out. Naturally the only mail carried was that of an official military nature or personal letters to and from the German troops.

"Fortress" covers from the islands normally bear the censor tape and cachets of the Frankfurt Primary Censor Office (code "e") and were usually routed through the Naval Post Office at Wiesbaden. They are postmarked between September 1944 and April 1945. The final supply flight to Guernsey took place during the night of 9/10 April 1945.

"Fortress" covers to the Channel Islands are very scarce, only eight are recorded, one into Jersey and seven into Guernsey.

Radio Message Cards

A further consequence of the Normandy landings in 1944 was that German troops in the Channel Islands made use of radio to send messages to relatives in their homeland. Each man was allowed one very brief standardised message a month to his next of kin. The Naval radio station at Wilhelmshaven received messages from several *Festungen* (fortified locations), including the Channel Islands, and special *Feldpost* postcards were prepared to forward these communications.

One such *Funknachrichtenkarte* (radio message card) was already preprinted with the origin *Dünkirchen–Kanalinseln* (Dunkirk–Channel Islands), either of which could be crossed out as appropriate.

These cards are very scarce. Those from Sark, of which only two are known, are the rarest.

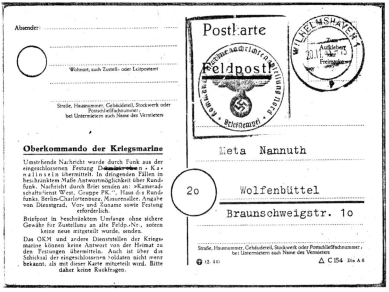

Radio Message Card of November 1944 from German Serviceman on Jersey

"ZURÜCK AN DEN ABSENDER" Roller Marking

During the final few months of the war much of the *Feldpost* mail addressed to German forces in the Channel Islands remained undelivered due to the infrequency, and eventually the termination, of the supply flights. When the American forces advanced and took the Frankfurt area, they recovered much of this mail in local post offices. A special roller marking "ZURUCK/AN DEN/ABSENDER" ("Return to sender") was prepared and struck on this mail which was then returned to sender in mid-1945. Very few examples of this marking have survived.

Feldpost Overprints

Several German definitives of the Hitler head series are known overprinted "Deutsche feldpost/Kanalinseln" in a Gothic typeface. These may have been essays printed in Jersey, but are more likely to be bogus. Others overprinted by hand "Kanal-Inseln/Feld Post" are definitely bogus.

Jersey Mail Cancelled in France

On 12 August 1940 a German *Feldpost* unit arrived at the *Feldpostamt* at Montmartin-sur-Mer with Jersey civilian mail, comprising some 1500 letters and 200 packets, which had not been cancelled on the island. For some unknown reason the Germans handed it over to the French postmistress, who having in mind the English families awaiting news, cancelled all the letters with the normal Montmartin-sur-Mer datestamps, and forwarded them with the French mail. Apparently two datestamps were used so that the large influx of mail could be dealt with quickly.

What happended to them after that is not known. The one surviving envelope addressed to France, bearing a 3d. Postal Centenary stamp (SG484), was returned to the sender in Jersey handstamped "RETOUR L'ENVOYEUR" and "INADMIS". A 2½d. Postal Centenary stamp (SG 483) also exists, cancelled on piece.

Both cancellations are single circles of 26mm diameter with "MONTMARTIN S/MER" at top, "MANCHE" at foot and the time and date in three lines across the centre.

The difference between the two handstamps is in the shape and spacing of the letters. The first type (**2A**), shown on the 2½d., stamp has broad letters closely spaced, while the second type (**2B**), cancelling the 3d. stamp, has very thin letters widely spaced. On Type **2A** the spacing on the left between "MONT" and "MANCHE" is 5mm, but on Type **2B** it is 3mm. The spacing on the right between "MER" and "MANCHE" is 6mm on Type **2A**, but only 3mm on Type **2B**.

Dienstpost

A *Dienstpost* functioned in the Channel Islands as it did in other German-occupied territories. Its purpose was to carry correspondence of an official nature which the authorities did not wish to entrust to the *Feldpost* or the civilian Post Office. Covers were handstamped in violet "DEUTSCHE DIENSTPOST" and were carried by military personnel.

Official Mail

German soldiers were supplied with green letter sheets headed "Feldpost", which went free of charge.

Letters from the German *Feldkommandantur* in Jersey had a two-line handstamp in black reading "FELDKOMMANDANTUR 515/MIL VER. GR.". A similar stamp was used in Guernsey.

Other marks used by the German *Feldkommandantur* are: a circular type with eagle in the centre inscribed "FELDKOMMANDANTUR 515" and a similar type inscribed "HAFENVEBERWACHUNGSSTELLE ST. HELIER".

Covers are known addressed to Germans in Jersey and bearing stamps cancelled with a circular handstamp with the swastika and eagle emblem in the centre and the inscription "DIENSTSTELLE/FELDPOSTNUMMER 40517", but these are undoubtedly philatelic. A genuine cover of 1944 is known from Guernsey to Vienna having this handstamp numbered 24200. It was registered from *Feldpost* 937.

Official mail sent by the island Commandant in Jersey carried a round handstamp reading "INSEL-KOMMANDANTUR JERSEY" (Type **3**) which had the word "STANDORTKOMMANDANTUR" typed across it. A swastika and eagle appeared in the centre. Various handstamps are also recorded reading "DIENSTSTELLE/INSELKOMMANDANTUR/JERSEY".

Fakes

In 1969–70 a number of covers appeared from Germany with various fancy boxed cachets "KANALINSELN", "LUFTWAFFE GUERNSEY", "LUFTWAFFE KANALINSELN", "KRIEGSMARINE JERSEY", and unframed "KANALINSELN" in various sizes. These are fakes and in many cases have *Feldpost* marks which were never in the Channel Islands.

Guernsey Mission in France

From 16 August 1940 the States of Guernsey and Jersey maintained a joint Purchasing Commission in France, with headquarters at the Villa Hirondel, Granville.

The Guernsey representative was provided with special blue envelopes bearing the two-line inscription "ETATS DE GUERNSEY/GRANVILLE". One such cover, addressed to the Aerated Water Co., Guernsey, is stamped with a German *Dienststelle* handstamp in black.

It is possible that a similar envelope may have been provided for the Jersey representatives, but none has yet been seen.

The Liberation

The Liberation of the Channel Islands was put in train when the German High Command accepted defeat in the Second World War and ordered active operations to cease at one minute past midnight on 9 May 1945. Victory-in-Europe (VE) Day was proclaimed in Britain for 8 May and Winston Churchill's speech on that day included the famous reference to the freeing of "our dear Channel Islands".

The local German Commandants in Guernsey and Jersey signed surrender documents on the morning of 9 May and British military and civilian detachments began arriving that afternoon. The main military forces moved into both islands on 12 May, when Royal Proclamations were made re-establishing the ancient institutions and privileges. A British military detachment went to Sark on 10 May and the German garrison was taken off as prisoners of war on the 17th. Troops from Guernsey crossed to Alderney on 16 May and prisoners of war were evacuated on the 20th. As a climax to these events the King and Queen visited Jersey and Guernsey on 7 June 1945.

Among the British forces arriving in the Islands at Liberation were Post Office officials with supplies of stamps and also of postal stationery cards inscribed "Re-occupation of the Channel Islands". These cards bore an "Official Paid" frank and were issued to all the islanders to enable them to write to their relatives free of charge. Although covers and cards can be found addressed to the British mainland and postmarked 9 May 1945 the first mails did not leave the Islands until the 15 May.

The period of British military government ended on 25 August 1945 when Lieutenant-Governors were once again installed in both Bailiwicks. For the operation of Field Post Offices during this period *see* Section 11.

(1)   (2A)   (2B)

(3)   (4)

Cat. No.	Handstamp/Description	Dates of use	Colour	Price on cover
GO1	Cover addressed to British Vice-Consul Lisbon with Lisbon backstamp	1940	—	£500
GO1a	ditto, but not forwarded to Portugal	1940	—	£200
GO2	ditto to Washington	1940	—	£150
GO3	Cover via Box 506 Lisbon (detained in France)	1940	—	£800
GO4	Censored cover from Ireland delivered in Jersey	1940–41	—	£250
GO5	ditto, but returned from Germany	1940–41	—	£150
GO6	Feldpost 405 (Jersey) (registered cover)	1941	Black	£500
GO7	Feldpost 712 (Jersey) (Type **1**) (reg. cover)	1941–44	Black	£400
GO7a	Manuscript 712 on cover	1941–44	—	£100
GO8	Feldpost 937 (Guernsey) (registered cover)	1941	Black	£400
GO8a	Feldpost 937a (registered cover)	1941–44	Black	£350
GO8b	Manuscript 937 on cover	1941–44	—	80·00
GO9	Feldpost, no code number (Jersey)	1941–44	Black	70·00
GO10	Feldpost, no code number (Guernsey)	1941–44	Black	70·00
GO11	Zurück	Aug.1944	Red	£120
GO12	Montmartin-sur-Mer (Type **2**)	12.8.40	Black *on cover*	£900
			on piece	£600
GO13	Deutsche/Dienstpost	1941	Violet	£200
GO14	Feldkommandantur 515/Mil. Ver. gr.	1942	Black	40·00
GO15	Feldkommandantur 515 (circular)	1942	Black	50·00
GO16	Hafenveberwachungsstelle/St. Helier	1940s	Violet	55·00
GO17	Insel-kommandantur/Jersey (circular) (Type **3**)	1942–43	Violet, black . .	60·00
GO18	Kriegsmarine/hafenüber/wachungstelle (on stamp)	1941	Violet	50·00
GO19	Dienststelle Feldpostnummer 24200	1944	Black	75·00
GO20	Dienststelle Inselkommandantur Jersey	1941–45	Violet, black . .	50·00
GO21	Geprüft dienstelle	1942	Red	70·00

Fortress Period

Cat. No.	Handstamp/Description	Dates of use	Colour	Price on cover
GO22	"Fortress" cover from Guernsey	1944–45	—	£400
GO23	"Fortress" cover from Jersey	1944–45	—	£450
GO24	"Fortress" cover from Sark	1944–45	—	£750
GO25	"Fortress" cover into Guernsey	1944–45	—	£1000
GO26	"Fortress" cover into Jersey	1944	—	£1500
GO27	ZURÜCK AN DEN ABSENDER roller marking (Type **4**) on cover addressed to Guernsey/Jersey	1945	—	£200
GO28	Ditto, cover addressed to Sark	1945	—	£350

Radio Message Card

Cat. No.	Handstamp/Description	Dates of use	Colour	Price on cover
GO29	via Wilhelmshaven and inscribed Kanalinseln	1944–45	—	£1200

Special Cover for Purchasing Commission

Cat. No.	Handstamp/Description	Dates of use	Colour	Price on cover
GO30	Etats de Guernsey/Granville	1941	—	£500

Cat. No.	Handstamp/Description	Dates of use	Colour		Price on cover
Postal Stationery					
GO31	Re-occupation card	1945	— ...	*unused*	6·00
				used	30·00
GO32	ditto, but with additional Guernsey or Jersey stamp	1945	—		5·00

German markings used on Alderney and Sark are listed in Section 13.

19. Red Cross Message Service

Through the Red Cross, civilians in the U.K. and overseas could send messages to friends and relatives in the Channel Islands and could receive replies, although by the time that arrangements were made in Jersey and Guernsey for handling these messages, a well-organised service on similar lines between the U.K. and Germany had already been in existence for about a year.

In Jersey *ad hoc* arrangements were made to deal with messages received in December 1940 and January 1941. A committee was set up subsequently under the Bailiff and Mr. C. J. d'Authreau, the Assistant Postmaster, was seconded from his duties in March 1941 to take charge of the receipt and dispatch of messages. He opened an office in Halkett Place, St. Helier, known as the Bailiff of Jersey's Enquiry and News Service.

In Guernsey an office to handle Red Cross messages was opened on 13 January 1941 with Mr. George A. Bradshaw in charge, assisted by Miss Leonie Trouteaud. Mr. Bradshaw gave his name to advice cards which his office posted to civilians in Guernsey to advise them that messages had been received and were awaiting collection. The cards were either sent inside window envelopes or on their own, but in either case were post free. The various types of card used are described and priced later in this Section. Mr. Bradshaw was deported in September 1942 and Miss Trouteaud then took charge.

U.K. residents could go to a Red Cross Bureau (usually situated in a Citizens' Advice Bureau, of which there was one in all the main towns) and leave a message of not more than twenty-five words. The messages were sent to Red Cross Headquarters in London, from there to the G.P.O. for censoring, then on to the Channel ports to be taken by sea to Lisbon where officials of the British Red Cross and of the International Red Cross dispatched the messages to Geneva, either by train via Spain and France or by sea via Marseilles.

When they arrived at Geneva the messages were checked by the International Red Cross, a cachet was applied, and the messages were put into window envelopes. The envelopes were put into boxes and sent to the headquarters of the German Red Cross in Berlin, where they were fed into the *Feldpost* system. Random censoring took place. Messages for the Channel Islands were sent from Berlin via Paris, where they were examined and had cachets applied by the French Commission of the German Red Cross. The German authorities in the Channel Islands advised the local authorities when the messages arrived and were available for collection. The same route (in reverse) was used for replies from the Channel Islands.

A Red Cross message from the U.K. to the Channel Islands would have the following marks:

(1) A British Red Cross local bureau cachet
(2) One or two British censor marks
(3) One or two International Red Cross Committee cachets
(4) One or two cachets applied by the French Commission of the German Red Cross
(5) One Guernsey or Jersey Red Cross cachet
(6) Date stamps as applied
(7) Chemical wash as applied.

The prices quoted are for forms showing the most common types of cachet. Those with the scarcer cachets command a premium, and prices for these can generally be calculated by adding to this basic price the price of the cachet. Although message forms of foreign origin are listed, cachets applied in foreign countries are excluded.

Late in the war, after the Allied invasion of France closed the land route from

Lisbon to Geneva, an arrangement was made between the British Red Cross, the German Red Cross and the International Red Cross Committee whereby messages arriving in Lisbon were transcribed on to a summary form which was forwarded to the Channel Islands by sea on the S.S. *Vega* (this ship is depicted on the 1s. 9d. Jersey "Liberation" commemorative stamp of 1970).

A very extensive range of official stationery was used in Geneva, Great Britain and other centres where Red Cross operations were conducted. That used by the I.C.R.C. was mostly numbered for reference purposes and items known to have been used on the Channel Islands service are listed in this section. They are generally very scarce.

Local leaflets and forms used in the Channel Islands were, in some cases, based on the British leaflets and are much sought after.

As the volume of Red Cross messages and correspondence grew there was an increasing need to resort to standard forms of instruction and reply. Various types of form were introduced and accorded reference numbers in the Foreign Relations FR/CL series.

The final leaflets in this category were those used by the British Postal Censors in the P.C. series. Each leaflet was printed on either white or cream paper of poor quality in various sizes covering different situations. When used they were normally stapled or pinned to the message form itself. Those known to have been used on the Channel Islands Red Cross Message service are included in this section.

In the following priced list of stationery and cachets, catalogue numbers are categorised:

Message forms................	RXF
Summary forms	RXS
Window envelopes	RXE
Bradshaw Advice Cards........	RXA
Cachets.....................	RXC
Leaflets	RXL

RED CROSS MESSAGE STATIONERY

From :

WAR ORGANISATION OF THE BRITISH RED CROSS
AND ORDER OF ST. JOHN

To :

Comité International
de la Croix Rouge   Foreign Relations
Genève   Department.

ENQUIRER
Fragesteller

Name ...... Mrs W. E. Howitt.

Christian name
Vorname
Address ...... RED CROSS MESSAGE BUREAU
             No 62?
             CITIZENS ADVICE BUREAU, COLWYN BAY

Relationship of Enquirer to Addressee ...... Daughter.
Wie ist Fragesteller mit Empfänger verwandt ?

The Enquirer desires news of the Addressee and asks that the following
message should be transmitted to him.
Der Fragesteller verlangt Auskunft über den Empfänger. Bitte um Weiter-
beförderung dieser Meldung.

Our thoughts will be you this Christmas.

Hope you are well. We are Well

Think ofe you a lot.   Love from us all.
                              Winnie.

Date ......   29 SEP 1941

ADDRESSEE
Empfänger

Name ...... Wingate

Christian name ...... George Fisher.
Vorname
Address ...... Lansdowne.
             Esplanade.
                    GUERNSEY.   C. I.

The Addressee's reply to be written overleaf.
Empfänger schreibe Antwort auf Rückseite.

RXF3a (*illustration reduced*)

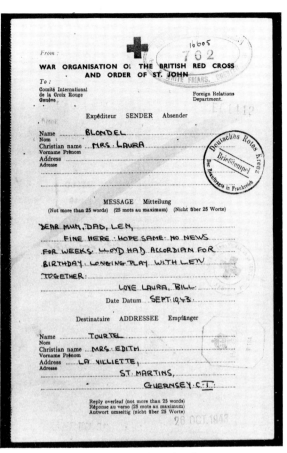

RXF4 (*illustration reduced*)

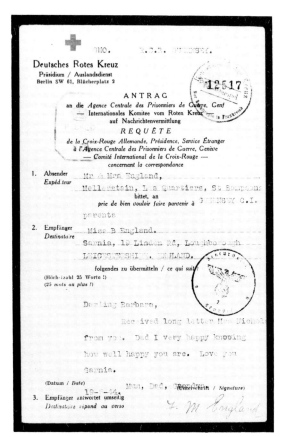

RXF5 (*illustration reduced*)

The Controlling Committee of the
States of Guernsey.

25/212

1941

A communication for you has been received through the International Red Cross *from Dorothy Bradney*.

If you will call at Elizabeth College between 10.30 a.m. and 12.30 p.m. on any morning, or between 2.30 p.m. and 5 p.m. on any afternoon (except Thursday), you can see the communication and send a reply not exceeding 25 words.

If you do not call within seven days of the above date, it will be concluded that you do not wish to send a reply.

GEO. A. BRADSHAW,
Red Cross Department.

IMPORTANT.—Please bring this Card with you.

RXA1a (*reverse*) (*illustration reduced*)

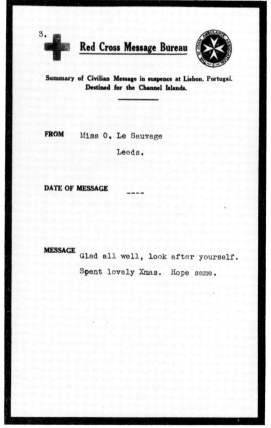

3.

Red Cross Message Bureau

Summary of Civilian Message in suspence at Lisbon, Portugal.
Destined for the Channel Islands.

FROM   Miss O. Le Sauvage

Leeds.

DATE OF MESSAGE   ----

MESSAGE
Glad all well, look after yourself.
Spent lovely Xmas. Hope same.

RXS1 (*illustration reduced*)

RXE1c (*illustration reduced*)

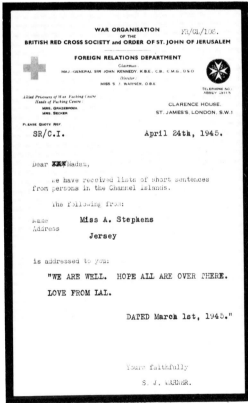

RXL28 (*illustration reduced*)

(1) Enquiry Forms from the United Kingdom

RXF1   Typescript form approx. 203 × 165mm. on white paper with the Form number E.F. (M) S/40 in top right corner and headed WAR ORGANISATION OF THE BRITISH RED CROSS/AND ORDER OF ST. JOHN / FOREIGN RELATIONS DEPARTMENT. / St. James's Palace, LONDON, S.W.1./ – ENQUIRY FOR MISSING RELATIVES. . £175

(2) Message Forms from the United Kingdom

RXF2   Printed in red on buff-coloured paper approx. 223 × 140mm. Headed "COMITE INTERNATIONAL DE LA CROIX-ROUGE/Palais du Conseil General/GENEVE (Suisse)" with number 61 in top right corner and printed instructions in the order of German, French, English. . . . . 10·00

RXF2a   As RXF2, but with accent over middle E of GENEVE in letterhead, no stop after OVERLEAF at bottom right, bracket after "familial" on reverse side, no stops after "schreiben" and "clearly" on reverse side etc. . . . . 10·00

RXF2b   As RXF2a, but printed instructions in the order French, German, English. . . . . 25·00

RXF3   Printed in red and black on buff-coloured paper approx. 229 × 145mm. Headed WAR ORGANISATION OF THE BRITISH RED CROSS/AND ORDER OF ST. JOHN and sub-headed "Prisoners of War,/Wounded and Missing/Department". Bilingual in at least three different printings. . . . . 5·00

RXF3a   As RXF3, but approx. 227 × 142mm. Sub-headed "Foreign Relations/Department". Bilingual. . . . . 3·00

RXF3b   As RXF3a, but instruction at foot of form is more central with the inscription "(Not more than 25 words)" added in both English and German. . . . . 4·00

RXF4   As RXF3a but approx. 228 × 148mm. with format differing slightly and the final instructions at foot of form reading "Reply overleaf (not more than 25 words)", trilingual (English, French and German) in three lines. . . . . 5·00

(3) Message Forms from the Channel Islands

RXF5   Printed in black, except for Red Cross emblem, on buff-coloured paper approx. 209 × 134mm. Headed "Deutsches Rotes Kreuz". Bilingual in German and French. At least eight sub-types known. . . . . 5·00

(4) Message Forms from other Countries

RXF6   Canadian form. Headed at top left "C.I.C.R." below Red Cross. Trilingual (English, French and German) £125

RXF7   Ceylon forms (two types). Headed "The Ceylon Branch of the British Red Cross Society". . . . . 80·00

RXF8   Middle East forms (8 types). Used for messages from Allied Middle East Forces. Various types of heading. . . . . 60·00

RXF9   New Zealand form. Headed "THE NEW ZEALAND RED CROSS SOCIETY/WELLINGTON, NEW ZEALAND". £150

RXF10   Southern Rhodesian forms (3 types). Headed "MESSAGE FORM" with Southern Rhodesian address at foot. £150

RXF11   Australian forms (3 types). Headed "AUSTRALIAN RED CROSS SOCIETY". £150

RXF12   Indian forms (3 types). Headed "Indian Red Cross, Croix Rouge De L'Inde" £150

RXF13   French forms (2 types). Headed "CROIX-ROUGE FRANCAISE" £150

RXF14   Irish forms (4 types). Headed "CUMANN CROISH DEIRGE NA LEIREANN" £125

RXF15   American forms (2 types). Headed "Comité International de la Croix-Rouge AMERICAN RED CROSS, WASHINGTON, D.C." £100

RXF16   Dutch forms (2 types) headed "Het Nederlandsche Roode Kruis" . . . £150

RXF17   South African forms (3 types). Headed by circular "The South African Red Cross Society" cachet £150

RXF18   Kenyan form. With address "Red Cross Message Bureau, Kenya, No. 1
P.O. Box 712, NAIROBI, Kenya Colony £200
RXF19   Greek form. Sub-headed "CROIX ROUGE HELLENIQUE" £200
RXF20   Italian form headed "Comité International de la Croix-Rouge – Genève.
Delegazione Napoli – Via Tasso 38" £200
     Message Forms from the Channel Islands are known sent to Argentina, Barbados,
Bulgaria, Colombia, Curacao, France, Lebanon, Switzerland, U.S.A. and Venezuela.
(*Price from* £30)

(5) Summary Form used at Lisbon
RXS1   Size 217 × 139mm. Headed "Red Cross Message Bureau/Summary of
Civilian Message in Suspence (sic) at Lisbon, Portugal/Destined for
the Channel Islands." . . . . 50·00

(6) Window Envelopes
     Prices are for clean, uncreased envelopes. Those with postal markings and/or cachets are
worth more.
RXE1   Grey, grey-green or blue-green paper. Size 149 × 120mm. Window
119 × 43mm with 4mm carmine border . . . . 8·00
RXE1a   As RXE1, but window border in blue . . . . 25·00
RXE1b   As RXE1, but Red Cross and motto above "COMITÉ......GENEVE"
instead of below it. . . . . 10·00
RXE1c   As RXE1b, but "No. 52" in very small print above upper right corner of
window . . . . 8·00
RXE1d   As RXE1c, but window border and printing in scarlet . . . . 12·00
RXE2   Size 162 × 115mm. Window 100 × 45mm with Red Cross and motto
alongside. . . . . 15·00
RXE3   As RXE1, but without window . . . . 25·00
RXE4   Grey-green or grey-blue paper. Size 155 × 125mm. Window with
black border and printing in red headed "BAILIFF OF JERSEY'S
(Channel Islands) ENQUIRY AND NEWS SERVICE" . . . . 75·00
     Other envelopes are known, but these carried official correspondence and are rare.

(7) Bradshaw Advice Cards
     All these cards were printed by the Camp du Roi printing works, RXA1/3 on white,
commercially printed postcards and RXA4/7c on coloured card. Three different versions
of text were used and they read as follows:

Text A

The Controlling Committee of the
States of Guernsey.

_____1941

     A communication for you has been received through the International Red
Cross
     If you will call at Elizabeth College between 10.30 a.m. and 12.30 p.m. on
any morning, or between 2.30 p.m. and 5 p.m. on any afternoon (except
Thursday), you can see the communication and send a reply not exceeding 25
words.
     If you do not call within seven days of the above date, it will be concluded
that you do not wish to send a reply.

GEO. A. BRADSHAW,
Red Cross Department.

IMPORTANT—Please bring this Card with you

Text B

The Controlling Committee of the
States of Guernsey.

———

A communication for you has been received through the International Red Cross, from

If you will call at Elizabeth College between 10.30 a.m. and 12.30 p.m. on any morning, or between 2.30 p.m. and 5 p.m. on any afternoon (except Thursday), you can see the communication and send a reply not exceeding 25 words.

If you do not call within seven days of the above date, it will be concluded that you do not wish to send a reply.

GEO A. BRADSHAW,
Red Cross Department.

IMPORTANT—Please bring this Card with you.

Text C

The Controlling Committee of the
States of Guernsey.

———

A communication for you has been received through the International Red Cross, from

If you will call at Elizabeth College between 10.30 a.m. and 12.30 p.m. on any morning, or between 2.30 p.m. and 5 p.m. on any afternoon (except Thursday), you can see the communication and send a reply not exceeding 25 words.

Please reply to this notice immediately. Even if you do not wish to answer the communication, let the Red Cross Department know or you will delay the return of many messages.

GEO. A. BRADSHAW,
Red Cross Department.

IMPORTANT.—Please bring this Card with you.

Camp du Roi Printing Works.

RXA1	Commercially printed postcard (139 × 88mm) ("POSTCARD/The address to be written on this side" printed on front in green) with Text A in black on reverse	35·00
RXA1a	As RXA1 but "IMPORTANT—Please bring this Card with you." printed at foot. "1941" at upper right printed in large italic type	25·00
RXA1b	As RXA1a but "1941" in small roman type	25·00
RXA2	Commercially printed postcard ("PRINTED PAPER RATE", underlined, printed on front) with Text B in deep blue on reverse	25·00
RXA3	Commercially printed postcard ("POSTCARD/THE ADDRESS TO BE WRITTEN ON THIS SIDE" printed on front in green) with Text B in black on the reverse	30·00

RXA3a	As RXA3, but with inscriptions on front in blue using larger type....	30·00
RXA3b	As RXA3a, but showing imprint "CAMP DU ROI PRINTING WORKS" at lower left corner of reverse..................................	30·00
RXA3c	As RXA3b, but lines of inscription on front closer together.........	30·00
RXA4	Printed on pink card. Address side blank. Text C on reverse.........	25·00
RXA4a	As RXA4, but address amended "38 High St." and opening hours "(between 10.00 a.m. and 12.30 p.m. / 2.00 p.m. and 4.30 p.m.)", both in manuscript.......................................	25·00
RXA4b	As RXA4a, but printed on white card. Some cards omit the "38" in the manuscript amendment of the address..........................	30·00
RXA5	Printed on pale yellow-brown card with printed address of 38 High Street. Similar to Text C with words "delay the return" underlined...	30·00
RXA5a	As RXA5, but printed on cream or green card with printer's imprint moved slightly to the right..................................	30·00
RXA5b	As RXA5, but printed on a green card with printer's imprint centred .	30·00
RXA5c	As RXA5b, but printed on green or pink card with address altered to 9 High Street and opening hours in afternoon terminating at 4.00 p.m., both in manuscript....................................	30·00
RXA5d	As RXA5b, but printed on blue, yellow-orange, cream or pink card with address altered to 1 Market Street and opening hours in afternoon terminating at 4.00 p.m., both in manuscript.....................	30·00
RXA6	Printed on green or grey card with printed address of 9-11, High Street between 10.00 a.m. and 1.00 p.m. or between 2.00 p.m. and 4.00 p.m. Printer's imprint central	30·00
RXA6a	As RXA6, but on green, pink, blue or orange card with address altered to 1, Market Street in manuscript..............................	30·00
RXA7	Printed on green, orange or grey card with printed address of 1, Market Street, (Artisans' Institute).................................	30·00
RXA7a	As RXA7, but printed on blue card with printer's imprint moved to left and in upper and lower case letters............................	30·00
RXA7b	As RXA7a, but printer's imprint in upper and lower case italic letters..	25·00
RXA7c	As RXA7a, but printed on orange card	25·00

CACHETS APPLIED TO RED CROSS MESSAGES

RXC4

RXC12

COUPON·RÉPONSE

RXC6

TIMBRE· RÉPONSE

RXC7

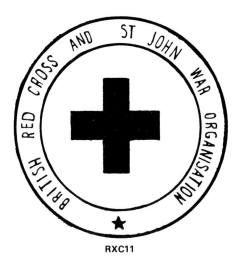

RXC11

RXC13

RXC16

RXC17

RXC18

The Controlling Committee of the
States of Guernsey

Jen. A. Bradshaw.

Red Cross Department.

RXC24

STATES OF GUERNSEY

RED CROSS BUREAU

RXC25

RXC26

RXC27 (*half-size*)

On behalf of the Bailiff
of Jersey's Enquiry and
News Service.

RXC29

RXC31

NOT TO BE USED FOR REPLY
POST OFFICE WILL SUPPLY
ADDRESS OF CITIZENS ADVICE BUREAU
WHERE MESSAGE FORMS ARE OBTAINABLE

RXC32

NOT TO BE USED FOR REPLY
POST OFFICE WILL SUPPLY
ADDRESS OF NEAREST RED
CROSS MESSAGE BUREAU WHICH
WILL DESPATCH A NEW MESS-
AGE FOR YOU.

RXC33

RXC35

RXC38

RXC39

RXC43

RXC45

(1) Cachets used by the International Red Cross at Geneva

RXC1	Double circle, 29mm diameter, reading COMITÉ INTERNATIONAL DE LA CROIX ROUGE—GENEVE. Red cross in centre	1·00
RXC2	As RXC1 but "de la" in lowercase letters	2·00
RXC3	Treble circle, 32mm diameter, otherwise similar to RXC1	10·00
RXC4	Treble circle, 34mm diameter, otherwise similar to RXC1	20·00
RXC5	Treble circle, 36mm diameter, otherwise similar to RXC1	6·00
RXC6	COUPON-REPONSE in single line, 34 × 3mm, in red (*two types*) . .	30·00
RXC6a	As RXC6, but 28 × 2mm	50·00
RXC7	TIMBRE-REPONSE in single line, 35 × 4mm	75·00

(2) Cachets used at the British Red Cross Headquarters

RXC8	Double circle, 52½mm diameter, reading BRITISH RED CROSS AND ST. JOHN WAR ORGANISATION with Red Cross in centre and 8-point asterisk at foot	15·00
RXC9	As RXC8, but 54mm diameter.	20·00
RXC10	As RXC8, but 57mm diameter.	12·00
RXC11	As RXC8, but 58mm and 5-point asterisk	25·00
RXC11a	As RXC8, but 60mm diameter and 5 point asterisk.	15·00

(3) Cachets used in Paris by the French Commission of the German Red Cross

RXC12	Single circle, 36mm diameter, eagle and cross in centre, with wording "Deutsches Rotes Kreuz—Der Beauftrage für Frankreich". Cross in red, rest of cachet in blue (can be found in violet due to mixing of inks) .	6·00
RXC12a	As RXC12, but "in" instead of "für"	50·00
RXC13	Boxed cachet 46½ × 21mm divided horizontally into two sections. "Deutsches Rotes Kreuz" in upper section and "Eing." and "Ausg." in lower section. Roman type. In red	40·00
RXC14	As RXC13, but in Fraktur (Gothic) type, in blue-green	£125
RXC15	As RXC13, but lower part of box removed. In red or blue.	4·00
RXC16	Single circle, 35mm diameter, reading "Deutsches Rotes Kreuz—Der Beauftragte in Frankreich" around outside and "Briefstempel" across centre between two horizontal lines. Fraktur (Gothic) type. Struck in red, crimson, green, light blue, bright blue, purple-brown, violet or grey-black	2·50
RXC17	As RXC16, but Roman type. In maroon, brown or blackish purple . . .	6·00
RXC18	Square, 39 × 39mm, containing single circle, 34mm diameter. Wording as RXC16. Roman type. Eagle at upper centre	8·00

(4) Cachets used in Berlin by the German Red Cross Headquarters

RXC19	As RXC18, but reads "Präsidium" at foot.	£150
RXC20	Two-line cachet reading "Deutsches Rotes Kreuz/Präsidium" in Fraktur (Gothic) type. Unboxed, size 44 × 12mm. Indigo/violet	£150
RXC21	Two-line cachet reading "Deutsches Rotes Kreuz" in Roman type over date. Purple	£125

Nos. RXC19 and RXC20 only occur on official stationery.

(5) Cachets used by the Guernsey Red Cross

RXC22	Typewritten. "The Controlling Committee of the States of Guernsey" with signature of Stamford Raffles in manuscript and "Information Officer" below	£150
RXC22a	As RXC22, but signature of George Bradshaw with "Red Cross Department" below.	25·00
RXC23	As RXC22a, but signature rubber-stamped	5·00
RXC24	As RXC22a, but both wording and signature rubber-stamped. Size 85 × 23mm	4·00
RXC25	Boxed cachet, 67½ × 24mm, reading STATES OF GUERNSEY/RED CROSS BUREAU. In black, blue, violet or green	3·00

(6) Cachets used by the Jersey Red Cross

RXC26	Embossed seal, 36mm diameter, with Arms of Jersey and wording S. BALLIVIE INSVLE DE JERSEYE . . . . *used on its own*	25·00

RXC27   Double circle, 55mm diameter, reading NACHFORSCHUNGS u.
NACHRICHTEN-UEBERMITTELUNGS-STELLE around outside. Red
Cross and DER BAILIFF VON JERSEY in centre £600
RXC28   Unframed three-line cachet, 55 × 11mm, reading ON BEHALF OF
THE BAILIFF/OF JERSEY'S ENQUIRY AND/NEWS SERVICE. In red,
blue, green or violet . . . .   5·00
RXC28a   As RXC28, but 47½ × 11mm . . . .   6·00
RXC29   Boxed cachet, 68 × 23½mm, reading as RXC28 but in upper and
lowercase letters. In red, green, blue or black . . . .   5·00
RXC30   REPLY, 16 × 5mm, in black, blue-black or red. . . . .   10·00
RXC30a   Four-line cachet reading "BAILIFF'S BUREAU/regrets your message
cannot be forwarded/on this occasion" £150

(7) British Censor Marks
RXC31   Octagonal cachet, 35 × 26½mm, containing Crown/PASSED and
P/number. Normally in red, but known in other colours . . . .   2·50
RXC31a   ditto, but with Crown/PASSED/T/number. . . . .   10·00
RXC31b   ditto, but with Crown/PASSED/W/number. . . . .   75·00
RXC31c   ditto, but with Crown/PASSED/PW/number . . . .   50·00
RXC31d   ditto, but with Crown/PASSED/IP/number. . . . .   75·00
RXC31e   MILITARY DEPUTY CHIEF FIELD CENSOR. . . . .   10·00

(8) British Instructional Marks
RXC32   Four-line unboxed cachet, 57 × 14mm, reading NOT TO BE USED
FOR REPLY/POST OFFICE WILL SUPPLY/ADDRESS OF CITIZENS
ADVICE BUREAU/WHERE MESSAGE FORMS ARE OBTAINABLE .   30·00
RXC32a   Wording as RXC32, but size 59 × 19mm. NOT TO BE USED FOR
REPLY in capitals, but rest of text in upper and lowercase letters . . . .   25·00
RXC33   Six-line cachet reading NOT TO BE USED FOR REPLY/POST OFFICE
WILL SUPPLY/ADDRESS OF NEAREST RED/CROSS MESSAGE
BUREAU WHICH/WILL DESPATCH A NEW MESS-/AGE FOR YOU.
Size 66 × 27mm. . . . .   25·00
RXC34   Five-line cachet reading "FURTHER MESSAGES FOR THE
ADDRESSEE/SHOULD BE ADDRESSED TO/RED CROSS BUREAU
201/WARWICK   HOUSE,   ST.   JAMES'S/LONDON   S.W.1.
ENGLAND" . . . .   40·00

(9) British Army Transit Marks
RXC35   Single   circle,   29mm   diameter,   reading   R.E.   RECORD
OFFICE/BRIGHTON. Date across centre . . . .   45·00
RXC36   Rectangular, 45 × 33mm, five-line boxed cachet reading "R.A.
(LIGHT A.A.)/RECORDS/DATE/IBEX HOUSE/MINORIES, E.C.3 . . .   45·00
RXC37   Rectangular, 45 × 25mm, four-line boxed cachet reading R.A.S.C.
RECORDS/DATE/ORE PLACE/HASTINGS . . . .   45·00

(10) German Civil Censor Marks
RXC38   Single   circle,   28mm   diameter,   reading   "Oberkommando der
Wehrmacht – Geprüft", with eagle, swastika, small wavy line to right
and code letter "b" for Berlin. In red . . . .   25·00
RXC38a   As RXC38, but without small wavy line to right of swastika. . . . .   30·00
RXC38b   As RXC38, but code letter "x" (Paris) in red . . . .   25·00
RXC38c   Similar to RXC38b, but 35mm diameter with code letters "n" and "h".
In black . . . .   50·00
RXC39   Single circle Gestapo censor mark, 34mm diameter, reading
"Zensurstelle-Geprüft" and with eagle and swastika in centre. . . . . . .   40·00
RXC40   As RXC38, but "Briefstempel" at foot of circle and no code letter . . .   £100
RXC41   Censor Tape – two horizontal lines with "Geöffnet", 24mm circle with
"Oberkommando der Wehrmacht" eagle and swastika and "x" below
between continuous parallel lines . . . .   15·00

(11) German Military Censor Marks
RXC42   Single circle, 20mm diameter, with capital "A" and small "b" applied
by Abwehr in Berlin . . . .   60·00

RXC43	Boxed cachet, 46 × 29mm, reading "Geprüft/Dienstelle/Feldpost Nr...."	50·00
RXC43a	As RXC43, but no number inserted	40·00
RXC44	Small boxed numbers (19 × 15mm) as 083, 279, 295, 833 etc	30·00

(12) Censor Marks applied at German Internee Camps on Red Cross Forms

| RXC45 | Biberach double circle, 34mm diameter, reading "Internierungslager Biberach/Riss" above, "Postüberwachung" below and "Geprüft" across centre | 80·00 |
| RXC46 | Laufen oval cachet reading "Ilag VII Geprüft" with code figure "4" in centre | 80·00 |

Censor marks from other countries eg Australia, Canada, Egypt, India, Kenya, New Zealand, South Africa, Southern Rhodesia, U.S.A., etc are also known on message forms
(*Price from* £10)

LEAFLETS

(1) Official Stationery of International Red Cross Committee Origin

RXL1	Letter No. 189 – in top right corner (222 × 137mm)	60·00
RXL2	Letter No. 696 – in top right corner (203 × 134mm)	60·00
RXL3	Letter No. 958 – in top right corner (220 × 138mm)	60·00
RXL4	Letter No. 959 – in top right corner (223 × 139mm)	75·00

(2) Official Stationery of British Origin

RXL5	Letter (204 × 126mm) headed WAR ORGANISATION/OF THE/ BRITISH RED CROSS SOCIETY and ORDER OF ST. JOHN OF JERUSALEM / FOREIGN RELATIONS DEPARTMENT / WARWICK HOUSE or CLARENCE HOUSE	25·00
RXL5a	Similar to RXL5, but larger (205 × 165mm). "CLARENCE HOUSE" only	35·00
RXL6	Letter (204 × 126mm) headed WAR ORGANISATION / OF THE / BRITISH RED CROSS SOCIETY and ORDER OF ST JOHN OF JERUSALEM only. Used in Algiers by the North African Commission	45·00
RXL7	Letter (212 × 140mm) similar to RXL5, but sub-headed PRISONERS OF WAR WOUNDED and MISSING/ALL COMMUNICATIONS TO BE ADDRESSED/OFFICER-IN-CHARGE with address 8, Sharia Malika Parida/Cairo	45·00
RXL8	Envelope (133 × 108mm) with emblems of Red Cross and St. John's in top left corner	35·00

(3) Instructional Leaflets

RXL9	Guernsey INSTRUCTIONS FOR REPLYING TO MESSAGES (128 × 87mm) with Red Cross Message Bureau/Market Street at lower right	20·00
RXL10	BAILIFF OF JERSEY'S ENQUIRY AND / NEWS SERVICE (110 × 70mm). "This is a reply to your enquiry and/you may keep the form."	30·00
RXL10a	As RXL10, but with additional words "Please return the envelope and this/slip for further use.	40·00
RXL11	Bailiff's Enquiry and News Office/"Morning News"/Halkett Place/ Jersey.–PARTICULARS OF MESSAGE. (128 × 105mm)	60·00
RXL12	Jersey. REVISED INSTRUCTIONS FOR REPLYING. (125 × 93mm) with wording in second paragraph "..Red Cross Office over Burton's within 48 hours..."	50·00
RXL13	Similar format to RXL12 except "Morning News" is substituted in place of "over Burton's"	50·00
RXL14	I.C.R.C. "Instruction for Reply Label" two-part gummed and perforated label in French (left-hand side 42 × 28mm)	50·00
RXL15	British FR/CL/6 – RED CROSS POSTAL MESSAGE SCHEME	10·00
RXL15a	British FR/CL/6A – RED CROSS MESSAGE SCHEME	15·00

RXL16	British FR/CL/13 – RED CROSS POSTAL MESSAGE SCHEME ...	10·00
RXL17	British FR/C/15a Postcard form of advice	25·00
RXL18	FR/CL/21 Reply to enquiry...........................	15·00
RXL19	British FR/CL/26b INSTRUCTIONS FOR REPLY	15·00
RXL20	British FR/CL/27 INVITATION TO SEND A REPLY	20·00
RXL21	British FR/CL/29 INSTRUCTIONS FOR REPLY....................	15·00
RXL21a	British FR/CL/29a INSTRUCTIONS FOR REPLY (two printings) ...	15·00
RXL21b	British FR/CL/29b INSTRUCTIONS FOR REPLY (two printings) ...	15·00
RXL21c	British FR/CL/29b as above with additional typescript "7) Postal Censorship regulations do not permit for snapshots or photos to accompany postal messages"....................................	30·00
RXL22	BRITISH – Instructions for Replying to Messages (No number) - two different types with underlining	10·00
RXL23	BRITISH INSTRUCTIONS FOR REPLY —stereo-typed 20-line instruction...	25·00
RXL24	British FR/CL/53 Enquiry re Channel Islanders deported	25·00
RXL25	British FR/CL/64 Acknowledgement of replies to inward Channel Islands messages and confirming despatch	35·00
RXL26	British FR/CL/95 Advice to delay answers to message form pending war situation developments.....................................	30·00
RXL27	British FR/CL/96 Small stereotyped form enclosed with message advising use of post for reply	25·00
RXL28	British FR/CL/108 Summaries of messages carried from Channel Islands by S.S. *Vega* in 1945	15·00

(4) British Censorship Leaflets

RXL29	P.C.11 printed form (98 × 51mm) on white or cream paper	15·00
RXL29a	As RXL29, but printed on blue paper	30·00
RXL30	As RXL29, but in stereo-typed form with several different layouts of wording...	10·00
RXL30a	As RXL30, but with the word "letter" crossed through and replaced by "message" and initialled by Censor...............................	15·00
RXL31	P.C.12 POSTAL CENSORSHIP – missing enclosures	30·00
RXL32	P.C.149 Communication with enemy or enemy held territory........	40·00
RXL32a	P.C.149 revised. Wording changed to a more vertical format	20·00
RXL32b	P.C.149 revised (in French)	40·00
RXL32c	P.C.149 (3rd revision) headed BRITISH POSTAL CENSORSHIP....	20·00
RXL32d	P.C.149 (4th revision) headed BRITISH POSTAL CENSORSHIP....	40·00
RXL33	P.C.176 REASONS FOR RETURNING A MESSAGE FORM (two types)	20·00
RXL34	P.C.206 SANCTION BY TRADING WITH ENEMY DEPARTMENT ..	25·00

20. Internee Mail Service

Starting in September 1942 some 2000 British-born Channel Islands residents were deported and interned in Germany. They joined a handful of other civilians from the Channel Islands who had been detained on the Continent during the rapid German advance in 1940.

Following the outbreak of war in 1939 the International Red Cross Committee had sought and obtained the consent of the belligerents to treat internees as prisoners of war. One of the results of this arrangement was that interned civilians were allowed both to send and to receive correspondence. Although it had been instrumental in obtaining the consent of the belligerents, the Red Cross was not responsible for ensuring that a mail service operated.

Article 36 of the 1929 Geneva Convention, which governed the transmission of P.O.W. mail (and by the later agreement the mail of internees also), provided for the exchange of mail by post, by the shortest route and without fee. The belligerent countries arranged amongst themselves, generally by the channel of the Protecting Powers, for the exchange of mail. In Europe, throughout the greater part of the war, the exchange took place through the Swiss postal service, in particular via Basle.

The first deportees left Jersey on 17 September 1942 and Guernsey on 21 September 1942, both groups destined for Germany. The journeys were interrupted and a number of stops were made. During these stops the internees were not permitted to leave the trains in which they were travelling.

Mail is known from temporary camps (*Frontstalag*) at Compiègne and St. Denis in France from a few Channel Islanders who were caught in France and interned before the 1942 deportations, also from some women who were interned there for a short while in 1943 before being moved to Biberach/Riss. Additional mail is known to and from Stalag VIF, Dorsten, in north-west Germany, where internees were held in transit for six to seven weeks.

Ultimately all Channel Islands deportees were, as far as is known, interned in one or other of the six following internee camps: Biberach/Riss (Ilag VB) in Württemberg; Wurzach/Allgäu (Ilag VC) in Württemberg; Laufen Obb (Ilag VII) in Upper Bavaria; Kreuzburg (Ilag VIIIZ) in Upper Silesia; Libenau in Württemberg; and Walzburg–Weissenburg (Ilag XIII) in Bavaria.

The majority of mail is from Biberach/Riss or Laufen, addressed either to the Channel Islands or to the United Kingdom. Mail from the camps was written on "free-issue" pre-printed cards or lettersheets, the senders being restricted to a maximum of one per week. Such cards postmarked at Tittmoning are believed to have originated at Laufen.

Correspondence to the camps was sent in plain, unstamped envelopes, generally with the added manuscript annotations "Interniertenpost" when from the Channel Islands or "Kriegsgefangenenpost" when from the United Kingdom, although "Interniertenpost" was sometimes used from the U.K. Fee-paid P.O.W. airletters are known from the U.K. and include the pre-printed $2\frac{1}{2}$d. envelopes and the plain 5d. envelopes.

Correspondence to and from the Channel Islands effectively ceased in June 1944, but mail is known to have been carried by the Red Cross vessel S.S. *Vega* during the winter of 1944–45.

All mails were subject to censorship, most mails of camp origins bearing either a cachet or censor mark and some additional German or British censor marks. Additional internee mail to the Channel Islands is known both from Italy and from the British camp on the Isle of Man which held German internees.

All the official *Interniertenpost* stationery, when used, bears certain markings which include postmarks, camp censor marks and camp cachets. The following listing allows for the card or lettersheet to bear a town or dumb cancel postmark, the cheapest variety of camp censor mark and the cheapest variety of camp cachet. Any stationery bearing an additional or more expensive mark is priced at the value of the dearest mark.

Items of mail to or from Channel Islanders in concentration camps, in civil prisons in Germany and France or in internment camps in Switzerland for escaped prisoners of war are known, but are very rare.

(Price per item from £250)

INTERNEE STATIONERY

Postcards. All cards of German origin are 149 × 96mm or 148 × 98mm and, with four exceptions, are of similar format. The camp name is usually pre-printed in the sender's panel at the left. The cards were used from late 1942 until 1945.

(For cards in pristine condition add 20%.)

Cat. No.		To the C.I.	To the U.K.
IP1	Biberach/Riss *Interniertenpost* postcard	20·00	8·00
IP2	Wurzach/Allgäu *Interniertenpost* postcard	40·00	20·00
IP3	Ilag VII (Laufen Obb) *Interniertenpost* postcard	20·00	10·00
IP4	Ilag VII (Laufen Obb) Christmas card (1943). Picture of camp and ''Christmas Greetings from Schloss Laufen''.	40·00	20·00
IP5	Ilag VII (Laufen Obb) Christmas card (1944). Line-drawing of inside of canteen and ''1944 A Merry Christmas and A Happy New Year Ilag VII 1945''.	45·00	20·00
IP6	Ilag VII (Laufen Obb) special bilingual Polish/English postcard. Used in 1943–44 to notify internees' relatives of the receipt of a parcel through the Red Cross	45·00	30·00
IP7	Liebenau *Interniertenpost* postcard	†	£100
IP7a	Kreuzburg *Interniertenpost* postcard	£100	50·00
IP7b	Tittmoning *Interniertenpost* postcard.	£100	50·00
IP8	Wurzach/Allgäu, Oflag 55VD, *Kriegsgefangenenpost* postcard (in German and French)	80·00	30·00
IP8a	ditto, but Biberach	40·00	15·00
IP9	''Universal'' *Kriegsgefangenenpost* postcard (in German only), from any internee camp	20·00	10·00
IP10	Postcard from Grande Caserne, Paris, used in 1941	£180	†

Lettersheets. All the lettersheets used were of the fold-over and tuck-in type, and the overall dimensions of those of German origin were 286 × 146mm. As they were printed on chalk-surfaced paper they are generally found in poor condition.

(For examples in fine condition add 20%.)

Cat. No.		To the C.I.	To the U.K.
IP11	Biberach/Riss *Interniertenpost* lettersheet	20·00	8·00
IP12	Wurzach/Allgäu *Interniertenpost* lettersheet.	40·00	20·00
IP13	Ilag VII (Laufen Obb) *Interniertenpost* lettersheet.	30·00	10·00
IP14	Ilag VII (Laufen Obb) provisional lettersheet. "Kriegsgefangenenpost" obliterated and "Jnterniertenpost" (*sic*) substituted	45·00	20·00
IP15	Kreuzburg *Interniertenpost* lettersheet.	£120	40·00
IP16	"Universal" *Kriegsgefangenenpost* lettersheet	30·00	10·00

Cat. No.		Unused	To Germany
IP17	*Interniertenpost* lettersheet from the Channel Islands, inscribed KANAL INSELN at foot.	£120	£250

Cat. No.		from	To the C.I.
IP18	Mail from Walzburg–Weissenburg	*from*	£200
IP19	British lettersheets of Isle of Man origin addressed to Guernsey.	*from*	£140

Airletters. The only airletters known to have been used are of British origin. They were first introduced on 21 July 1941 and were sold at 3d. each, including 2½d. postage (the European rate). Three types exist.

Cat. No.	To Germany
IP20 2½d. British airletter inscribed in English, French and German	40·00

Covers. This category includes all mail carried in commercial envelopes or newspaper wrappers, etc. Each piece would be expected to carry one, or more, of the following: an adhesive postage stamp where applicable, a town or dumb cancellation postmark, and the cheapest variety of censor mark, where applicable. Any cover bearing an additional or more expensive mark is priced at the value of the dearest mark (*see* the priced list of postmarks, censor cachets, camp cachets and instructional marks below).

Cat. No.		Price
IP21	From a German camp to Germany	£100
IP22	From Germany to a German camp	£100
IP23	From the U.K. to a German camp (free rate)	20·00
IP24	From the U.K. to a German camp (5d. airmail rate)	50·00
IP25	From a U.K. Isle of Man camp to Guernsey (5d. airmail rate)	£150
IP26	From the Channel Islands to a German camp	£100
IP27	Newspaper wrappers (1d. rate)	£100
IP28	Fee-paid internee mail of Italian origin from *isolati* (British citizens living at liberty) addressed to the Channel Islands. . . . . *from*	£200

Unofficial Stationery. In the periods of shortage during and immediately after the war, hand-made cards were produced by both internees and the camp authorities. These cards, hand written, are of the same format as the Official cards. They are only known from Ilag VII, Laufen.

Cat. No.		Price
IP29	Ilag VII (Laufen Obb)	£120

MARKINGS

Postmarks, censor cachets, camp cachets and instructional marks. Because the operation of the mail service was the responsibility of the belligerents, nearly all pieces of mail bear a postmark from the place of origin, most of which are of no significance. One of the exceptions is mail of Channel Island origin, addressed to German camps, which does not usually bear a postmark. This may be recognised by the lack of both an adhesive postage stamp and a country of origin censor mark.

IPC10

IPC14

IPC18

IPC16

IPC31

 Geöffnet Geöffnet

IPC44

IPC46

RETURNED FROM CONTINENT IN UNDELIVERED MAILS

IPC53

Cat. No.		Price on entire

(1) German Postmarks

IPC1   German town cancel, with name of town and code. Double circle, 28mm diameter . . . . 25·00

IPC2   German "dumb" cancel (no place name shown), 28mm diameter. Used on Biberach mail . . . . 25·00

IPC2a   As IPC2, but used on Dorsten mail (Sept–Nov 1942) . . . . 80·00

IPC3   As IPC2 but 29mm diameter and used on Kreuzburg mail . . . . 80·00

IPC4   TITTMONING town cancel with code "a" at foot, 28mm diameter. Used from 5 to 13 April 1943 . . . . 80·00

(2) French Postmarks

IPC5   PARIS GARE DU NORD—PROVINCE A, single circle, 26mm diameter, used only during May 1944 . . . . £180

IPC6   POSTE AUX ARMES, single circle, 27mm diameter, only known used 28 April 1945 on mail from Biberach/Riss. This date is *after* the liberation of Biberach/Riss by U.S. forces but *before* the liberation of the Channel Islands. Mail was processed by the French £120

Cat.	Price
No.	on entire

(3) Internee Camp Censor Marks

IPC7   Double circle, 33mm diameter, reading "Internierungslager Biberach/ Riss-Postüberwachung" around outside and "Geprüft" across centre. In violet, used from September 1943 to February 1945 .... 20·00

IPC8   "D22" code, 5mm high. Censor mark used at Biberach/Riss. In blue-black or violet, used on mail received from the U.K. from late 1944 onwards .... 30·00

IPC9   Double oval, 38 × 24mm, reading "Ilag VII–Geprüft" and with code number in centre. In violet or blue-violet. Used from June 1941 to November 1944 .... 20·00

IPC10 Single circle, 32mm diameter, reading "Ilag VII–Geprüft" and with code number in centre. In violet or blue-violet. In use from November 1042 to November 1944 .... 20·00

IPC11 Similar to IPC10 but "Ilag" misspelt JLAG, and in capitals. Code number "13" in centre. In violet or blue-violet. Used during October 1944 only 40·00

IPC12 Double circle (outer circle has "cogwheel" effect), 29mm diameter. Code "2" in centre. Used at Kreuzburg in Spring 1944 .... 80·00

IPC13 Triangle, 22mm high, reading "Ilag VIII/Geprüft" and code number. Used at Kreuzburg in the latter half of 1944 .... 80·00

IPC14 Shield type, 29mm high, reading "Ilag VIII/Geprüft" with code number. In scarlet. Used at Kreuzburg in Spring 1944 .... 80·00

IPC15 Single circle, 33mm diameter, reading "Oflag VD/geprüft" and code number in centre. In violet. Used until early 1943 .... £100

(4) Internee Camp Cachets

IPC16 Single circle, 33mm diameter, reading "Internierungslager— Biberach/ Riss", and with eagle over swastika in centre. In violet. Used in December 1942 and December 1943 .... 50·00

IPC17 "Internierungslager/Biberach/Riss" in Fraktur (Gothic type) in two lines, size 59 × 9mm. In violet. Used from early 1942 .... 60·00

IPC18 As IPC17, but smaller type and in one line 56 mm long. In violet. Used in first half of 1943 .... 20·00

IPC19 "Zivilinternierungslager Biberach/Riss" in single line cachet, 61mm long. In violet. Used during second half of 1944 .... 40·00

IPC20 "Biberach an der Riss" in single line, 34mm long. Used during second half of 1944 .... 30·00

IPC21 As IPC16, but reading "Wurzach" at foot. Used in December 1942 .... 50·00

IPC22 "Internierungslager Wurzach (Württ.)", 64mm long, similar to IPC18. In violet. Used early 1943 to 1944 .... 60·00

IPC23 Similar to IPC16, but reading "Jlag VII" [*sic*] at top £120

IPC24 "Jlag VIII" [*sic*], 24mm long. In violet. Used in November 1942 and August 1943 .... 40·00

IPC25 "Laufen/Obb.", 49mm long. In violet. Used in November 1942 .... 40·00

IPC26 "Ilag VIII Z", 24mm long. Used at Kreuzburg in second half of 1944... 85·00

(5) Internee Camp Instructional Marks

IPC27 "Jnternierten-Post" [*sic*], 67mm long. Used on mail from Laufen in November 1942 and August 1943 .... 30·00

IPC28 "Nicht im Ilag VIII", 35mm long. In violet. Used in April 1943 .... 80·00

(6) Transit Camp Censor Marks

IPC29 Double circle, 27mm diameter (outer circle with "cogwheel" effect), reading FR. STALAG/122/GEPRUFT. In scarlet. Used during 1943.. £150

IPC30 As IPC29, but with code "9" at foot. In violet. Used in 1943 .... £150

IPC31 Diamond-shaped cachet, 58 × 28mm, reading "Frontstalag 122/ Geprüft". In violet £150

Cat. No.		Price on entire

IPC32   Boxed cachet, 39½ × 15½mm, reading GEPRÜFT with code number "6"
below. In violet. Used at Compiègne in 1943 .... £150

IPC33   As IPC32, but 41 × 19mm and with code number "2". In crimson. Used
at St. Denis in 1944 .... £150

IPC34   As IPC32, but 40 × 18mm and code number "3". In crimson. Used at
St. Denis in 1944 .... £150

IPC35   As IPC30, but 30mm diameter and code number "8". In violet. Used at
St. Denis in July 1943 .... £150

(7) British Censor Marks

Cachet RXC31 (*see* Section 19) is known on internee mail, also a censor label designated
P.C.90, reading OPENED BY EXAMINER, etc.

(*Price* £13)

A double-circle DEPUTY CHIEF CENSOR mark (21mm diameter) in black has been seen
on post-liberation mail.

(*Price* £80)

Additional British censor marks struck in the Isle of Man internee camps are known.

(*Price on mail addressed to Guernsey from* £80)

(8) German Censor Marks

Cachets RXC38 and RXC38b (*see* Section 19) are known on internee mail, as well as
similar cachets with code letters for different points of application. Indeed, the majority of
German censor marks are identifiable from these code letters (fourteen different codes are
known, but not all were used on Channel Islands internee mail).

(*Price* £18)

IPC36   As RXC38b (*see* Section 19) but coded "y" for Bordeaux. In black. Only
seen used on mail from Isle of Man internee camps to Guernsey..... £150

IPC37   Similar to IPC36, but 35mm diameter and coded "c" for Cologne. In red   30·00

IPC38   Similar to IPC36, but 35mm diameter and coded "e" for Frankfurt-am-
Main. In red .... 20·00

IPC39   Similar to IPC36, but 35mm diameter and coded "d" for Munich. In red
or blue... 20·00

IPC40   Munich individual censor mark. Two-, three- or four-digit code number
in rectangular box, 27 × 15mm. In red. Usually present in pairs (i.e.
two different code numbers) as the censors made a double check ... 20·00

IPC41   As IPC40, but 12 × 8mm... 20·00

IPC42   Similar to IPC40/41, but 9 × 4mm, containing numeral code (Frankfurt-
am-Main censor mark). In red or black........................... 20·00

IPC43   "Geprüft/Dienststelle Feldpost 45190" (Paris censor mark), in two lines
46mm long. In red. Used until December 1942 on internee mail from
the U.K. to Guernsey... £120

IPC44   Continuous censor tape 40mm wide. Coded "e" (for Frankfurt-am-
Main) and printed in violet. Used on internee mail from the U.K. to
Guernsey... £150

IPC45   Continuous Frankfurt-am-Main censor mark, comprising single-circle
cachets (19mm diameter) 79mm apart, linked by six parallel horizontal
lines. Cachets read "Geprüft/Oberkommando der Wehrmacht", with
code "e" and eagle and swastika in centre. In deep red. Used on
internee mail from the U.K. to Guernsey £150

(9) Transit Marks

Cachet RXC1 (*see* Section 19) is known struck in red at Geneva on internee mail from
November 1944.

IPC46   Single-circle cachet, containing code "Ab" (Berlin). Known 16mm,
20mm or 21mm diameter and in black, violet or red................ 80·00

Cat. No.		Price on entire

IPC47 Similar to IPC46, but coded "Ae" (Frankfurt-am-Main). Diameter 19mm, 20mm or 21mm. In red or red-violet . . . . 50·00

IPC48 Similar to IPC46, but coded "Ax" (Paris). Diameter 19mm or 20mm. In red or red-brown . . . . 50·00

IPC49 Hexagonal Madrid airmail transit mark, 30mm across, reading CORREO AEREO/MADRID and date. In black. Used on internee mail from the U.K. Isle of Man camp to Guernsey £130

IPC50 Boxed cachet, 56 × 26mm, reading BRITISH RED CROSS/AUSTRIA and cross. Used by British Red Cross commission in Austria on liberation mail from Ilag VII in 1945. In dull pink £120

(10) Instructional Marks

Cachet PW9 (*see* Section 21) has been seen used on internee mail as well as on P.O.W. mail.

IPC51 Rectangular boxed cachet, 62 × 18mm, reading UNDELIVERED FOR REASON STATED/RETURN TO SENDER . . . . 30·00

IPC52 Rectangular boxed cachet, 74 × 17mm, reading "This letter/postcard has been returned by the/International Red Cross Committee at Geneva/who were unable to forward it". In violet. Used in conjunction with IPC51 . . . . 50·00

IPC53 Rectangular boxed cachet, 75 × 18mm, reading RETURNED FROM/CONTINENT IN/UNDELIVERED MAILS. In violet . . . . 50·00

IPC54 Rectangular boxed cachet, 32 × 11mm, reading RETOUR / A L'ENVOYEUR. In black. Used in Paris in July 1944 . . . . 50·00

21. Prisoner of War Mail

First World War

A P.O.W. Camp for German prisoners was opened at Blanches Banques in Jersey on 20 March 1915. For a few weeks, until an individual censorship cachet was provided, a standard type reading "POST FREE/PRISONERS OF WAR/P.C." in a single circle was used. This can be found in black or magenta and the only proof of its use in Jersey is the name and address of the P.O.W. written on the back. It is also known used during 1917 on two items.

(Price on cover £120)

In April 1915 a double-circle stamp with "JERSEY" at the top, "CHANNEL ISLANDS" at the bottom and "P.C." in the centre was introduced. It is known in red for most of 1915 and then in violet. Covers usually bear, in addition, an oval black stamp inscribed "PRISONERS OF WAR/INFORMATION BUREAU" with a crown in the centre and the London "Official Paid" datestamp.

(Price on cover £100)

Mail from England sent to prisoners-of-war in the Jersey camp received a double-circle with "P.C." in the centre and no other marks.

(Price on cover £100)

Second World War

During the Second World War responsibilty for the prisoners of war mail service rested with the belligerents, and the basic details have been outlined in Section 20 on internee mails.

Three distinct periods exist, the first being immediately after the Occupation, the second lasting until the end of the war, and the third following the cessation of hostilities. During the first period mails are known from British servicemen caught on the Islands and held in France. During the second period mails exist from many of the 150 German P.O.W. camps; additionally mails are known from Italian P.O.W. camps. Finally, during the third period, mail is known addressed to a German serviceman held as a P.O.W. on Jersey.

Most of the mail originated in German camps and the following are the German names for the different types of camp: *Stammlager* or *Stalag*, prisoner of war camp; *Offizierlager* or *Oflag*, officer camp; *Marinelager* or *Marlag*, naval camp; *Luftlager* or *Stalag Luft*, air force camp; *Durchgangslager* or *Dulag*, transit camp; *Straflager* or *Stralag*, penal camp. The camps were identified by a code which was either a Roman numeral/alpha or an Arabic numeral (the Roman numeral was that of the German military district or *Wehrkreis*). From 1939 to 1945 an attempt was made to keep all locations secret and censorship regulations dictated that only "dumb" cancels (that is, those not showing the place of origin) were to be used on P.O.W. mail; nevertheless, covers bearing town cancels do exist.

Each German camp had its own censor office which stamped all mail. The handstamps used were non-uniform, indeed within individual camps stamps were often of completely different form. The stamps usually bear the camp number and the individual censor's number and are known in a variety of colours.

Post Occupation Mails in July 1940. Two pieces are known. The first, from Cherbourg addressed to Jersey, is marked "P.G." (*Prisonnier de Guerre*) and also "Inadmis/Retour a L'Envoyeur". After being returned to sender it was smuggled in by a Jersey fisherman. The second, from Granville, was carried to Jersey by a ship's pilot. It is marked "Geprüft" in red manuscript and handstamped "Dienststelle/ Inselkommandantur/Jersey" in violet.

(*Price* £180 *each piece*)

Late 1940 to May 1945. Both inward and outward P.O.W. camp mail exists. The stationery used was similar to that for the internee mail service.

Cat. No.		Price
PW1	P.O.W. card or lettersheet from a *Stalag*	30·00
PW2	P.O.W. card or lettersheet from an *Oflag*	40·00
PW3	P.O.W. card or lettersheet from a *Marlag*	45·00
PW4	P.O.W. card or lettersheet from a *Luftlager*	45·00
PW5	P.O.W. card or lettersheet from a *Dulag*	50·00
PW6	P.O.W. card or lettersheet from a *Stralag*	60·00
PW7	Cover from the Channel Islands to a German P.O.W. camp	80·00
PW8	German town cancel on P.O.W. card or lettersheet	50·00
PW9	BRITANNIQUE, 42mm long, unframed. In violet or red on mail to a German camp... *cover*	£100
PW10	SHORT AND LEGIBLE LETTERS WILL RECEIVE PRIORITY, in two lines 48mm long. In deep blue .... *cover*	40·00
PW11	Boxed cachet, 68 × 15mm, reading PAS DE LONGUES LETTRES/ECRITURE TRES LISIBLE. In violet .... *cover*	40·00
PW12	BESETZTES GEBIET, single-line cachet in red. Applied by the German authorities to mail originating in occupied territory.......... *cover*	40·00
PW13	P.O.W. card from an Italian camp to Jersey or Guernsey (scarcer than German cards) .... *from*	£100

Post-war Mails. After the surrender of the Channel Islands in May 1945, large numbers of German prisoners of war fell into Allied hands, of which some were held on the Islands.

Mail from Germany to P.O.W.'s in Camp 802 on Jersey is very scarce

(*Price from* £340)

Two letters from German P.O.W.'s in Camp 802 are also known (*Price from* £300)

22. Aerial Propaganda Leaflets

During the Second World War allied propaganda leaflets were dropped over every occupied country. The Channel Islands were not forgotten and examples of leaflets dropped there make interesting reading. They are keenly sought after by collectors of Channel Islands postal history material. Two classes of leaflet were dropped, the first in English for the information and comfort of the civilian population and the second in German for the demoralisation of the occupying forces.

Leaflets for Civilians. In the first group are four leaflets, but only three were actually dropped. The first is headed "News from England" in Gothic letters, and is dated September 1940. It is inscribed "Distributed by the R.A.F." and has as its main feature a message from King George VI. It is numbered 600/1 and was dropped on the night of 23/24 September 1940.

The second is somewhat similar, but bears the inscription "News from England" in Roman letters and is dated 30 September 1940. It is also inscribed "Distributed by the R.A.F." and "For the Channel Islands". It is numbered 600/2 and was dropped between 7/8 and 15/16 October 1940.

The third leaflet is a rather attractive one entitled "The Archbishop of York speaks to the people of the Channel Islands" and is printed in red and black. Its four pages contain the sermon preached by the archbishop on Sunday 31 January 1943 in St. Martin-in-the-Fields Church, and broadcast by the B.B.C. Home Service. The archbishop took as his text the words from Isaiah. "Comfort ye, comfort ye my people, saith your God". The leaflet also has pictures of the archbishop and of St. Martin-in-the-Fields. It is numbered J1 and was dropped on 4/5 March 1943.

The fourth leaflet, which for some reason was never dropped, bears on one side the Royal Arms and in bold capitals "To the inhabitants of the Channel Islands", and on the other side a statement made in the House of Commons by the Home Secretary, Mr. Herbert Morrison, on Tuesday, 12 December 1944. The statement deals with the sending of medicine, soap and food parcels to the islanders. The leaflet is numbered J2.

Leaflets for Occupation Forces. The second group of leaflets consists of a series of over 300 prepared by S.H.A.E.F (Supreme Headquarters Allied Expeditionary Forces) and dropped almost daily, by the British and American Air Forces, behind the enemy front line and over isolated garrisons in the Channel Islands and elsewhere. These are the famous *Nachrichten* newspapers which gave the German forces latest details of the Allied war effort. Not every one of the series was dropped over the Channel Islands and it is, in any case, virtually impossible to obtain all of them, so those interested are advised to include a representative selection. The leaflets actually dropped on the Islands between 31 August 1944 and May 1945 were numbers 136, 137, 138, 143, 145, 147, 148, 150, 151, 152, 155, 156, 158, 159, 160, 161 and an un-numbered "Extrablatt" (dropped 5/6 May 1945).

Eight issues of the famous *Le Courrier de L'Air* series were dropped over the Islands between 26/27 November 1941 and 25/26 March 1944, together with other leaflets in French.

A miniature German newspaper, *Front und Heimat* (Front and Home) was dropped over the Channel Islands by the *Luftwaffe* for the German forces after they were cut off from France by the Allies.

A 12-page, sepia-coloured, illustrated booklet in English headed "We Protest", and with a picture of Field-Marshal Montgomery on the front, was distributed in Jersey by the Germans one night in 1944 after the Allied landing in Normandy. It purported to be a leaflet prepared by Allied soldiers, protesting at the politicians' presentation of the German soldier as a weakling. The text is rather crude and contains one or two obscene words.

Included in the disseminations for the German troops by the Allies were certain items of "black" propaganda, i.e purporting to come from German sources. No details of these have been given officially, but known to have been dropped over Jersey on 9 September 1944 were small booklets entitled *Stiegel der Holzhauer*. These had the appearance of genuine German stories, but included a great deal of information, with illustrations, describing how to "go sick" so as to avoid fighting. It is interesting to note that similar information was dropped by the Germans on Allied troops in Italy. Fake 50 Reichspfennig Forces vouchers were dropped over Guernsey and Sark in September 1944, the reverse being printed with a verse emphasizing their worthlessness.

Cat. No.	Leaflet	Price
PL1	*News from England*, 600/1	8·00
PL2	*News from England*, 600/2	12·00
PL3	*The Archbishop of York*, etc., J1	30·00
PL4	*To the inhabitants*, etc., J2	50·00
PL5	*Nachrichten* newspaper *from*	3·00
PL6	*Le Courrier de L'Air*	3·00
PL7	*L'Amerique en Guerre*. Double sheet. (Three editions dropped between October and December 1943)	5·00
PL8	*Pourquoi cette photo vous regarde*. Single sheet. (7 November 1941)	10·00
PL9	*Francais—Quand nos Avions Viennent*. Single sheet (7 January 1942)	5·00
PL10	Fake 50 Reichspfennig Forces voucher (Three versions, each with a different verse in German on reverse) (6 September 1944)	40·00
PL11	*Stiegel der Holzhauer*. Booklet on how to feign illness (9 September 1944)	30·00
PL12	*Front und Heimat*. Miniature newspaper	4·00
PL13	*We Protest*. Booklet	20·00
PL14	*Entente Cordiale*	15·00

Other leaflets are reported to exist, together with further items from the French series which may not have been used over the Channel Islands.

23. Parcel Post Labels

Parcel post labels were introduced by the British Post Office on 1 August 1883. Sixteen different types (plus sub-types) have been issued, but not all are known used in the Channel Islands.

Most types show the name of the office, the head office, the telegraphic code address, with special panels in which details of the postage, registration and insurance could be entered, the adhesives stuck and the datestamp applied. Often the adhesives were cancelled with a different marking from the datestamp.

For example, the postage stamp might be cancelled with a double-ring parcel post marking (e.g. Jersey Type **J63**) and the space provided for "Office Stamp" or "Date Stamp" could show a sub-office c.d.s. (listed in Section 14).

The labels are mostly scarce or very scarce. They were affixed to the parcel, but they more often occur without stamps than with, either because the stamps were stuck elsewhere on the parcel or because they were later soaked off.

No. PP4

No. PP5

Eight different types are so far recorded for the Channel Islands. differing in details of wording in the upper parts. Those listed as PP7 and PP8 are unnamed and must, of course, be used with a Channel Islands c.d.s. The labels are of importance to specialists because they show examples of some of the scarcer sub-office datestamps; also because they often bear postage stamps not usually found on cover.

Prices are for labels only or for those adhesives of little value. The value of high denomination stamps must be added to that of the label when these appear.

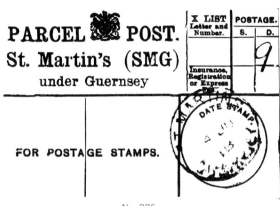

No. PP6

Cat. No.	Distinguishing wording, etc.	Dates of use	Price
PP1	PARCELS POST	1883	90·00
PP2	PARCEL POST; italic *For Postage Stamps*	1884–95 ...	40·00
PP3	Postage box headed S.D.; no space for Registration, etc.	1887–1905 .	25·00
PP4	Space provided for Registration	1891–1905 .	25·00
PP5	Space provided for Registration and Express (two types)	1900–13 ...	20·00
PP6	Space provided for Registration, Express or Insurance Fee (two types)	1909–20s	20·00
PP7	Label 50 × 40mm; coat of arms; no printed office name	1918–30s ..	15·00
PP8	Label 35 × 42mm; no coat of arms; no printed office name	1938–50s ..	10·00

Sub-Offices. The earlier labels were printed in versions specifically for the sub-offices and ALL are scarce or rare. Only about 100 have been recorded for Jersey and 60 for Guernsey, with not more that 13 from any one office. From most offices only two or three examples are known. Labels are known from the following places listed in ascending order of scarcity:

Jersey. Rouge Bouillon: Havre des Pas: David Place, St. Aubins: Georgetown: Beaumont, St. Brelade's Bay: Cheapside, Millbrook, Samares, La Rocque, First Tower: Colomberie, Beresford St., Gorey Village, Grouville: Five Oaks, Carrefours Selous, Gorey: St. Martin's, St. Owen's, St. Peter's, Town Mills.

Guernsey. Vale Road, Sark, Les Gravees: Market Place: St. Peter-in-the-Wood: Câtel, St. Sampson's, Alderney: St. Martin's, The Vale: Cobo, L'Islet, St. Andrew's: Forest, Mount Row.

Customs Duty Parcel Post Labels

On 1 November 1895 the British Post Office instituted a service whereby dutiable goods like tobacco sent from the Channel Islands to Britain could have charges prepaid with postage stamps. Special green labels with separate spaces for the stamps paying postage and those paying customs duty were introduced and a handling charge of 1s. per parcel was made. The system was also used for prepayment of purchase tax in due course and it ceased to function on 30 June 1971, G.B. stamps being then no longer valid on the Islands. A single example of No. CP10 is known used with stamps of the Guernsey independent postal administration.

No. CP9

The labels measure 89 × 108mm and are scarce. Victorian and Edwardian labels have the stamps paying postage cancelled with a datestamp and those paying duty cancelled with a double-ring rubber stamps normally used as a parcel-post cancellation. Later issues have all the stamps cancelled with the same datestamp.

The labels in the upper part read "PARCEL POST" (either side of a coat of arms) below which is "JERSEY (JE)", "GUERNSEY (GU)" or "ALDERNEY (ACK)" with details of postage and registration or express fees in boxes to the right. Below these are boxes for postage stamps to be affixed and office datestamp to be applied. Below the boxes is the caption "Amount prepaid for Customs Dues.../(Stamps for this be affixed below)".

An Alderney label of 1936 is known overprinted for use in Jersey by means of a rubber stamp with JERSEY in a box. Perhaps the remaining Alderney stock was transferred to Jersey to meet a temporary shortage.

Cat. No.	Distinguishing wording, etc.	Dates of use	Price
Jersey			
CP1	Fee paid on/Registration; also "Office Stamp" (upper and lowercase)	1896	80·00
CP2	Fee paid on/Registration; also OFFICE STAMP	1901	50·00
CP3	Registration and/Express Fees; also OFFICE STAMP	1903	40·00
CP4	Registration and/Express Fees; also DATE STAMP	1913–17 . . .	35·00
CP4a	ditto, but with St. Edward's Crown	1954–59 . . .	35·00
CP4b	As CP4a, but with "JE5" in top left corner	1950s	40·00
Guernsey			
CP5	Registration and/Express Fees; also OFFICE STAMP	1905	60·00
CP6	ditto, but with DATE STAMP	1911	50·00
CP7	ditto, but with DATE STAMP and arms of George V	1914	40·00
CP8	Registration/ and Express/Fees; also DATE STAMP	1910	50·00
CP9	ditto, but with arms of George VI	1952–56 . . .	40·00
CP10	ditto, but with St. Edward's Crown	1970	£100
Alderney			
CP11	Name in upper and lowercase	1910	£150
CP12	Name in capitals	1936	£100
CP13	As CP12 overprinted JERSEY by rubber stamp	1936	£100

There are also typographical differences in the labels especially Nos. CP5/6 and the coat of arms was changed at the beginning of each new reign. The prices are for examples with low value stamps affixed. High value stamps, as often used, will considerably enhance the prices.

The usual Parcel Post cancel on the stamps is the double-circle type with the name across the middle, **J63** and **G56**, but occasionally **G57** or a sub-office cancel is found and these are worth more.

Forged Edward VII Stamp. The London stamp dealer, George Lowden (trading as George Ellis) was convicted in 1913 for selling photo-lithographed copies of the King Edward VII £1 green. These are on thinner paper than the genuine, have a roughly impressed crown watermark and are slightly deeper in colour.

Each has a forged Jersey postmark, because the £1 Edward was frequently used for payment of customs duty as mentioned above.

Lowden had 2679 copies for sale, but most were destroyed after the case.

(*Price of forgery* £200)

Keep this Catalogue up to date month by month with

STANLEY GIBBONS UNIVERSAL
The complete collecting system.

If your collection include booklets, first day covers or presentation packs as well as stamps, you will undoubtedly have faced the problem as to how best to mount them all up. This problem is now solved – thanks to the Stanley Gibbons Universal System.

The advantage of the Universal is that it is based on a standard 22 ring binder with a choice of twelve different leaf formats; thus enabling stamps, covers, entires, booklets and presentation packs to be included either in the same album or in a series of matching albums. There are three different stamp albums, a cover album, a booklet album and a presentation pack album in the Universal range as well as extra binders and packs of leaves in all twelve formats.

The Universal Stamp Album
is available with either white unfaced, white faced or black faced leaves.

The Universal Cover Album
contains 13 leaves, 12 double pocket and 1 single pocket; the latter taking covers up to 8½in × 10½in.

The Universal Booklet Album
with six different leaf types available. Stitched, folded, "Prestige" and the latest "window" style booklets can be included in the same album.

The Universal Presentation Pack Leaves
Yes – presentation packs too can now be mounted alongside basic sets and covers – once again two different leaf formats are offered – single or double pocket.

All Universal Albums and binders
are available in a choice of dark red, deep blue or brown grained PVC, gold blocked on the spine and presented in a smart slip box.

For further details visit your favourite stamp shop or, in case of difficulty write to:

Stanley Gibbons Publications Ltd.,
5 Parkside,
Christchurch Road,
Ringwood, Hampshire BH24 3SH
Telephone 0425 472363

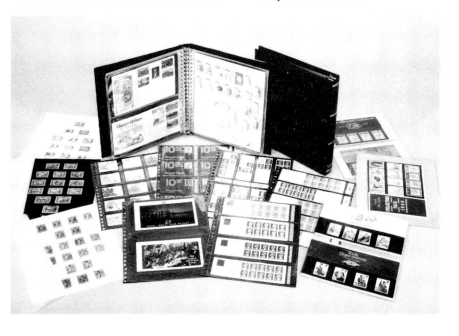

COVER ALBUMS

With cover collecting growing in popularity all the time we are proud to offer a comprehensive range of albums to meet the needs of first day cover collector and postal historian alike. All leaves have black card inserts to set off your covers to best advantage.

1. THE NEW PIONEER COVER ALBUM

A fully padded PVC Binder in a choice of black, green or red. Holds up to 40 covers in a high capacity, low priced album, ideal for the beginner.

2. THE MALVERN COVER ALBUM

Another great value album suitable for collectors at all levels. The 4-ring arch fitting binder contains 19 double-pocket leaves, 1 single-pocket leaves and holds up to 78 covers in all. Available in blue, green or red.

3. THE NEW CLASSIC COVER ALBUM

A compact de-luxe album with 20 crystal clear leaves offering full protection for up to 40 covers and two clear fly leaves to hold an index of notes. Available in black, red or blue and supplied in a protective slip box.

4. THE UNIVERSAL COVER ALBUM

The cover album which allows stamps, booklets and presentation packs to be housed all together – see page 379 for details.